D1598367

The Grim Years

The Grim Years

Settling South Carolina, 1670–1720

John J. Navin

THE UNIVERSITY OF
SOUTH CAROLINA PRESS

© 2020 University of South Carolina

Published by the University of South Carolina Press
Columbia, South Carolina 29208

www.uscpress.com

Manufactured in the United States of America

29 28 27 26 25 24 23 22 21   10 9 8 7 6 5 4

Library of Congress Cataloging-in-Publication Data
can be found at http://catalog.loc.gov/.

isbn: 978-1-64336-054-6 (hardback)
isbn: 978-1-64336-055-3 (ebook)

To Paul and Margaret Navin

Where every man is enemy to every man . . . In such condition there is . . . continual fear, and danger of violent death; And the life of man, solitary, poor, nasty, brutish, and short."

Thomas Hobbes, *Leviathan*

CONTENTS

Illustrations

Acknowledgments

I am greatly indebted to the many scholars who have published works on the founding and early development of Barbados and South Carolina. As my notes attest, these researchers and authors paved the way for myself, as well as anyone who hopes to provide a fair reckoning of South Carolina's history. I am humbled by their respective efforts and hope that I have not in any way misrepresented their findings.

It has been my great privilege to have several esteemed historians as colleagues and mentors. At Brandeis University, I studied under David Hackett Fischer and have profited from his advice and example ever since. At Coastal Carolina University I worked alongside the late Charles W. Joyner, a scholar admired by every person with a serious interest in African American history. Whatever positive things that may be said about this work are due in part to the influence of these two historians; the flaws are mine alone.

I want to thank Richard Brown at the University of South Carolina Press for his insight and guidance. I also appreciate the efforts of the editors and production staff at USC Press and the anonymous outside readers who helped shape the final draft. Nicholas Butler at the Charleston County Public Library has been a great ally and source of information on early Charleston, and Steven D. Tuttle and Charles Lesser at the South Carolina Department of Archives and History provided valuable assistance. Those institutions have been essential to this study, as has the South Carolina Historical Society and its publications.

I am indebted to Robert Figueira for his editorial assistance on an article published in 2013 that was the precursor to chapter 2 (Navin, "Servant or Slave? South Carolina's Inherited Labor Dilemma"). Special thanks to Ken Townsend for reviewing the entire text and providing candid feedback, and to Joseph Breault, a meticulous scholar, for his help with the documentation. I could not have completed this work without the support provided by Coastal Carolina University and its marvelous staff and resources at Kimbel Library. Finally I want to thank Karen Marie Loman, who assisted in the research for this book, and our daughter, Sarah Marie Navin, *wordsmith extraordinaire*, for her assistance in preparing the final draft.

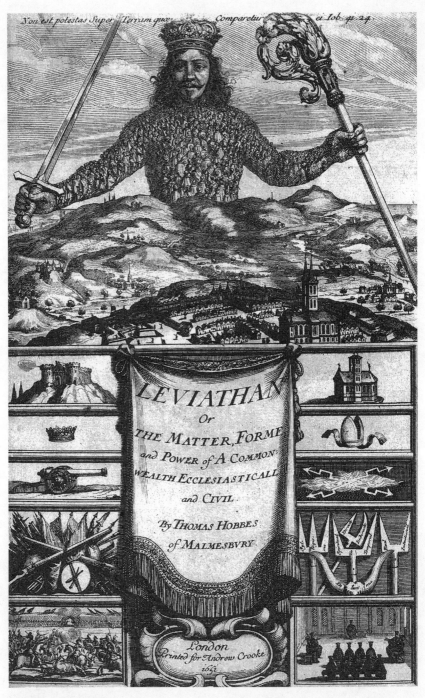

The frontispiece of the book *Leviathan* by Thomas Hobbes; engraving by Abraham Bosse, 1651. Wikimedia Commons Image Database.

Introduction

PORTENTS AND VISIONS

In 1651 philosopher and political theorist Thomas Hobbes penned *Leviathan*, his dark vision of an unregulated society. Hobbes, shocked by the execution of Charles I, whom he supported, envisioned a world of unceasing poverty, violence, and death. In the absence of an absolute sovereign, there would be no law, and "where no Law, no Injustice." Competition for power and wealth would go unchecked; the condition of man would become "a condition of War of every one against every one." Unfettered by notions of right and wrong, every man would have "a Right to every thing: even to one another's body." Hobbes believed this to be the case among "the savage people in many places of America [who] . . . have no government at all; and live at this day in that brutish manner, as I said before."[1] Hobbes did not know how mistaken he was regarding Native American society, nor did he imagine that the nightmarish scenario he described would materialize, for a time, in a colony called Carolina.

In 1666, fifteen years after the publication of Hobbes's treatise, John Locke, physician and future champion of natural rights, encountered Anthony Ashley Cooper—member of Parliament, privy councilor, and minister of state who would soon be named 1st Earl of Shaftesbury. An influential but highly controversial Whig, the earl was a schemer, an opportunist, and a visionary.[2] Despite the rancor his actions provoked, Shaftesbury's writings, in retrospect, seem enlightened. They presaged an era that celebrated reason,

1. Thomas Hobbes, *Leviathan: Or, The Matter, Form, and Power of a Common-Wealth Ecclesiastical and Civil* (London: Printed for Andrew Crooke, 1651), 62–64. The "nature of war," according to Hobbes, "consisteth not in actual fighting; but in the known disposition thereto." Ibid., 62.

2. In 1666 Anthony Ashley Cooper was addressed as 1st Baron Ashley; he acquired the title of 1st Earl of Shaftesbury in 1672. His allegiances and political fortunes vacillated during the English Civil War and continued to do so after he encountered Locke.

skepticism, freedom of thought and religion, and a general lifting of the human condition. In Locke, Shaftesbury sensed a kindred spirit, an individual who foresaw the collective potential of stable government, commercial enterprise, and common purpose.[3] He enlisted Locke to help lay the groundwork for a self-sufficient land-based society—one that might pose a solution to England's economic, demographic, and religious problems.[4] That grandiose vision would collide with reality in a colony called Carolina.

℘

On December 5, 1740, a Spanish privateer cruising off the "bar of Carolina" seized a schooner coming out of Charles Town. One person on board was "a little negro of 10 or 12," who reported that "the largest and best part of Carolina," namely the city's waterfront, had burned. According to the youngster, the inferno lasted for two weeks and the colony's powder magazine had

---

In 1643 he declared for Charles I and was appointed president of the king's council of war for the county of Dorset; the next year, he declared for Parliament and led a brigade of horse and foot that helped capture several Royalist towns and garrisons. [Osmund Airey, "Anthony Ashley Cooper, Baron Ashley and 1st Earl of Shaftesbury," DNB 1887.] Historian John Spurr notes that "few politicians have been so reviled by contemporaries as false and self-interested . . . and yet simultaneously recognized as crucially important to the age's great struggles over religious and constitutional principles." John Spurr, ed., *Anthony Ashley Cooper, First Earl of Shaftesbury 1621–1683* (Surrey: Ashgate Publishing, 2011), 1.

3. An "aristocratic capitalist," Shaftesbury's colonial blueprints were infused with strains of republicanism. Thomas Leng, "Shaftesbury's Aristocratic Empire," in Spurr, ed., *Anthony Ashley Cooper*, 102. Shaftesbury was dismayed by some of Locke's later views, but his grandson, the third Earl of Shaftesbury, later wrote of the philosopher: "No one has done more towards the recalling of philosophy from barbarity, into use and practice of the world, and into the company of the better and politer sort; who might well be ashamed of it in its other dress. No one has opened a better or clearer way to *reasoning.*" Shaftesbury to [anon.], Feb. 24th, 1706–7, in Anthony Ashley Cooper, Earl of Shaftesbury, *Letters of the Earl of Shaftesbury, author of the Characteristicks, collected into one volume* (Glasgow: 1746), Eighteenth Century Collections Online; Gale.

4. The extent to which John Locke helped formulate the *Fundamental Constitutions* is unclear; as secretary to Anthony Ashley Cooper, he certainly participated in the document's creation. However, certain elements also appeared in the Carolina charters of 1663 and 1665, so many historians believe that the *Fundamental Constitutions* were the result of a collaboration between Locke and Shaftesbury and the other proprietors.

blown up.⁵ The child may have overstated the duration of the fire, but its impact on the city's residents was indisputable—the blaze consumed more than three hundred dwellings and commercial buildings. Hugh Bryan, a prominent planter, wrote a letter conveying "melancholy News" of the disaster: "How deplorable is the Condition of many there, that are in a few Hours reduc'd to want of Bread! Surely God's just Judgments are upon us ... O! that this fiery Dispensation may now lead us to Repentance, and truly humble us before GOD, that the Fury of his Anger may turn away from us, and that we be not utterly consumed!"⁶

Bryan went on to catalog South Carolina's recent tribulations; they included drought, disease, slave insurrections, and a failed assault on the Spanish stronghold at St. Augustine. These had all taken their toll; but, in Bryan's view, not since the 1715 Yamasee War had so many colonists been cast into such dire circumstances at one blow.⁷ Three weeks after the fire, Reverend George Whitefield visited the charred city and reminded its inhabitants of the fate of Sodom and Gomorrah. The renowned preacher "endeavour'd to

5. "Letters of Manuel de Montiano: Siege of St. Agustine [*sic*]," No. 248, Florida, Jan. 2, 1741. *Collections of the Georgia Historical Society*, vol. 7, part 1 (Savannah: Georgia Historical Society, 1909), 68–70.

6. "A Letter from Mr. Hugh Bryan to a Friend," November 20, 1740, in *The South Carolina Gazette*, January 15, 1741. Eliza Lucas Pinckney described Bryan as "much deluded by his own fancys and imagined he was assisted by the divine spirrit [*sic*] to prophesy." According to Pinckney, Bryan predicted that "Charles Town and the Country as farr as Ponpon Bridge should be destroyed by fire and sword, to be executed by the Negroes before the first day of next month." Eliza Lucas Pinckney to Mrs. Cheesman, c. March 1742; to Miss Mary Bartlett, March 1742; entry dated March 11, 1741/2, in *The Letterbook of Eliza Lucas Pinckney, 1739–1792*, ed. Elise Pinckney (Chapel Hill: University of North Carolina Press, 1972), 27–30; Harvey H. Jackson, "Hugh Bryan and the Evangelical Movement in Colonial South Carolina," *The William and Mary Quarterly* 43, no. 4 (October 1986): 606–10.

7. When Bryan's letter appeared in the *South Carolina Gazette*, local authorities were appalled at his apocalyptic interpretation of events. On March 17, 1741, a Grand Jury presented a Public Grievance against his writings, which allegedly contained "sundry enthusiastic Prophecys, of the destruction of Charles Town, and deliverance of the Negroes from their Servitude." The grievance noted that "by the Influence of ye said Hugh Brian, great bodys of Negroes have assembled together on pretence of religious worship, contrary to ye Laws, and destructive of ye Peace." Bryan was arrested for libel and his writings were suppressed; he soon retracted his statements and admitted that he was "not guided by the infallible spirit but that of delusion." MS. Council Journal, vol. 8, 13, cited in Herbert Aptheker, *American Negro Slave Revolts* (New York: Columbia University Press, 1943), 190fn.

shew what were the Sins which provoked God to punish the Israelites in that Manner" and "drew a Parallel between them and the Charlestown People."[8] Whitefield's power of persuasion was unrivaled, but as Charles Town's residents cleared the rubble and tallied their losses, they were either too distracted or too far corrupted to take such jeremiads to heart. Commerce was the lifeblood of the colony and the seaport's inhabitants had to restore the city's infrastructure of docks, wharves, warehouses, shops, offices, and private homes as quickly as possible.

Twenty-five years earlier, Yamasee warriors and their Native American allies had nearly driven South Carolinians into the sea. Anglican minister Francis Le Jau, who huddled behind Charles Town's defenses with other refugees from frontier settlements, insisted that "the Evil Spirit of Covetiousness & self Interest" were "the true & Immediate Causes of our Desolation."[9] As Indians advanced toward lowcountry settlements in 1715, people on both sides of the conflict were maimed or killed; dwellings, crops, and livestock were destroyed; the number of homeless and destitute colonists soared; and the colony's very survival was briefly in question.[10] Although a quarter-century separated the Yamasee War from the fiery destruction of Charles Town's waterfront in 1740, men of the cloth found the causes strikingly similar. In both cases, the conduct of the South Carolinians—particularly their avarice—had

8. George Whitefield, *A Continuation of the Reverend Mr. Whitefield's Journal, from a few Days after his Return to Georgia to his Arrival at Falmouth on the 11th of March 1741 . . . The Seventh Journal* (London: W. Strahan for R. Hett at the Bible and Crown in the Poultry, 1741), 76.

9. Le Jau to the Secretary, August 23, 1715, in *The Carolina Chronicle of Dr. Francis Le Jau, 1706–1717*, Frank J. Klingberg, ed., *University of California Publications in History*, vol. 53 (Berkeley: University of California Press, 1956), 166. The conflict known as the Yamasee War was part of a much broader and longer-lasting frontier war waged by the Yamasee, Creek, Catawba, and several other Native American groups from 1715 to 1728. Larry E. Ivers, *This Torrent of Indians: War on the Southern Frontier, 1715–1728* (Columbia: University of South Carolina Press, 2016), vii.

10. According to Peter McCandless, the "Lowcountry" extends from Cape Fear in North Carolina to northern Florida, "and inland from the Atlantic about 70 to 80 miles." See Peter McCandless, *Slavery, Disease, and Suffering in the Southern Lowcountry* (New York: Cambridge University Press, 2011), 4. Others subdivide eastern Carolina into the "low country"—a "labyrinth of tidal flats, salt marshes, and lagoons"—and two coastal zones: an "outer coastal plain, or Tidewater region," and an inner or "upper" plain. David G. Bennett and Jeffrey C. Patton, ed., *A Geography of the Carolinas* (Boone, NC: Parkway Publishers, 2008), 20.

invited God's wrath. But just as the 1740 conflagration did not deter colonists from their selfish, acquisitive ways, neither did the Yamasee War.[11]

Since its founding in 1670, Charles Town had served as a vital but perilous outpost of England's expanding empire. Throughout the era of proprietary rule and beyond, violence, disasters, disease, and recklessness reaped a grim harvest in South Carolina.[12] Adversity killed some, impoverished others, and caused an unknown number to abandon the colony, yet the quest for mammon remained a driving force that sustained growth and production. Between 1670 and 1720, a cadre of ambitious men established commercial operations or rice plantations that by mid-century would return spectacular profits, the bulk of which they reinvested in the colony in one form or another.[13] The fortunes they amassed, the trade they generated, and the infrastructure they developed would all be indications that the Earl of Shaftesbury's vision for Carolina was becoming reality, at least in part.[14] Mere survival was not the goal of these nascent capitalists. In that pregnant space, in those lowest of provincial lands, the pursuit of profit superseded and exacerbated the precariousness of existence. Interlopers, conquerors, and colonizers, the first lowcountry planters were fixed not on competency (some pale glimmer of

11. The Yamasee War greatly diminished the Indian slave trade in South Carolina, but not because colonists objected to it on moral grounds.

12. In 1698, the residents of Charles Town endured an outbreak of smallpox, an earthquake, and a major fire. The next year, the townspeople dealt with yellow fever and a damaging hurricane. Emma Hart, *Building Charleston: Town and Society in the Eighteenth-Century British Atlantic World* (Charlottesville: University of Virginia Press, 2010), 29.

13. South Carolina's inability to attract and keep sufficient numbers of European immigrants enabled some colonists to acquire property more easily (as well as the elevated status that large landholdings engendered), but the reluctance of whites to join the colony engendered the "acute anxieties" associated with the slave system that met their labor demands. Louis Roper, *Conceiving Carolina: Proprietors, Planters, and Plots, 1662–1779* (New York: Palgrave Macmillan, 2004), 3.

14. This introduction and the chapters that follow focus on the southern part of Carolina, in this case, the area below the Cape Fear River. Colonists drifting south from Virginia or other northern origins originally settled the part of the province that became North Carolina. Their circumstances, needs, and priorities were far removed from those of the merchants, planters, and others around Charles Town. In 1691, the Lords Proprietors granted Governor Philip Ludwell the power to appoint a deputy for the northern portion of the Province. Because elected representatives from North Carolina were unable to travel to Charles Town on a regular basis, they met in their own Assembly. In 1710 the proprietors appointed a separate governor for North Carolina, thereby sanctioning the official separation of Carolina into two colonies.

Calvinist endeavor) but on prosperity.[15] Theirs was a vision of immense personal wealth—a marker of liberty, intellect, and merit. These founders— proselytes of a new creed—linked self-aggrandizement to the greater good.

Despite this prevailing spirit of covetousness, few men grew rich in South Carolina during the first fifty years of settlement. Numerous wealthy individuals emigrated from England, Barbados, and other places, but until the rice boom of the 1730s and '40s, the colony had very few thriving plantations.[16] Settlers used their land and servants or slaves (if they had any) to produce foodstuffs for their own consumption, and cattle, pork, beef, corn, and cedar for export to Barbados.[17] Merchants struggled to get ahead, though men linked to the Indian and deerskin trades—and then to the trade in Indians themselves—had a clear leg up on the rest.[18] Artisans and tradesmen strove to establish a customer base, all the while fending off a descent into poverty.[19]

15. New England Puritans strove for "competency," or sufficiency. It defined "a middling way of life, not an indulgent one." Conspicuous wealth and an appetite for "luxuries" or material possessions "for their own sake" were not only discouraged, but were also considered sinful. Joseph A. Conforti, *Saints and Strangers: New England in British North America* (Baltimore: Johns Hopkins University Press, 2006), 42.

16. Edward Randolph visited South Carolina in 1697 and 1698; his report to the Board of Trade implied that the African method of processing rice with a mortar and pestle was being used—"They have now found out the true way of raising and husking rice." Judith Ann Carney, *Black Rice: The African Origins of Rice Cultivation in the Americas* (Cambridge: Harvard University Press, 2001), 84.

17. S. Max Edelson, *Plantation Enterprise in Colonial South Carolina* (Cambridge: Harvard University Press, 2006), 49. Many independent planters evaded land laws established by the Lords Proprietors, dispersing across the Lowcountry away from the "scrutiny of elites"; there they built plantations on waterways that lured them progressively deeper into the interior (Ibid., 46). In 1700 John Lawson traveled up the Santee River and visited a "colony of French Protestants" who "live as decently and happily, as any Planters in these Southward parts of America." The seventy Huguenot families were a "temperate industrious People." John Lawson, *A New Voyage to Carolina; Containing the Exact Description and Natural History Of That Country* . . . (1709), quoted in Molly McClain and Alessa Ellefson, "A Letter from Carolina, 1688: French Huguenots in the New World," *The William and Mary Quarterly*, 3rd series, 64, no. 2 (April 2007): 387.

18. Jack Greene describes Charles Town's mercantile community as "small and financially weak" before the 1740s. After 1750 an "enterprising, aggressive, and seasoned" group of merchants presided over the Lower South's "increasingly kinetic economic pace." Jack P. Greene, *Pursuits of Happiness: The Social Development of Early Modern British Colonies and the Formation of American Culture* (Chapel Hill: University of North Carolina Press, 1988), 146.

19. Between 1670 and 1720, 101 different artisans were mentioned in Charles Town records; 16 arrived in between 1670 and 1679, 9 between 1680 and 1689, 30 between

As men vied for the best town lots, the best lands, the best partnerships, and tried to determine which crops, goods, and methods would turn a profit, competition and misfortune weeded out the weak. To get ahead, entrepreneurs were more than willing to exploit Africans, Native Americans, and even their fellow colonists. Between 1670 and 1720, many of the hardships that South Carolinians endured stemmed from the actions of individuals who enriched themselves at the expense of everyone and everything they touched, much as Thomas Hobbes had predicted.[20]

Throughout the colony's first half-century, Charles Town's population included legions of paupers, many of them women and children who would eventually come to depend on St. Philip's parish for food and shelter. A wide range of diseases ensured that the colony always had an abundance of chronically ill individuals. In the early 1700s, rice plantations gradually appeared along lowcountry rivers and swamps, but South Carolina's countryside continued to be dotted with hardscrabble farms where ordinary men and women struggled to make ends meet.[21] Even lower on the economic ladder were landless servants, many of whom had labored for seven years to gain a pittance—if they survived. Yet they were not the worst off. Fifty years after the *Carolina* made landfall, two-thirds of the province's population consisted of enslaved Africans, poor beyond measure and likely to flee or, when pushed to the limit, to revolt. To the south, Spanish adversaries in St. Augustine plotted Charles

---

1690 and 1699, 23 between 1700 and 1709, and 23 between 1710 and 1720 ("Index of Artisans," Museum of Early Southern Decorative Arts, Winston-Salem, NC). An analysis of thirty artisan probate records for the years 1730 to 1749 shows that 37 percent owned no slaves, 32 percent owned one to four slaves, 24 percent owned five to nine slaves, and 7 percent owned ten or more slaves. [Charleston County Inventories, 1730–1800, Charleston County Public Library, in Hart, *Building Charleston*, 30, 103.] During the proprietary era, fewer artisans lived in Charles Town than after 1730, and both the percentage owning slaves and the number of slaves owned would likely have been lower.

20. Hobbes, *Leviathan*, 62–64. Henrietta Johnson, perhaps the earliest female painter in North America, created pastel portraits of leading South Carolinians between 1707 and 1725. The list of notables who posed for her included Colonel William Rhett, Colonel Daniell (deputy governor), Mrs. Robert Brewton, Anne Broughton (daughter of the lieutenant governor), the wife and three daughters of Jacques Du Bosc, Colonel John Moore and his wife, and Frances Moore Bayard. Jan Onofrio, "Johnston, Henrietta, (?–1728/1729)," *South Carolina Biographical Dictionary*, 2nd ed., vol. 1 (St. Clair Shores, MI: Somerset Publishers, Inc., 2000), 412.

21. In 1700 the colony's plantations were "still largely clustered along the banks of the few rivers near Charlestown ... Planters took up scarce upland tracts surrounded by wetlands they denigrated as wastes." Edelson, *Plantation Enterprise*, 15.

Town's destruction; to the west, Native Americans contemplated revenge for a thousand wrongs. With enemies on every side—and even within the colony—death had a thousand faces. Lowcountry rice planters would one day be counted among the richest men in the world; but between 1670 and 1720, the lives of many colonists were solitary, poor, nasty, brutish, and short.[22]

℘

The southeast had not always been associated with calamity. Before the slave trade devastated indigenous tribes, before Africans converted swamplands into fields of rice, and before the machinations of lowcountry planters and merchants bent on wealth and power, Muskogean-, Siouan-, Yuchi-, Algon-quian-, and Iroquoian-speaking peoples, who coexisted in a region of natural abundance, inhabited the Carolina landscape.[23] Buffeted by Atlantic winds and waves on its eastern edge and bounded by the formidable Appalachian range to its west, Carolina boasted a seemingly infinite variety of birds, in-sects, plants, animals, minerals, and waterways. European explorers de-scribed the area between Virginia and Florida in glowing terms, keen on the opportunity to exploit its resources. Jean Ribault said that the country "is the fairest, fruitfullest and pleasantest of all the world . . . incomparable land, never yet broken with plow irons."[24] Juan de la Vandera compared Carolina to Andalusia, a region of hills, rivers, and lush valleys.[25] William Hilton and his companions saw "as good Land, and as well Timbered, as any we have seen in any other part of the world, sufficient to accommodate thousands of our Eng-lish Nation."[26] Robert Horne reported that "Carolina is a fair and spacious

22. Hobbes, *Leviathan*, 62.

23. Europeans considered property a "hallmark of civilization and modernity" and thought that the concept did not exist among Native Americans. Allan Greer's work demonstrates the inaccuracy of that view; his work highlights the diversity (and occa-sional incoherence) of "indigenous and Euro-American property systems" in the early modern period. Allan Greer, *Property and Dispossession: Natives, Empires and Land in Early Modern North America* (Cambridge: Cambridge University Press, 2018), 2.

24. Jean Ribault, "The Whole and True Discovery of Terra Florida" (1563), in Michael P. Branch, ed., *Reading the Roots: American Nature Writing Before Walden* (Athens: University of Georgia Press, 2004), 41–43.

25. "Relacion escrita por Juan de la Vandera," in E. Ruidiaz y Caravia, *La Florida su Conquista y Colonizacion por Pedro Menendes de Aviles* (Madrid: 1893), ii, 485, quoted in Woodbury Lowery, *The Spanish Settlements within the present limits of the United States, 1513–1561* (New York: G.P. Putnam, 1911), 295.

26. William Hilton, "A Relation of a Discovery by William Hilton, 1664," in Alexander S. Salley, Jr., ed., *Narratives of Early Carolina 1650–1708* (New York: Barnes & Noble, 1911), 53.

Province ... doubtless there is no Plantation that ever the English went upon, in all respects so good as this."[27] Robert Sandford and his fellow travelers found Carolina "soe excellent a Country for both Wood, land and Meadowes" that it "Exceed[s] all places that we knowe."[28]

Ironically nature's bounty went untouched by the first Europeans that visited Carolina. In 1521 Pedro de Quexos and Francisco Gordillo set an ugly precedent that other intruders would follow. The two Spanish captains steered their respective vessels to the area of the Santee River, lured "about sixty-odd people" on board, and carried their human cargo back to Hispaniola where they intended to sell them into slavery.[29] Quexos, a licensed man-stealer, was free to follow his own avaricious instincts but Gordillo had been assigned to explore the area north of Florida. When he returned with captives, Gordillo's superior—Lucas Vasquez de Ayllón, a judge in the Royal Audiencia in Santo Domingo—ordered that the Indians be repatriated. Gordillo fell into disfavor but his slave raiding activities had far-reaching consequences. Based on the description of Carolina that Gordillo provided, Ayllón gained the consent of Charles V to establish a Spanish colony on the mainland. In 1526 he was at the head of an ill-fated expedition that made landfall somewhere along the Carolina or Georgia coast. The first setback was the loss of his flagship along with the bulk of the colony's provisions and supplies. Within a matter of months, disease, starvation, mutiny, arson, a slave uprising, and warfare with local Indians devastated the fledgling colony of San Miguel de Gualdape. Of the

27. Robert Horne, "A Brief Description of the Province of Carolina" (1666), in Salley, ed., *Narratives*, 66.

28. Robert Sandford, "A Relation of a Voyage on the Coast of the Province of Carolina," (1666), in Salley, ed., *Narratives*, 91, 108. Sandford's companions were confident that "a Colony of English here planted, with a moderate support in their Infant tendency, would in a very short time improve themselves to a perfect Common Wealth."

29. Exactly how many Native Americans were taken is unknown. Historian Woodbury Lowery said 150 were seized. [Lowery, *The Spanish Settlements*, 156.] Samuel Eliot Morison stated that seventy were taken. [Samuel Eliot Morison, *The European Discovery of North America: The Northern Voyages A.D. 500–1600* (New York: Oxford University Press, 1971), 332.] In 1526 Pedro de Quexos testified during a trial that "about sixty" people were captured. [June 2, 1526.] "Replies by Pedro de Quijos [Quexos] to interrogatories administered on behalf of Matienzo," in Shea Papers, Georgetown University Library, cited in Margaret F. Pickett, Dwayne W. Pickett, *The European Struggle to Settle North America: Colonizing Attempts by England, France and Spain, 1521–1608* (Jefferson, NC: McFarland & Co., 2010), 232, n14.] There is no record of the captives being returned to Carolina; some perished when one of the ships was lost at sea, prompting many of the surviving captives to refuse food. Those who reached Hispaniola were employed as servants. William J. Rivers, *A Sketch of the History of South Carolina to the Close of the*

500 to 600 colonists who boarded Ayllón's six ships in midsummer, only 150 made it back to Hispaniola in the fall. Ayllón was not one of the survivors.[30]

European interest in the area north of Florida intensified in the second half of the sixteenth century. In 1559 a Spanish fleet under the command of Angel de Villafane carried 230 settlers to the Carolina coast, but the expedition came to naught when a hurricane battered the vessels as they searched for a promising site for their colony.[31] Three years later, Jean Ribault, a French naval officer, constructed a rude fort at Port Royal, entrusted twenty-six volunteers with its defense, erected a stone pillar to establish French dominion, and then sailed away. The next year, sensing their abandonment, the men Ribault left behind despaired. "Undone by their owne selves," the company was torn asunder by "partialities and dissentions." After putting their commander to death, all but one set out for France, 3,500 miles distant, in a boat fashioned from timbers, pine resin, and Spanish moss. For sails, the mutineers used shirts and sheets. Adrift in their makeshift coffin, many died of starvation.[32] Some survived and joined René de Laudonniére's colonizing expedition to St. John's River in Florida. There they were among the 132 French settlers massacred by Spanish troops under Pedro Menéndez de Avilés in the autumn of 1565.[33]

Proprietary Government by the Revolution of 1719; With an Appendix Containing Many Valuable Records Hitherto Unpublished (Charleston: McCarter & Co, 1856), 16.

30. Pickett, *European Struggle*, 24–27. The settlement may have been as far north as the Cape Fear River or as far south as the Savannah River. Historians disagree whether the number of original colonists was 500 or 600; there is, however, a consensus that only 150 survived.

31. Lawrence Sanders Rowland, *Window on the Atlantic: The Rise and Fall of Santa Elena, South Carolina's Spanish City* (Columbia: South Carolina Department of Archives and History, 1990), 8.

32. One soldier named LaChère was executed and devoured by his boatmates. René Goulaine de Laudonnière, *A notable historie containing foure voyages made by certaine French Captaines into Florida*, in Richard Hakluyt, *Principal Navigations, Voyages, Traffiques and Discoveries of the English Nation*, ed., Edmund Goldsmid, vol. 13 [America], Part 2 [1599].

33. Before he established Charlesfort, Ribault planted the French colors on the St. John's River near modern-day St. Augustine. French Huguenots established a colony at the site; in 1565 Spain's monarch, Philip II, called for their extermination. Pedro Menéndez de Avilés and his men carried out the massacre. When Ribault shipwrecked on the Florida coast, Avilés executed the Frenchman and members of his crew as Protestant heretics. Ribault was singled out for especially audacious treatment: "His face

Though Ribault's settlement at Charlesfort lasted only a year, it gave the Spanish a handy footprint for Santa Elena, a colony established in 1566 that served as the capital of La Florida and as the starting point for a series of ventures into the interior. Settlers built homes, a church, boardinghouses, and a tavern, and soldiers erected a fort at Santa Elena and at several places further inland. Disease, inept leadership, and chronic food shortages took a toll on the colony. Beset by internal problems and hostilities with the neighboring Guale and Edisto tribes, the Spanish abandoned Santa Elena in 1576. Native Americans who had suffered at the hands of the invaders—and even more so from the diseases they brought—quickly burned the empty forts and dwellings. One year later, in the wake of an abortive French effort to establish a colony on the ruins, Spanish soldiers and colonists reappeared and rebuilt Santa Elena. Over the course of a decade this revitalized settlement thrived; forty houses and a new fort occupied the fifteen-acre site. Then, in the summer of 1587, renewed problems with local Indians and concerns about Sir Francis Drake's fleet and Sir Walter Raleigh's men at Roanoke prompted Spanish officials to order the destruction and abandonment of the settlement.[34]

When Charles I assumed England's throne in 1630, indigenous tribes were the only inhabitants of the vast tract between Virginia and Spanish Florida. Europeans had come and gone; the land had spit them out like foul gristle not suited to the palate of North America. Despite the moldering remains of abandoned French and Spanish settlements, Carolina remained a landscape that promised untold riches to men who knew how to exploit it. Based on the 1497 voyage of John Cabot, England laid claim to the entire eastern seaboard and beyond. In 1629 Charles I named Robert Heath, his attorney general, "lord predominant" of a tract in North America that encompassed all land between the 31–36° parallels of latitude. This enormous parcel, which Charles named the "Province of Carolana," stretched from Virginia to Florida and west to the Pacific Ocean. Despite its potential, Heath virtually ignored the province, perhaps because he was already a charter member of the Council for New England and a councilor of the Virginia Company. Heath eventually became Lord Chief Justice, but during the English Civil War, his loyalty to the king cost him his property and nearly his life. Impeached for

---

with his beard ... his eyes, nose, and ears they cut off when he was dead and sent them all to the Isles of Peru to exhibit them." Roger Schlesinger and Arthur P. Stabler, eds., trans., *Andre Thevet's North America: A Sixteenth-Century View* (Kingston and Montreal: McGill-Queen's University Press, 1986), 152.

34. Eugene Lyon, *Santa Elena: A Brief History of the Colony, 1566–1587* (Columbia: University of South Carolina Institute of Archaeology and Anthropology, 1984), 3–16.

high treason, Heath fled to Calais, where he died seven months after Charles I was executed.[35] During the Interregnum (1649–1660), the Province of Carolina barely existed as far as Oliver Cromwell and other Englishmen were concerned.

Not until 1664 did English cartographers use "Carolina" to designate the contested terrain where the French and Spanish had planted their flags and their doomed colonies the previous century.[36] That tribute to the late Charles I was made possible by the Restoration of the monarchy in England in 1660. The ascent of Charles II to the throne was a miracle of divine intervention in the eyes of some Englishmen, but others, including the new king, recognized the role played by certain individuals in restoring the "natural and divine order."[37] Eager to solidify his base of support, Charles II found ways to reward the men who had put him in power. One such gesture was the creation of the Company of Royal Adventurers Trading to Africa, the latest in a long line of slave-trading initiatives supported by successive English monarchs.[38] Another noteworthy demonstration of the king's appreciation and largesse was a grant for the "Province of Carolina," which he gave to eight enterprising Englishmen, some of whom had played a significant role in his accession. In the eyes of these new "Lords Proprietors," the vast wilderness north of Spanish

35. Charles I also gave Heath the Bahamas Islands; the grant excluded Roanoke Island and the territory the Virginians explored since 1607. Heath was also connected to commercial enterprises involving lead mines in the East Midlands. Paul E. Kopperman, "Heath, Sir Robert (1575–1649)," *Oxford Dictionary of National Biography*.

36. A 1657 map by Nicholas Comberford was later amended to include the "North Part of Carolina," but not until Joseph Moxon's *Americae Septentrionalis Pars* (1664) was Carolina situated in a geographic space on a published map. Robert Horne's 1666 map, *Carolina Described*, portrayed the province as a "distinctive place that stretched well to the south of Albemarle Sound." S. Max Edelson, "Defining Carolina: Cartography and Colonization in the North American Southeast, 1657–1733," in *Creating and Contesting Carolina: Proprietary Era Histories*, ed. Michelle LeMaster and Bradford J. Wood (Columbia: University of South Carolina Press, 2013), 28–29. Some historians assert that Jean Ribault originally named the region Carolina in honor of Charles IX of France. In 1682, Thomas Ashe said the name could have been derived from either monarch. Thomas Ashe, *Carolina, or a Description of the Present State of that Country* (London, 1682), in Salley, ed., *Narratives*, 140.

37. J. R. Jones, *Country and Court* (Cambridge: Harvard University Press, 1979), 115, 138.

38. William Andrew Pettigrew, *Freedom's Debt: The Royal African Company and the Politics of the Atlantic Slave Trade, 1672–1752* (Chapel Hill: University of North Carolina Press, 2013), 22. Charles reorganized the enterprise as the Company of Royal Adventurers in 1663. Ibid., 23.

Florida was opportunity writ large—resources waiting to be extracted, inhabitants waiting to be exploited, and proceeds waiting to be spent.[39] Such outcomes would not occur deus ex machina; they would stem from the actions of planters, merchants, and traders—bold adventurers and entrepreneurs who ascribed to the notion, later articulated in Bernard Mandeville's *Fable of the Bees* (1705), that avarice and other private vices could prove beneficial to society at large:

> Thus every Part was full of Vice,
> Yet the whole Mass a Paradise;
> Flatter'd in Peace, and fear'd in Wars,
> They were th' Esteem of Foreigners,
> And lavish of their Wealth and Lives,
> The Balance of all other Hives.
> Such were the Blessings of that State;
> Their Crimes conspir'd to make them Great:
> And Virtue, who from Politicks
> Had learn'd a Thousand Cunning Tricks,
> Was, by their happy Influence,
> Made Friends with Vice: And ever since,
> The worst of all the Multitude
> Did something for the Common Good.[40]

There would be no shortage of vice in Carolina. But like the insects in Mandeville's *Fable*, the colonists could generate "publick benefits" that extended to the entire hive, namely to England and her other colonies—at least in theory.

---

39. Louis Roper asserts that the Lords Proprietors were not "overly concerned with securing a financial return from their province"; Shaftesbury and the Colleton family were the only proprietors who operated plantations in Carolina. Roper acknowledges that the proprietors attempted to monopolize the lucrative Indian trade, but he claims that it was "in order to facilitate frontier peace." Roper, *Conceiving Carolina*, 9.

40. Bernard Mandeville, "the Grumbling Hive: or, knaves Turn'd honest" (1705), lines 155–56, 167–68. Mandeville's "Grumbling Hive" first appeared under its full title in 1714; nine years later it reappeared in *The Fable of the Bees: or, Private Vices, Publick Benefits*. The latter work gained notoriety when it was implicated in "an intense controversy about the nature of politics, modern commerce and their contemporary moral consequences." Mandeville challenged the notion that men were naturally sociable and beneficent—a view embedded in the 3rd Earl of Shaftesbury's *Characteristics* (1711 and 1714). In 1724 the Grand Jury of Middlesex declared Mandeville's *Fable* a public nuisance and recommended that the author be prosecuted. Bernard Mandeville, *The Fable of the Bees and Other Writings*, ed., E. J. Hundert (Indianapolis: Hackett Publishing, 1997), xvii–xix.

As colonists boarded ships for the southern part of the Carolina grant, a cynic might point out that the intended settlement was named after an unscrupulous monarch who alienated his subjects, waged a bloody war against Parliament, was declared a "Tyrant, Traitor, Murderer and public Enemy," and lost his head in 1649.[41] Pessimists could remind prospective settlers that misery had proved to be a shared attribute across the colonial landscape. The 118 colonists who arrived at Roanoke in 1587 literally vanished within three years. In Jamestown, 440 of the 500 settlers perished during a winter in which starving men disinterred corpses to sate their appetites. English magistrates sent vagrants and convicted criminals to Virginia to repopulate the foundering colony.[42] Plymouth's firstcomers, only half of whom survived the first six months, placed their dead in a common grave to conceal their losses from "skulking" Indians. Massachusetts Bay Colony's puritan vanguard found itself "in great straits" from disease and want of provisions. Only eight of Quebec's twenty-eight founders were alive after the first winter. In New Netherland, Dutch colonists claimed to be surrounded by "savage and wild" natives who served "nobody but the Devil."[43]

The colony established at Charles Town, in the southern part of Carolina, would resemble none of these. Prosperous and impoverished, beleaguered and belligerent, and insular and expansive, it was a place where virtually everyone was expendable and where calamities interrupted but seldom deterred the pursuit of profit. During its first half-century of existence, South Carolina would prove unique in remarkable, important, and sometimes terrible ways.

Scholars have produced a plethora of books and articles about the early history of South Carolina. Things that made the colony distinctive—its Barbadian influence, the *Fundamental Constitutions*, the conflict with Spanish

41. Having rejected a proposed constitutional settlement and secretly negotiated for the Scots to invade England, Charles I was charged with treason and placed on trial by the Puritan "Rump Parliament." At his execution at Whitehall on January 30, 1649, the doomed king told the crowd, "I am the martyr of the people . . ." ["The Execution of Charles I, 1649," *EyeWitness to History* website, 2003.] During the reign of Charles II (1660–1685), nine of the men who signed his father's death warrant would be hanged, drawn, and quartered for their actions.

42. The first prisoner banished to Virginia by the Court of Bridewell was sentenced to transportation on October 2, 1607, less than five months after the colony was established. London's homeless poor continued to be shipped to Virginia into the 1700s. Stephen J. Nagle and Sara L. Sanders, ed., *English in the Southern United States* (New York: Cambridge University Press, 2003), 36.

43. "Letter of rev. Jonas Michaelius (1628)," in *Narratives of New Netherland, 1609–1664*, vol. 8, ed. John Franklin Jameson (New York: Charles Scribner's Sons, 1909), 126.

Florida, its racial demographics, the quarrel and break with the Proprietors, the disease environment, rice culture and the plantation system, the emergence of a lowcountry merchant and planter gentry—have been at the center of these works. These are important topics and this study is meant to shed new light on them. But few historians have focused on the hardships that people of all ethnicities and all stations in life endured during the first fifty years of South Carolina's existence—years of misery caused by climate, disasters, pathogens, greed, and recklessness. Between 1670 and 1720, as a cadre of men rose to political and economic prominence, ordinary colonists, enslaved Africans, and indigenous groups were victimized by circumstances over which they had no control.

One

Barbadian Precedents

In 1781 a prominent slave owner noted, "In a warm climate, no man will labour for himself who can make another labour for him."[1] That observation, offered by Thomas Jefferson in his *Notes on the State of Virginia*, had staying power. In the American South, it characterized a succession of tobacco growers, rice barons, and cotton planters. Jefferson's maxim also had geographic breadth. It reflected circumstances in the West Indies, where a privileged few accumulated fortunes based on the ceaseless toil of the unfree majority. There, on the tiny island of Barbados, English sugar planters honed a system of exploitation that was replicated throughout the Caribbean and on the North American mainland. They demonstrated that large-scale landownership, plentiful cheap labor, and production of an agricultural staple could produce immense riches—especially if one was not squeamish about the emotional and physical distress of one's workers.

The unrelenting pace and high mortality that characterized Barbados's plantations meant that only the most desperate or powerless individuals planted, harvested, and processed the sugarcane; precious few people labored in those sweltering fields by choice. In the mid-seventeenth century, Barbadian landowners shifted from white servants to enslaved Africans as their primary workforce. The implications of that change—a deliberate, open-ended reliance on the exploitation of black men and women—would play out not just in the Caribbean but also in the American South where Jefferson and his fellow slave owners feared that "a revolution of the wheel of fortune, an exchange of situation" might occur.[2] In the language of the slaves, the bottom rail might one day come out on top.

☙

---

1. Thomas Jefferson, *Notes on the State of Virginia*, Query XVIII, in *The Writings of Thomas Jefferson*, ed. Paul L. Ford (New York: G.P. Putnam, 1892–99), 4: 232.
2. Ibid.

A topographicall Description and a measurement of the Yland of Barbados in the West Indyaes: With the Mrs. Names of the Severall plantacons [map], in Richard Ligon, A true & exact history of the island of Barbados. London: Printed for H. Moseley, 1657. Rare Books Collection, The Latin American Library, Tulane University.

Barbados dangles on the tip of the Caribbean like God's afterthought. The easternmost landfall in the Lesser Antilles, the island was plucked clean of its Arawak inhabitants by Spanish raiders in the sixteenth century. Those who were not captured either perished or fled long before 1625, when Captain John Powell steered the *Olive* to its shores to restock his water and provisions. The ship was on its return voyage from Brazil, where one of Powell's sponsors, Sir William Courteen, had financial interests in a Dutch tobacco colony in Guiana.[3] Upon his return to London, Powell's favorable description of Barbados prompted Courteen, a formidable presence in Anglo-Dutch commerce, to form a syndicate to promote settlement on the island. The members envisioned a colony of hirelings who would grow tobacco for export; operational costs should prove modest compared to the investors' potentially enormous profits. Capitalizing on the labor of others was hardly a new concept: landowning gentry had been doing it for centuries. More recently English capitalists had invested in enterprises that relied on the labor of colonists in places such as Virginia, Bermuda, and Plymouth.

No sooner had Courteen and his partners set their colonization scheme in motion than the resumption of war between Holland and Portugal diverted their attention to privateering ventures.[4] The syndicate profited from the capture of a Portuguese vessel in the Channel in 1626, fueling their collective interest in similar opportunities. When the first group of English settlers

3. A merchant, financier, and colonial entrepreneur, Courteen funded the construction of more than twenty ships and employed between four thousand and five thousand mariners. His investment in the Barbados colony was valued at £12,000.

John C. Appleby, "Courteen, Sir William (c.1568–1636)," in *Oxford Dictionary of National Biography*, ed. H. C. G. Matthew and Brian Harrison (Oxford Oxford University Press, 2004); online ed., ed. Lawrence Goldman, January 2008. In a 1901 article, Reverend George Edmundson noted that the firm Courten (*sic*) and Company constituted a partnership between John Money, a London merchant, and brothers William and Peter Courten. William settled in London and became a naturalized Englishman, but Peter continued to live in Zeeland, making the company Anglo-Dutch. Edmundson claims the Dutch element was predominant, for its books were kept in Middleburg, and Peter also served as director of the Dutch West India Company. In a 1660 petition, Henry Powell identified "Sir Peter Courten" as one of the investors in the voyage of the John and William to Barbados. See "The Dutch in Western Guiana," in *The English Historical Review*, ed. S. R. Gardiner and Reginal L. Poole, vol. 16, 1901 (London: Longmans, Green and Co., 1901), 640–75.

4. The Dutch–Portuguese War that commenced in 1602 pitted the Dutch East India Company and the Dutch West India Company against the far-flung Portuguese Empire. In the conflict Portugal received aid from Spain, ostensibly making England an ally to the Dutch.

finally set sail for Barbados in the *William and John* the following year, their voyage was interrupted by a chance encounter with a Portuguese ship. In the resulting battle, Captain Henry Powell—brother of John—and his crew proved victorious and took ten enslaved Africans as part of their prize. These captives—seized in Africa by their countrymen, sold to slave traders and then taken as booty on the high seas—would be the first blacks pressed into service in Barbados. Thousands more would follow.

Assisted by Powell's newly acquired slaves, the eighty settlers who arrived on the *William and John* went about the business of constructing shelters and clearing fields. At that juncture, most of the island's white inhabitants were mere employees: they received wages from Courteen's syndicate but no grants of land.[5] Despite the example set in Virginia, Courteen and his partners seemed oblivious to the role of headrights in attracting and keeping planters.[6] Instead, they continued to recruit hired hands, preserving title to the land and reserving the lion's share of anticipated earnings for themselves. The syndicate should have looked to Plymouth Colony, where, after several lean years laboring under the "common course and condition," colonists had become far more productive after switching to a system of private landownership.

Time after time the investors and their representatives in Barbados would demonstrate their eagerness to persuade or compel others to work long and hard on their behalf. Shortly after making landfall at Barbados, Powell sailed to the Dutch trading post at Guiana to obtain "all things that was to be gotten

5. Appleby, "Courteen, Sir William (c.1568–1636)," in *Oxford Dictionary of National Biography*.

6. A "headright" was a grant of land used to encourage settlement and to reward the importation of laborers and family members by early colonists. On Barbados, a total of 771 grants placed 67,929 acres (80 percent of the island) in private hands between 1627 and 1638; these figures do not include ten thousand additional acres granted to a syndicate of London merchants. Eventually, much of the land would be allocated by headright at the rate of ten acres for each dependent white servant—the so-called ten-acre men needed for militia purposes. Richard B. Sheridan, *Sugar and Slavery: An Economic History of the British West Indies, 1623–1775* (Kingston, JA: Canoe Press, 1974), 83; and Michael Craton, "Property and propriety: Land tenure and slave property in the creation of a British West Indian plantocracy, 1612–1740," in *Early Modern Conceptions of Property*, ed. John Brewer and Susan Staves (London: Routledge, 1996), 523–24, n20. Land-rich colonies in the American south offered early colonists even larger headrights, typically fifty acres for themselves and an additional fifty acres for each family member or servant that accompanied them. Carolina's proprietors used headright grants to control settlement by linking the size of a grant to the number of dependents (free, slave, and indentured) capable of cultivating it. Edelson, *Plantation Enterprise*, 94.

for the planting of this Island."[7] Captain Gromwegle, governor of the out-post, served as intermediary between Powell and local Arawak Indians, who provided corn, cassava, sweet potatoes, plantains, bananas, citrus fruits, and melons. Whether it was the Dutch or the Arawak who provided the Barbadi-ans with crucial tobacco plants is not clear, but they were included in the mix. According to Powell, three "cannoes" of Indians expressed their desire "to goe with me as free people . . . and that I should allow them a piece of land, the which I did, and they would manure those fruits, and bring up their children to Christianitie."[8] Later depositions indicated that the Arawaks went at Cap-tain Gromwegle's bidding and upon the promise that, should they choose to leave Barbados after two years, they would be transported back to Guiana and awarded £50 worth of axes, bills, hoes, knives, looking-glasses, and beads. In a "horrid breach of faith," the thirty-two Arawaks that Powell brought to Barbados were enslaved against their will.[9] This betrayal foreshadowed the conduct of Carolina entrepreneurs in their dealings with various southeast-ern tribes.

English investors provided Barbados with continued financial and ma-terial support: within two years, Courteen and his partners expended more than £10,000 and sent as many as 1,500 additional settlers to the island.[10]

7. Powell and Gromwegle both fought in the West Indies on behalf of Spain. See Nicholas Darnell Davis, *The Cavaliers & Roundheads of Barbados, 1650–1652: with some account of the early history of Barbados* (London: Argosy Press, 1887), 67. By the time of Barbados's settlement, the Dutch West Indies Company, working from its base on the Essequibo River, had commercial interests in the region's dyes, tobacco, cotton, coffee, and sugar. David Scott Hammond, *Tropical forests of the Guiana Shield: Ancient Forests in a Modern World* (Cambridge, MA: Cabi Publishing, 2005), 409.

8. *Report and Accompanying Papers of the Commission appointed by the President of the United States, "To investigate and report upon the true divisional line between the Republic of Venezuela and British Guiana."* Vol. 1, United States Commission on Boundary between Venezuela and British Guiana (Washington: Government Printing Office, 1897), 183, fn. 2.

9. According to Nicholas Darnell Davis, one of these Indians escaped on a Dutch ship and returned to Essequibo in 1631. The Dutch governor, Gromwegle, who had en-couraged the Arawaks to go to Barbados, was compelled "to marry a Carib wife to fortify himself against the wrath of the Arawaks, and afterward had to make valuable presents to the latter to retain their goodwill to the Dutch." Sir George Ayscue liberated some of the Indians, but it was not until 1664 that the surviving Arawaks were freed. Davis, *Cavaliers & Roundheads*, 67.

10. Jan Rogozinski, *A Brief History of the Caribbean from the Arawak and the Carib to the Present* (New York: Penguin, 1994), 68.

Thanks to its location on the extreme eastern periphery of the Caribbean, the fledgling colony was untouched by war during its critical founding period (unlike English settlements elsewhere in the region).[11] However, internal tranquility was quite another matter. Just one year after Sir William Courteen and his associates founded the colony, a royal grant of Barbados and the rest of the "Caribbee Islands" to James Hay, 1st Earl of Carlisle, trumped their claim.[12] The island's new owner allocated ten thousand acres to a hastily formed company of London merchants and gave land allotments of one hundred acres to sixty-four independent landowners who would generate revenues for him and for themselves, though they had to provide their own capital and workforce.[13] The arrival of the latter in 1628 led to infighting between the "Leeward men" at Holetown and the newer "Windward men," who settled around "the Bridge" (Bridgetown afterward). The following decade saw continued conflict in which the two factions met in armed combat and resorted to burning each other's crops. The political situation on Barbados was equally chaotic: prosecutions for treason, mutiny, and rebellion led to several executions. Between 1627 and 1630, seven individuals held the title of governor or deputy governor; none won the support of both factions and several were sent back to England in irons. On top of it all, few Barbadians prospered. Planters produced tobacco so bitter that they satisfied their personal cravings with product from Virginia; the island's other cash crops fared almost as badly.

Despite economic hardship and continuing disorder on Barbados, new settlers flocked to the island. In 1635 one-fifth of all the emigrants sailing westward from London were destined for Barbados; during the next four years the

11. Barbados lay ninety miles east of the principal islands in the Lesser Antilles; prevailing westerly winds discouraged the approach of ships sailing from the South American mainland or Leeward Islands. Even so, a Spanish naval force under the command of Admiral Don Fadrique de Toledo did overwhelm heavily armed English settlements at St. Kitts and Nevis in 1629.

12. The Earl of Carlisle had outmaneuvered the sponsor of Courteen's syndicate, James Ley, 1st Earl of Marlborough, for possession of St. Kitts and Barbados. The latter would become a royal colony in 1663. "Colonial administrators and post-independence leaders in Barbados (1627–2000)," in *Oxford Dictionary of National Biography*, online ed., ed. Lawrence Goldman, January 2011.

13. Carlisle's planters owed him forty pounds of cotton annually. See Sir Robert Hermann Schomburgk, *The History of Barbados* (London: Longman, Brown, Green, and Longmans, 1848), 262. Approximately half of Barbados's 166 square miles were parceled out to the colonists who arrived in the 1620s.

population advanced sevenfold.[14] A decade after the Earl of Carlisle made the first land grants to individuals, only one-fifth of the island's 106,000 acres remained unclaimed. The size of grants had dwindled somewhat after 1630, but the average allotment for the first decade was just over ninety-six acres. This included allocations made as part of a headright system that awarded ten acres to new planters for each servant they brought—a less generous version of the strategy used to lure prospective settlers to land-rich colonies along the eastern seaboard of North America. In addition to outright grants and the dispensation of "freedom dues" for former servants, some acreage went to newcomers who purchased as much land as they could afford.[15] By 1640 the island could boast an estimated ten thousand inhabitants, a population comparable to Virginia and Massachusetts. Approximately one-quarter of those Barbadians were landowners, large and small; the rest were mainly indentured servants. The population also included several hundred African slaves but at that juncture they accounted for less than 10 percent of the total.

The prospect of laboring in a tropical climate dissuaded many Englishmen and Englishwomen from committing to four to seven years of servitude in the Caribbean. But hard times at home and misinformation—augmented by promises of free passage, free land when indentures expired, and future self-sufficiency—were enough to induce thousands to sign contracts with agents representing Barbados planters. A goodly number of servants were adolescents whose parents or guardians committed them to years of toil on the faraway island. In the seventeenth century, there were simply too few jobs and not nearly enough land to feed England's 4.8 million inhabitants. Poverty, rising crime rates and widespread homelessness helped induce 175,000 men, women, and children to immigrate to North America and an even greater number—some 210,000—to English possessions in the Caribbean before the century was out. In the 1650s, the peak period of outmigration, Barbados

14. Richard S. Dunn, *Sugar and Slaves: The Rise of the Planter Class in the English West Indies, 1624–1713* (New York: Norton, 1973), 56; Nicholas Canny, ed., *The Oxford History of the British Empire: Volume 1: The Origins of Empire* (New York: Oxford University Press, 2001), 222.

15. Hilary Beckles, *White Servitude and Black Slavery in Barbados 1627–1715* (Knoxville: University of Tennessee Press, 1989), 5. "Freedom dues" were awarded to servants who completed their terms of service. They varied by time and place, but they often included clothing, tools, or firearms and, in some cases, grants of land. Because of the intense competition for land in Barbados, servants did not receive land as part of their freedom dues after the introduction of sugar in the 1640s.

was the destination for 70 percent of the male servants and 65 percent of the female indentured servants.[16]

Not all fieldworkers on Barbados migrated there by choice. From the colony's inception, slavery and involuntary servitude were parts of everyday life on the island. Unlike the first blacks that arrived quite by chance in Virginia in 1619, the ten Africans who fell in with Barbados's first settlers were not freed after a standard period of indenture. In 1636 the Barbados Council resolved that, unless a previous contract stipulated otherwise, Africans and Indians transported to the island as laborers should serve for life. Native Americans from other Caribbean islands and the coast of South America did trickle in to Barbados in coming years but never constituted a significant population on the island. Some even came from as far away as New England. In late 1638 Governor John Winthrop of Massachusetts noted that Captain William Pierce of Salem had recently returned from Barbados with the first shipment of African slaves obtained in exchange for Indians captured in the Pequot War. Four decades later New Englanders attempted the same strategy with Indians taken in King Philip's war, but they proved troublesome, and in 1676 the Barbados Assembly resolved "to prevent the bringing of Indian slaves, and as well to send away and transport those already brought to this island from New England and adjacent colonies."[17]

Barbados also became a prison without walls for thousands of whites transported to the island against their will. In 1625 the same year that Henry Powell claimed Barbados for England, a royal proclamation called for the overseas banishment of "dangerous rogues." This merely gave sanction to a long-standing practice: the deportation of undesirables to distant lands. Among them were prisoners of war, political and religious dissidents, convicts, orphans, "rogues, thieves, whores and idle persons" deported by local authorities, and anyone who stood in the way of English expansion and exploitation in the British Isles.[18] The importation of such servants occasionally devolved into quasi-slavery, for many of those who arrived as a result of military and political conflicts in England, Scotland, and Ireland had their indentures sold in Barbados at auction. English slave traders sometimes

16. David Galenson, *White Servitude in Colonial America: An Economic Analysis* (Cambridge: Cambridge University Press, 1981), 82.

17. Jerome Handler, "Amerindians and their Contributions to Barbadian Life in the Seventeenth Century," *The Journal of the Barbados Museum and Historical Society* 35, no. 3 (1977): 189–90; Ron Wellburn, *Roanoke and Wampum: Topics in Native American Heritage and Literatures* (New York: Peter Lang Publishing, 2001), 28.

18. Abbot Emerson Smith, *Colonists in Bondage: White Servitude and Convict Labor in America, 1607–1776* (Gloucester, MA: Peter Smith, 1965), 136–74.

found it more profitable to purchase indentured men, women, and children in Bristol for £4 and sell them in Barbados for £10 to £35 rather than compete with the Dutch in the African trade.[19] Many people in seaside communities in the British Isles were kidnapped outright—"Barbadosed" in contemporary parlance—by unscrupulous traders. As many as fifty thousand Irish were deported to Barbados and Bermuda in what one historian has termed an "ethnic cleansing" of the land.[20] Some found themselves on vessels so crowded that epidemics were inevitable; the ship that carried Thomas Rous in 1638 lost 80 of its 350 passengers to disease.[21]

Citizens of other nations were spirited away to Barbados as well. According to a letter addressed to the French West India Company, in 1640 two English scalawags deceived two hundred young Frenchmen and transported them from a coastal town in Brittany to Barbados, where they were "engaged" by planters for five to seven years at the rate of £900 for each. Despite efforts by the governor of Guadeloupe to secure their release, the captives remained on the island until the entire group was alleged to have "died from the effects of the climate."[22] Three years later a Dutch trader offered to sell fifty Portuguese captives to Barbados planters. However, the terms of his proposal apparently ignored the distinction between involuntary servitude and lifelong slavery, violating the sensibilities of at least one influential islander. Feigning interest in the transaction, Philip Bell, governor of Barbados, ordered the prisoners to be brought on shore; he then released them and castigated the Dutchman for trying to sell white men and Christians. Just a few years later, the increased demand for laborers that attended the sugar boom seems to have tempered the Barbadians' moral squeamishness.[23] After his troops stormed the Irish fortifications at Drogheda in 1649, Oliver Cromwell reported to Parliament that the rebel officers were "knocked in the head, every tenth man was executed, and the rest shipped to Barbados" where they were forced into servitude. Other combatants in the vicinity were spared "as

19. Sean O'Callaghan, *To Hell or Barbados: The Ethnic Cleansing of Ireland* (Dingle, Co. Kerry, Ireland: Brandon, 2000), 86. The transport of human cargo from the British Isles to Barbados gave traders the added advantage of returning to England with sugar as their cargo.

20. Ibid., 9.

21. Rous to Archibald Hay, May 26, 1638, Hay Papers, quoted in Dunn, *Sugar and Slaves*, 57.

22. Père Du Tertre, *Histoire générale habitées les François* (Paris: 1667–71), tom. ii, 465–66, cited in Thomas Southey, *Chronological History of the West Indies*, vol. 1 (London: Longman, Rees, Orme, Brown, & Green, 1827), 285.

23. Schomburgk, *History of Barbados*, 144.

to their lives only"—their property and freedom having been forfeited—and "shipped likewise for the Barbados." Cromwell's fourth son, Henry, regarded the deportation of hundreds of thousands of Irish in the previous century as "a great benefit to the West Indies sugar planters, who desired men and boys for their bondsmen, and the women and Irish girls in a country where they had only Maroon women and Negresses to solace them."[24]

Following the Battle of Worcester in 1651, Oliver Cromwell ordered that the defeated Scots be "sold as slaves to the plantations of the American isles."[25] In 1655 a Court of Oyer and Terminer banished seventy "freeborn Englishmen" captured in a failed uprising against the Lord Protector's rule; they were "sold uncondemned into slavery" in Barbados for 1,550 pounds of sugar each. According to a 1659 petition for their relief, the former "divines, officers and gentlemen" were forced to grind sugarcane, attend furnaces and labor in the fields on "that scorching island." Despite the fact that Barbados's governing Council remained loyal to the king during the English Civil War, the Royalist exiles were ill-treated by their owners—"bought and sold from one planter to another, or attached like horses or beasts for the debt of their masters, being whipped at the whipping post as rogues, and sleeping in sties worse than hogs in England."[26] A 1661 deposition by Captain John Cole of Stepney disclosed that in March 1656 he transported prisoners ("80 men and one youth") from England to Barbados where they were to be disposed of "at the best rate in exchange for commodities"; his share was 6 percent of the profits.[27]

Even those servants who voluntarily signed indentures to gain passage to Barbados often met disappointment and ill treatment, inclining many toward the spirit of discontent that pervaded the workforce. Visitors noted the abuse that servants suffered and the desperation of many to escape the island. Not

24. Letter of Henry Cromwell, 4th, *Thurloes' State Papers*, quoted in John Prendergast, *The Cromwellian Settlement of Ireland* (Baltimore: Genealogical Publishing Com., 2009), 89.

25. Davis, *Cavaliers and Roundheads*, 82–83 fn. In retaliation Scottish Highlanders reportedly executed their prisoners of war since "they had no Barbados to send them to." Ibid., 42.

26. "England's Slavery, or Barbados Merchandize. Represented in a petition to the high and honourable court of Parliament, by Marcellus Rivers and Oxenbridge Foyle, Gentlemen, on behalf of themselves and three-score and ten more of freeborn Englishmen, sold uncondemned into slavery" (London, 1659), in Schomburgk, *History of Barbados*, 284.

27. "Deposition of John Cole of Stepney, Middlesex, mariner, age 39, and late Commander of the 'John' of London," in *Lord Mayor's Court of London, Depositions Relating to Americans, 1641–1736*, ed. Peter Wilson Coldham (Arlington, VA: National Genealogical Society, 1980), 81.

surprisingly, forced labor and intolerable living conditions generated resistance and sporadic violence. During a visit to Barbados in 1634, Henry Colt noted the crowds of servants lingering at the waterfront, hoping to stow away on a departing vessel. Few succeeded, of course, so they registered their dissatisfaction in other ways, stealing goods, hiding in the "thickets," and occasionally burning cane fields. In 1634 an uprising took place in which servants resolved to kill their masters and sail from Barbados.[28] An even more dangerous and widespread revolt, in which servants aimed to take over the island, occurred in 1647; eighteen were executed in its aftermath.[29] Richard Ligon noted that the planters built strongly fortified houses with "bulwarks and bastions" to defend themselves in case there should be "any uproar of commotion on the island, either by the Christian servants or negro slaves."[30] It would not take long for the latter group to become the greater threat to Barbados planters thanks to their sudden obsession with a lucrative but labor-intensive new commodity—sugar.

In the mid-1640s, Barbados planters began to abandon tobacco, indigo, ginger, and cotton crops in favor of sugarcane—a staple with seemingly limitless demand throughout Europe. Dutch interlopers who had developed their expertise on Brazilian plantations that they had seized from the Portuguese tutored the Barbadians. In disseminating the secrets of sugar production, the savvy Dutch generated numerous revenue streams: they would provide vital equipment and then transport, process, and market the sugar grown on Barbados. Because intensive cultivation would require significantly more laborers than the island held at that point, Dutch slave traders also stood to gain by providing thousands of Africans to augment and eventually replace white servants in the fields.

Sugar was not a poor man's crop: the most successful planters were those with substantial lands, a large workforce and the financial resources to pur-

28. In 1634 settlers headed for the new colony of Maryland made anchor at Barbados and found the planters "all in arms." The servants had "conspired to kill their masters and make themselves free, and then handsomely take the first ship that came, and so go to sea." A servant revealed the plot and it was foiled. "A Briefe Relation of the Voyage Unto Maryland by Father Andrew White," in *Narratives of Early Maryland, 1633–1684*, ed. C. C. Hall (New York: Charles Scribner's Sons, 1910), 34.

29. Sir Henry Colt, "The Voyage of Sir Henrye Colt Knight to the Ilands of the Antilles ...," in *Colonising Expeditions to the West Indies and Guiana, 1623–1667, Publications of the Hakluyt Society*, 2nd series, vol. 56, ed. Vincent T. Harlow (London, 1925), 54–102.

30. Richard Ligon, *A True History and Exact History of the Island of Barbados*, ed. Karen Ordahl Kupperman (London, 1657; reprinted Indianapolis: Hackett Publishing, 2011), 22; Dunn, *Sugar and Slaves*, 69.

chase sugar boilers and other equipment necessary to convert raw sugarcane to crystalline sugar and molasses. Because more acres under cultivation meant more revenues, the process of land consolidation greatly accelerated on Barbados. The island's wealthier inhabitants, some of whom were Royalist newcomers seeking refuge from war-torn England, vied for any parcels that became available; these were frequently the dividends or freedom dues awarded to smaller planters who died, departed, or simply could not compete effectively with their larger neighbors. Sir James Drax, one of Barbados's original settlers, amassed an 850-acre plantation; another planter's 800-acre estate reportedly included no less than forty separate lots originally assigned to individual settlers.[31] In 1647 Thomas Modyford and his brother-in-law invested £7,000 for a half share in William Hilliard's plantation, which had been valued at £400 just seven years earlier.[32]

As more and more planters converted to sugar production, land prices soared, as did income. Father Antoine Biet, a French priest who visited Barbados in 1654, commented that sugarcane was planted in the countryside "as far as the eye can see."[33] Just ten years after the introduction of sugar to the island, visitor Henry Whistler noted that Barbados was "one of the richest spots of ground in the world" and its gentry "live far better than ours do in England."[34] A London pamphlet entitled *Trade Revived* claimed that the sugar boom had "given to many men of low degree vast fortunes, equal to noblemen."[35] In 1666 Barbados was adjudged to be seventeen times richer than before the introduction of sugar; planters had by then become so devoted to the crop that they opted to import foodstuffs from North America and Ireland rather than grow their own.[36]

31. Sloane 3662, folio 62, cited in Davis, *Cavaliers & Roundheads*, 80 fn. Due to his Dutch connections, Drax had played a major role in the introduction of sugar cultivation to Barbados.

32. Nuala Zahedieh, "Modyford, Sir Thomas, first baronet (c.1620–1679)," in *Oxford Dictionary of National Biography*, ed. H. C. G. Matthew and Brian Harrison (Oxford: OUP, 2004); online ed., ed. Lawrence Goldman, January 2008.

33. Jerome S. Handler, ed., "Father Antoine Biet's Visit to Barbados in 1654," *Journal of the Barbados Museum and Historical Society*, 32 (1967): 66.

34. "Extracts from Henry Whistler's Journal of the West India Expedition," in *The Narrative of General Venables*, ed. C. H. Firth (Camden Society, 1900), 146.

35. "Trade Revived," [pamphlet] quoted in *Leigh Hunt's London Journal* 1, no. 29 [Oct. 15, 1834] (London: Charles Knight, 1834): 227.

36. Nearly two decades earlier, Richard Vines informed Governor John Winthrop of Massachusetts that Barbadians would "rather buy food at very deare rates than produce it by labour, soe infinite is the profit of sugar works." [Richard Vines to John Winthrop,

At first, the great effort involved in conversion from tobacco and cotton to sugarcane fell primarily upon the shoulders of white servants, but this grew more problematic over time. As described earlier, military, and political affairs in England, Scotland, and Ireland provided Barbados planters with thousands of additional laborers during the opening decade of the sugar boom. However, many of these proved to be even more vulgar, shiftless, and uncooperative than the servants who had voluntarily entered indentures in the 1620s and '30s. The island's workforce had already established an unsavory reputation for intoxication, thievery, lewdness, and sloth; the influx of outcasts, felons, captives, and political prisoners in the 1640s and '50s only exacerbated those problems. Irish servants were held in especial contempt, "derided by the negroes, and branded with the Epithet of 'white slaves.'"[37] The Barbados Council in 1644 considered *An Act for the Prohibition of Landing of Irish Persons*, but not all the island's pariahs were from the Emerald Isle. Vagabonds of all descriptions continued to be transported to the island; young scalawags in the British Isles were known to be whipped through the streets and then transported to Barbados.[38] In one visitor's estimation, the island was "the dunghill whereon England doth cast forth its rubbish . . . Rogues and whores and such like people are those which are generally brought here."[39]

Planters attempted to control matters by enforcing rigid discipline: following several years' residency in Barbados, Richard Ligon said, "I have seen

---

July 19, 1647, *Winthrop Papers, 1498–1649* (Boston, 1929–1947) Massachusetts Historical Society Collections, 4th series, vol. 5, 172.] Barbadians' collective commitment to production of one cash crop, using slave labor, foreshadowed South Carolina's rice and cotton industries. However, the abundance of land meant Carolina planters were not constrained to a rigid monoculture pattern; they could also produce foodstuffs and secondary exports such as indigo, diversifying to a degree that the Barbadians could never imagine. Thus the plantation system developed by sugar planters was imperfectly mimicked in the Southeast, though it might be argued that rice and (later) cotton planters improved on the Barbadian model by making self-sufficiency a hallmark of plantation efficiency.

37. Hilary Beckles, "A 'Riotous and Unruly Lot': Irish Indentured Servants and Freemen in the English West Indies, 1644–1713," *William and Mary Quarterly*, 3rd series, 47, no. 4 (October 1990): 511.

38. Schomburgk, *History of Barbados*, 144 fn.

39. Firth, "Extracts from Henry Whistler's Journal," 146. Antoine Biet considered lewdness to be the greatest of all the vices that prevailed in Barbados, saying, "It is a horrible thing to think about: adulterers, incest and all the rest." He viewed drunkenness as a particular problem "among the lower classes." Handler, "Father Antoine Biet's Visit," 68.

such cruelty done to servants as I would not think one Christian could ever have done to another." Moreover, the sugar barons' intense competition for land consumed the acreage that servants coveted as freedom dues; their prospects on the island were as bleak as they would have been in England, or worse. Disease was another major problem; according to Ligon, a 1647 epidemic struck down so many inhabitants that islanders were compelled to throw corpses into "the swamp." He observed that in Barbados, "sicknesses are there more grievous, and mortality greater by far than in *England*."[40] At mid-century as many as three out of four whites perished within two years of their arrival, usually from malaria or yellow fever.[41]

ᘓᘓ

By the 1660s the abusive treatment, scant opportunities, and appalling death rate of servants on Barbados were so widely known that English emigrants steered away from the island, opting instead for more promising destinations in the English West Indies (most notably Jamaica) or on the American mainland.[42] In addition, the termination of hostilities and improved economic conditions in England meant that fewer young men and women were inclined to become indentured servants, especially if the associated "freedom dues" were inconsequential. The Barbados Assembly attempted to alleviate the situation by passing the first comprehensive statute "for the good governing of Servants, and ordaining the rights between Masters and Servants." The legislation did little to attract white servants to the island. In a petition drafted in 1675, Barbadian sugar planters bemoaned the fact that in former times they were "plentifully furnished with Christian servants" from England and Scotland but "now we get few English, having no lands to give them at the end of their time, which formerly was their main allurement."[43] This only hastened a transition that was already underway—the shift to a predominately African workforce.

40. Ligon, *True History and Exact History*, 25, cited in Schomburgk, *History of Barbados*, 80.

41. Rogozinski, *Brief History of the Caribbean*, 71. Richard Sheridan claims the island was free of malaria; see Sheridan, *Sugar and Slavery*, 126.

42. The Barbadian diaspora also included destinations in Surinam, St. Lucia, St. Kitts, and Nevis. Justin Roberts and Ian Beamish, "Venturing Out: The Barbadian Diaspora and the Carolina Colony, 1650–1685," in *Creating and Contesting Carolina*, ed. LeMaster and Wood, 49–50.

43. "Grievances of the Inhabitants of Barbados" (November 25, 1675), cited in Hilary Beckles, *White Servitude and Black Slavery in Barbados, 1627–1715* (Knoxville: University of Tennessee Press, 1989), 10.

Though the first Africans on Barbados arrived at the colony quite by chance, those who followed were acquired by barter or outright purchase. Until the 1640s there was little demand for slaves: conditions and events in England fostered an ample supply of indentured servants, both voluntary and involuntary. The insubstantial revenues stemming from the planting of tobacco, indigo, and cotton hardly necessitated the importation of large numbers of Africans. Also, given the prohibitive cost of enslaved Africans in the first half of the seventeenth century and the likelihood that disease, malnutrition, and overwork might kill them within a matter of months, white indentured servants initially seemed the wiser choice despite the problems they caused. The cost of passage for a servant was only £6 to £7, so planters could recover their investment in just two years; every year of service beginning with the third was pure profit.[44] A servant's untimely demise, should it come, had limited financial ramifications: he or she was a short-term investment, not a purchase for life. But the emergence of sugar as the island's main crop changed everything; the number of slaves—fewer than one thousand in 1640—climbed to twenty thousand by 1655, nearly equal to the white population.[45] According to *Leigh Hunt's London Journal*, Barbados planters "found it impossible to manage the cultivation of sugar by white people in so hot a climate" and the example of Portuguese sugar plantations in Brazil "gave birth to the negro slave trade."[46] In 1654 Antoine Biet noted Barbados planters' investment in their captive workforce: "Their greatest wealth are their slaves, and there is not one slave who does not make a profit of more than one hundred *ecus* each year for his master. Each slave does not cost four *ecus* per year for his upkeep."[47] The following year Henry Whistler observed that most Barbados's gentry had "100 or 2 or 3 [hundred] slave apes who they command as they please." He described the latter as "miserable Negroes born to perpetual slavery, they and their seed." According to Whistler, "Some planters will

44. Beckles, *White Servitude and Black Slavery*, 2.

45. Russell Menard argues that slavery was expanding rapidly before the island's "sugar boom," but there can be no doubt that sugar and slavery grew in tandem on Barbados and elsewhere in the West Indies. Menard offers a "rough guess" that "at least one thousand slaves arrived on the island during the 1630s." Russell R. Menard, *Sweet Negotiations: Sugar, Slavery, and Plantation Agriculture in Early Barbados* (Charlottesville: University of Virginia Press, 2006), 30–31. Richard Ligon observed on several occasions that Barbadian planters worked servants harder than slaves because the labor of the former was only available for the term of their indentures. Ligon, *True and Exact History*, ed. Kupperman, 21.

46. *Leigh Hunt's London Journal* 1, no. 29 [Oct. 15, 1834]: 227.

47. Handler, ed., "Father Antoine Biet's Visit," 66.

have thirty more or less about four or five years old. They sell them from one to the other as we do sheep."[48] In 1645 planter George Downing informed his cousin, John Winthrop Jr. that Barbadians had bought "no less than a thousand negroes" that year, and "the more they buy, the better able they are to buy, for in a year and a half they will earn (with God's blessing) as much as they cost."[49]

During Barbados's sugar boom, the trade in slaves was a lucrative and expanding business. The Dutch had supplanted the Portuguese as the preeminent slave traders and supplied Barbados planters in the 1630s and '40s but two decades of Anglo-Dutch conflict beginning in 1652 gave impetus to English endeavors.[50] Several years after the restoration of the monarchy in 1660, Charles II granted a charter to the Royal Adventurers to Africa, a company whose members included royalty as well as prominent aristocrats and merchants. Their ships and those of private traders ensured a plentiful supply of Africans to islands in the West Indies. With the creation of the Royal African Company in 1672, the sale of enslaved blacks to sugar planters on Barbados, St. Christopher, Nevis, Antigua, Montserrat, and Jamaica enriched a new coterie of investors, including James, Duke of York and future king of England.[51] The frequent appearance of RAC ships and smugglers who competed with them guaranteed favorable prices for Africans in Barbados, especially since the island, situated ninety miles east of its closest neighbor, St. Lucia, was often the slavers' first port of call.

48. Firth, ed., "Extracts from Henry Whistler's Journal," 146.

49. *Winthrop Papers*, Massachusetts Historical Society Collections, 4th series, vol. 4, 536.

50. When Barbados was settled in 1627, England had already been involved in the slave trade for more than half a century; Stuart monarchs would increase the nation's complicity in the trade. John Hawkyns, the first Englishman to engage the Spanish military in the Americas, conducted slave trading voyages in the 1560s underwritten in part by London merchants, English noblemen, the Lord Mayor of London, and Queen Elizabeth. He carried 1,500 to 2,000 Africans from Guinea into slavery in the Caribbean. [Nick Hazlewood, *The Queen's Slave Trader: John Hawkyns, Elizabeth I, and the Trafficking in Human Souls* (New York: Harper Collins, 2004), 312.] Sir Robert Rich, later the Earl of Warwick, was one of the founders of the Company of Adventurers to Guinea and Benin, a group largely composed on London merchants. In 1632 Charles I granted a license to another slave-trading syndicate.

51. Chartered in 1672 to deliver slaves to the English colonies "on a large scale," the Royal African Company transported approximately 120,000 Africans to the English West Indies over the next four decades. Dunn, *Sugar and Slaves*, 231–33.

High volume and low purchase prices encouraged sugar planters to invest in slaves rather than pay the passage for indentured servants which had risen from £6 in the 1630s to £12 by mid-century. At that point an African male deemed in his prime could be purchased for £30; a female in her prime cost £25. Because planters needed significant capital to purchase slaves in quantity, the changeover from white to black laborers was a gradual process, so many plantations had biracial workforces for years or even decades. In fact during the 1640s and '50s, when indentured servants were still in plentiful supply, many planters acquired both white and black laborers.[52] Twenty-one servants and nine slaves tended to Sir Anthony Ashley Cooper's 205 acres in 1646; Thomas Modyford, by contrast, had twenty-eight servants and 102 enslaved Africans on the five-hundred-acre plantation he managed in 1647. A decade later John Read, a planter of more limited means, had twenty-one servants and twenty-five slaves laboring on his seventy-five acres.[53]

This racial mixing did lead to problems: many Europeans objected to working alongside Africans, especially considering that the slaves, "being subject to their masters forever," were "kept and preserved with greater care than the servants." Some whites ran away rather than work in gangs that included blacks; others demanded unilateral termination of their indentures.[54] In 1654 one visitor observed that servants were "badly treated," receiving only potatoes as their diet—the same fare given to slaves. In the fields the overseers acted "like those in charge of galley slaves," prodding servants with sticks to hasten their efforts. Another contemporary stated that servants "have the worser lives, for they are put to very hard labour, ill lodging, and

52. Skin color and cultural markers (especially language) linked white servants and their masters, but these commonalities were often overshadowed by differences in socioeconomic status, nationality, and religion. This was especially the case in the 1640s and 1650s as Barbados's planter elite emerged and the servant population became increasingly composed of Irish Catholics. Peter Wood maintains that in Carolina, "custom, language, and religion naturally made Europeans prefer to have other Europeans working with and under them." This ignores many differences that separated rather than united servants and masters. Moreover, servant uprisings in Barbados (and later, Virginia) and the Africanization of the workforce on Barbados and in the American South raise serious questions about Wood's claim. Peter H. Wood, *Black Majority: Negroes in Colonial South Carolina from 1670 through the Stono Rebellion* (New York: W. W. Norton, 1974), 40.

53. Dunn, *Sugar and Slaves*, 68.

54. William Roger Louis, Alaine M. Low, and Nicholas P. Canny, *The Oxford History of the British Empire: The Origins of Empire* (New York: Oxford University Press, 1998), 228.

their diet very slight."[55] The arrival of Royalist gentry fleeing England may have benefited some servants: Richard Ligon's 1657 description of Barbados stated that "as discreeter and better natured men have come to rule there, the servants' lives have been much better." While most planters remained quick to lash out at any worker who compromised their operations, some recognized that unrestrained fury posed a danger to all. Colonel Henry Drax, one of the island's wealthiest landowners, told his overseer that a man who was unable to control his passions, "especially with servants," was not fit to judge or command.[56] The ongoing test of wills between profit-minded masters and resentful servants, many of whom were not in Barbados by choice, meant the possibility of rebellion was omnipresent, especially among the lowly Irish.

Some planters were well ahead of the curve in the transition to an enslaved labor force. Menard estimates that in 1643, the year of Barbados's first sugar crop, there were already six thousand Africans on the island.[57] One reason to purchase slaves despite their higher cost was the steadily deteriorating relationship between the planters and servants on Barbados. A breach of faith occurred when Barbadian planters ignored the reciprocity that traditionally accompanied the master-servant relationship in England.[58] Many individuals

55. Handler, ed., "Father Antoine Biet's Visit," 66; Ligon, *True and Exact History*, ed. Kupperman, 51–52.

56. Peter Thompson, ed., "Henry Drax's Instructions on the Management of a Seventeenth-Century Barbadian Sugar Plantation," *The William and Mary Quarterly*, 3rd Series, 66, no. 3 (July 2009): 588.

57. Menard, *Sweet Negotiations*, 31.

58. Susan Dwyer Amussen, *Caribbean Exchanges: Slavery and the Transformation of English Society, 1640–1700* (Chapel Hill: University of North Carolina Press, 2007), 128. In a landmark article, sociologist Alvin Gouldner describes the norm of reciprocity and its contribution to the stability of social systems. "It can be hypothesized that a norm of reciprocity is universal," states Gouldner, but from the standpoint of a "purely economic or utilitarian model," the only motive for an exchange is "the anticipated gratification it will bring." Under those conditions, "Each may then feel that it would be advantageous to lay hold of the other's valuables without relinquishing his own." In such a model, distrust becomes rampant. Gouldner adds, "At least since Hobbes, it has been recognized that under such circumstances, each is likely to regard the impending exchange as dangerous and to view the other with some suspicion." When internalized, the norm obliges the one who has first received a benefit—in this case, the labor of an indentured servant in Barbados—to repay it at some time. But economics and utilitarianism were driving forces in Barbados, and sugar planters gave servants little reason to expect the type of reciprocity that once typified social relations in England. Alvin W. Gouldner, "The Norm of Reciprocity: A Preliminary Statement," *American Sociological Review* 25, no. 2 (April 1960): 161–78.

had indentured themselves voluntarily, but the conditions they encountered on the island meant their servitude had to be "maintained by the systematic application of legally sanctioned force and violence."[59] Of course the brutal subjugation of fellow Englishmen or Irish was problematic since even servants were entitled to certain rights under common law. Colonial courts and assemblies could intervene on a servant's behalf and occasionally did so. Thus masters sometimes had to restrain themselves or face possible legal consequences.

Faced with the resistance that emanated from servants' sense of rights, both inherent and contractual, and with the need to act within legal bounds when motivating or correcting individuals, some planters undoubtedly preferred workers who could be routinely exploited and punished without restraint. Enslaved Africans fit that bill. They lacked the rights that British servants claimed. They could be compelled to work at whatever pace the master or overseers set or face the consequences. Slaves had to settle for whatever food, clothing, and shelter were dispensed, no matter how inadequate. Courts and lawmakers were unlikely to intervene on their behalf. African slaves lacked solidarity, at least at the outset, and had no indentures that limited their terms of service. In short, some planters were probably willing to pay more for workers over whom they had absolute power. And as Lord Acton famously observed: "Power tends to corrupt, and absolute power corrupts absolutely."[60] The absence of any restraints that might protect slaves from sadistic whites was blatant when Father Antoine Biet visited Barbados in 1654: "They treat their Negro slaves with a great deal of severity. If some go beyond the limits of the plantation on a Sunday they are given fifty blows with a cudgel ... If they commit some other slightly more serious offense they are beaten to excess, sometimes up to the point of applying a firebrand all over their bodies which makes them shriek with despair."[61]

Biet was "horrified" by the scars on one female slave's body. On another occasion, he felt compelled to intercede on behalf of a black laborer who had stolen a pig. The overseer had the thief placed in irons and whipped by fellow slaves daily for a week, after which he cut off one of his ears, roasted it, and

59. Beckles, *White Servitude and Black Slavery*, 5.

60. Lord Acton, "Letter to Bishop Mandell Creighton, April 5, 1887," in Lord Acton, *Historical Essays and Studies*, by John Emerich Edward Dalberg-Acton, ed. John Neville Figgis and Reginald Vere Laurence (London: Macmillan, 1907), appendix; accessed from http://oll.libertyfund.org. Though Acton's observation came more than two centuries after the introduction of African slavery on Barbados, it seemed especially cogent regarding affairs prior to the establishment of Enlightenment principles.

61. Handler, ed., "Father Antoine Biet's Visit," 66–67.

forced him to eat it. He planned to do the same to the slave's nose and other ear, but the clergyman "pleaded so well with the overseer that the Negro was freed from his torment." Biet acknowledged that "one must keep these kinds of people obedient" but maintained that "it is inhuman to treat them with, so much harshness."[62]

Most planters realized that discipline, a vital part of the emerging plantation complex, required a blend of severity and good judgment. Colonel Drax gave his overseer specific advice on how and when to punish a slave: "You must never punish either to satisfy your own anger or passion, the end of punishment being either to reclaim the malefactor or to terrify others from committing the like fault." Drax considered the theft of molasses or sugar to be a crime of the most serious nature—one that called for extreme measures, "there being no punishment too terrible on such an occasion as doeth not deprive the party of either life or limbs."[63] He cautioned that there should be no delay in executing the sentence, given slaves' tendency to hang themselves to avoid punishment. Richard Ligon attributed these suicides to the Africans' belief that death would be followed by a resurrection, whereby "they shall go into their own Country again and have their youth renewed." For this reason, he explained, they made it an "ordinary practice" to hang themselves "upon any great fright or threatening of their Master."[64] Colonel Humphrey Walrond, a prominent Barbadian angered by the suicides of several of "his best Negroes," decapitated one of his slaves and set the head atop a pole: "Having done that, caused all his *Negroes* to come forth and march round about this head and bid them look on it . . . he then told them, that they were in a main error in thinking they went into their own Countries after they were dead; for, this man's head was here, as they all were witnesses of; and how was it possible the body could go without a head. Being convinced by this sad yet lively spectacle, they changed their opinions; and after that, no more hanged themselves."[65]

Walrond arrived in Barbados in the mid-1640s at the outset of the sugar boom; in the 1650s his insistence that the island's fast-growing population of servants and slaves threatened the safety of all planters caused considerable consternation. His argument was not without merit: a conspiracy by indentured servants had been thwarted in late 1633 and a more serious revolt by indentured whites was narrowly averted in 1649. By then the servants'

62. Ibid., 67.
63. Thompson, ed., "Henry Drax's Instructions," 588.
64. Ligon, *True and Exact History*, Kupperman, 17.
65. Ibid., 51.

collective suffering had "grown to a great height"; no longer able to endure the "intolerable burdens they labored under," the majority plotted to "fall upon their Masters, and cut all their throats and by that means make themselves not only freemen but Masters of the Island."[66] For the planters, the nightmare scenario was that white and black laborers might join forces and take control of the island. In 1655 Irish servants and slaves were reportedly "out in rebellion," though the uprising was limited in scope.[67] Over time it would become clear that the planters' interests were best served by taking steps to foster a racial divide, reducing the likelihood of biracial collusion at the bottom of Barbados society. However, in the 1640s and 1650s the importation of thousands of workers, white and black, rendered such measures difficult: planters literally needed laborers by the boatload for their expanding sugar plantations. Richard Ligon's 1657 description of Barbados included the observation that "We breed both Negroes, Horses and Cattle . . . and yet the increase will not supply the moderate decayes which we find."[68]

Following his three-year stint on the island from 1647 to 1650, Ligon noted that many people questioned why Barbados's blacks, being "more than double" the number of Christian inhabitants, did not commit "some horrid massacre" and become "Masters of the Island." He attributed the slaves' inaction to that point to three reasons. First, they were not allowed to touch or handle any weapons. Second, they were "held in such awe and slavery" that "they are fearful to appear in any daring act; and seeing the mustering of our men and hearing their Gun-shot (that which nothing is more terrible to them), their spirits are subjugated to so low a condition as they dare not look up to any bold attempt."[69] The third reason, "which stops all designs [plans] of that kind," according to Ligon, was that the slaves on Barbados were "fetch'd from several parts of *Africa*, who speak several languages, and by that means one of them understands not another." The exodus of small landholders and former servants from the mid-1640s onward undermined whatever

66. Ibid., 44–46.

67. In 1686 Barbados planters were alarmed by rumors about a "rising designed by the Negroes"; they planned to join with the Irish servants "to destroy all masters and mistresses." The rumors eventually proved false, but the sense of alarm was genuine. See Jerome Handler, "Slave Revolts and Conspiracies in Seventeenth-Century Barbados," in *New West Indian Guide* 56 (1982), no: 1/2, Leiden, 20. In 1692 another slave conspiracy involved the enlistment of "four or five Irish men" who were supposed to open the doors of the fort to the rebel slaves. Ibid., 26–27.

68. Ligon, *True and Exact History*, quoted in Hilary Beckles, *Natural Rebels: A Social History of Enslaved Women in Barbados* (New Brunswick: Rutgers University Press, 1989), 90.

69. Ligon, *True and Exact History*, Kupperman, 57.

security the island's planters may have drawn from such reassurances. The departure of thousands of former proprietors who had been "wormed out of their small settlements by their more subtle and greedy neighbors" left the island's remaining planters more vulnerable to slave insurrection.[70] White Barbadians narrowly averted disaster in 1659 when a major slave conspiracy was exposed at the last minute. The leader, an African alleged to have been a Prince in his own country, was promptly executed and white patrols hunted down "straggling negroes" and conducted searches for spears, lances, clubs, and knives.[71]

Given the rebellious nature of many indentured servants and the continuing importation of potentially murderous African slaves, the island's leaders looked for some way to ensure planters' collective safety. The solution they derived—one that would be replicated by Barbadians who migrated to other slaveholding colonies—was to mollify the white laborers with certain concessions and protections while exerting greater control of the black majority through intimidation, ongoing scrutiny, and subjugation backed by brute force. In 1661 this strategy was articulated via two pieces of legislation: *An Act for the good Governing of Servants and ordeyneing the rights between Master and Servants* and *An Act for the better ordering and governing of Negroes*, often referred to as the "Barbados Slave Act."

The 1661 act concerning white indentured servants ensured their continued subordination but placed limits on the type and extent of punishments that a master could employ. It also established minimum allotments of food and clothing for servants and gave them the right to appeal in the courts if they were mistreated. If they were accused of any serious crime(s), servants were entitled to trial by jury. While calling on masters to take a "continual strict course" in dealing with servants' "unruliness, obstinacy and refractioness," the *Act for the good Governing of Servants and ordeyneing the rights between Master and Servants* did placate some white laborers by making a clear distinction between indentured servitude and outright slavery.[72]

A scandalous milestone in the history of racial discrimination, the 1661 *Act for the better ordering and governing of Negroes* established a legal foundation for the oppression of the island's black population. Revised and expanded in 1676, 1682, and 1688, the 1661 act would serve as the model for similar

---

70. *Cal. S.P. Col. 1661–1668, 528–30*, cited in Sheridan, *Sugar and Slavery*, 132.

71. Carla Gardina Pestana, *The English Atlantic in an Age of Revolution, 1640–1661* (Cambridge and London: Harvard University Press, 2004), 203.

72. Robin Blackburn, *The Making of New World Slavery: From the Baroque to the Modern, 1492–1800* (London: Verso, 1998), 249–50.

legislation passed in Jamaica, Antigua, and South Carolina. The preamble described Africans as a "heathenish, brutish and an uncertain, dangerous kind of people." Though the act acknowledged that slaves were "Men, though without the knowledge of God," it equated them with "goods and Chattels." The new law afforded masters total authority over their slaves, including the right to punish them as they saw fit. Should an offending slave die because of such "correction," the master faced no legal consequences; fines could be assessed if an owner wantonly murdered his slave or that of another planter. The Assembly aimed to control the growing population of slaves without exposing individual blacks to "the Arbitrary, cruell and outragious wills of every evill disposed person."[73]

Among the act's twenty-three clauses or articles were those that confined slaves to the plantation of their owner (blacks with written passes were an exception) and one that called for planters to flog any slave who visited his plantation without a pass. Should a slave "offer any Violence to any Christian," a severe whipping was administered for the first offense. A second infraction resulted in slitting of the nose, facial branding, and another whipping. A third offense invited "greater corporall punishment" at the discretion of the Justices. Ten clauses pertained to runaway slaves—a real concern because in planters' minds they opened the door to theft, arson, and general insurrection. The death penalty awaited any black disposed toward mutiny or rebellion. The *Act for the better ordering and governing of Negroes* included few provisions meant to protect slaves; it was taken for granted that planters had a personal stake in their slaves and therefore would not harm them without just cause.[74] In theory it made sense, but reality often proved otherwise.

One threat to the planters' collective security was the continuing problem of runaway slaves. Prior to the deforestation of Barbados (which was largely accomplished by the 1680s), runaways hid out in the island's woods and caves. An English visitor reported "many hundreds of rebel Negro slaves in the woods" and a map of Barbados published in 1657 depicts white riders

73. Barbados Act for the better ordering and governing of Negroes, Sept. 27, 1661, Barbados MSS Laws, 1645–1682, C.O. 30/2/16–26, quoted in Dunn, *Sugar and Slaves*, 238.

74. This sentiment was echoed in a 1789 Parliamentary report on the slave laws in the West Indies; it stated that the owner's "interest in their [slaves] Preservation, might perhaps have been judged a better Security for their good Treatment, than any Sanction of Legislative Authority." David Barry Gaspar, "With a Rod of Iron: Barbados Slave Laws as a Model for Jamaica, South Carolina and Antigua, 1661–1697," in *Crossing Boundaries: Comparative History of Black people in Diaspora*, ed. Darlene Clark Hine and Jacqueline McLeod (Bloomington: Indiana University Press, 1999), 346–48.

on horseback firing guns at black fugitives. That same year, the Assembly requested the governor to appoint a day for the "general hunting" of runaways who were "committing murders, robberies, and divers other mischiefs." Fortunately for the planters, the island's small size, relatively flat terrain and disappearing forests prohibited any long-standing maroon communities from forming as they would on larger islands such as Jamaica. A law passed in 1661 allowed armed patrols to seize fugitive slaves "either alive or dead" and stipulated that one thousand pounds of sugar would be the reward for the return of any slave who had been in hiding for more than twelve months.[75]

A plot even more dangerous than that which inspired the 1661 *Act for the better ordering and governing of Negroes* was "miraculously discovered" in 1675 when a domestic slave informed her mistress of a conspiratorial conversation she overheard. Upon a prearranged signal "in the dead time of the night," slaves all over the island were to set fire to the cane fields and cut the throats of their masters. According to one account, the blacks were to kill all whites "within a fortnight" except for the "fairest and handsomest women" who would be "converted to their own use." Seventeen slaves implicated in the plot were seized and hastily arraigned before a panel of four militia officers; eleven of the seventeen were beheaded, the remaining six were burned alive. In accordance with the planters' strategy of intimidation, the bodies of the beheaded conspirators were dragged through the streets and then burned alongside those unfortunates who were set to the stake. Five other slaves hanged themselves rather than face similar punishments. As the investigation and arraignments continued, twenty-five more blacks were executed for their role in the conspiracy. According to the governor's subsequent report, the scheme was three years in the making and had been "cunningly and clandestinely" communicated "over most of the plantations."[76]

In the wake of the "Grand Conspiracy of the Negroes," the Barbados Assembly took steps to fortify the island's militia and to eliminate deficiencies in the 1661 slave act. New language stiffened the penalties for assaults on whites and for theft or malicious destruction of property. The legislation also attempted to curb unregulated travel that afforded slaves "more opportunity of contriving mischief and rebellion." Certain provisions called for regular

75. Beauchamp Plantagenet, *A Description of the Province of New Albion* (London: 1648), quoted in Handler, "Slave Revolts and Conspiracies," in *New West Indian Guide* 56 (1982), no: 1/2, Leiden, 8–9. The map appeared in Richard Ligon's *True History and Exact History of the Island of Barbados*, published in London in 1657.
76. *Great Newes From the Barbados. Or, a True and Faithful Account of the Grand Conspiracy of the Negroes Against the English* (London, 1676), 9–12, quoted in Handler, "Slave Revolts and Conspiracies," 14–16.

searches of slave quarters for runaways or contraband such as drums, horns, clubs, wooden swords, or other "mischievous weapons."[77]

Despite the threat that enslaved Africans posed to white inhabitants of Barbados, many planters believed that blacks were more productive and better suited to fieldwork than white indentured servants. In 1676 the governor stated that the planters there had "grown weary" of Irish servants: "They prove commonly very idle and they do find by experience that they can keep three blacks who work better and cheaper than they can keep one white man."[78] Some planters considered tasks such as spreading manure, digging cane holes, and weeding fields to be degrading and therefore inappropriate for white laborers when blacks were readily available. In addition, some planters feared that demeaning work and oppressive discipline might provoke retaliation by whites, particularly those who had been forced into servitude. Colonel Henry Drax informed his overseer that if he had his way, he would employ only slaves: "I shall not leave you many white servants . . . the fewer the better."[79]

By the mid-1670s Africans constituted 60 percent of the inhabitants on Barbados (though not by choice). Natural increase contributed slightly to the increase in the island's black population, but the life of a slave on a sugar plantation was dreadful; throughout the seventeenth and eighteenth centuries, deaths outnumbered births. The arrival of a hundred enslaved Africans did not foster a corresponding increase in the population; many were simply purchased to replace those who had died.[80] Anticipating that 3 percent to 5 percent of his slaves would perish each year, Colonel Drax offered to replace "those that shall be deceased" or to simply provide "a yearly recruit of 10 or

77. *A Supplemental Act to a Former Act for the Better Ordering and Governing of Negroes*, April 21, 1676, CO 30/2, 114–25, in Handler, "Slave Revolts and Conspiracies," in *New West Indian Guide* 56 (1982), no: 1/2, Leiden, 17.

78. Vincent Todd Harlow, *A History of Barbados: 1625–1685* (New York: Negro Universities Press, 1969), 309.

79. Thompson, ed., "Henry Drax's Instructions," 587.

80. This was no short-term phenomenon; between 1708 and 1735, Barbadians imported eighty-five thousand slaves. Due to the extremely high mortality on the island, the net increase in slaves at the end of that period was only four thousand. A 1757 publication, *An Account of the European Settlements in America*, estimated that five thousand slaves needed to be imported annually to sustain Barbados's population of eighty thousand slaves. Information compiled by Griffith Hughes, a Barbadian cleric, revealed that "the whole term of a negro life may be said to be there but sixteen years!" Anthony Benezet, *Some Historical Account of Guinea: With an inquiry into the rise and progress of the slave trade* (London: J. Phillips, 1788), 78.

15." A fellow planter placed slave mortality at a slightly higher rate; he estimated that a workforce consisting of one hundred Africans would cease to
exist in less than two decades unless replacements were purchased on an ongoing basis.[81]

In 1680 Barbados's sugar crop was more valuable than the combined exports of all the British colonies in North America.[82] More than half of the
island's arable land was in the hands of just 175 large planters; not coinci-
dentally, they also owned more than half of the 38,782 slaves. Nineteen of
these planters owned two hundred or more slaves, and eighty-nine owned
one hundred; they comprised the rising master class that had been pushing
small landholders off the island since the 1640s.[83] One consequence of that
process of consolidation and the concomitant importation of slaves was a
troubling disparity in the island's racial composition: a census compiled by
Governor Atkins in 1680 revealed that there were twice as many blacks as
whites on Barbados.[84] Two decades earlier, planters had started showing
signs of nervousness about the growing number of Africans; the Council
responded by offering subsidies for the importation of white servants and
passing new legislation designed to improve their treatment.[85] The measures
proved ineffective and Barbados experienced continuous outmigration of
whites to the Leeward Islands, especially Jamaica, which the British had captured from the Dutch in 1655.[86]

81. Thompson, ed., "Henry Drax's Instructions," 585; Edward Littleton, *The groans
of the plantations, or, A true account of their grievous and extreme sufferings by the heavy impositions upon sugar and other hardships relating more particularly to the island of Barbados*
(London: Printed by M. Clark, 1689), 6, 18, quoted in Dunn, *Sugar and Slaves*, 323.

82. Eric Eustace Williams, *Capitalism and Slavery* (Chapel Hill: University of North
Carolina Press, 1944), 25; Richard S. Dunn, "The Barbados Census of 1680: Profile of
the Richest Colony in English America," *The William and Mary Quarterly*, 3rd Series, 26,
no. 1 (January 1969): 4.

83. Large estate owners constituted no more than one-quarter of the island's white
population. Another quarter belonged to "an intermediate class of officeholders, small
merchants, professionals, estate managers, and small estate owners who produced cotton and foodstuffs on less than one hundred acres or hired out slaves." The rest were
poor whites, families with ten acres or less, who lived in poverty on the margins of the
plantation system. Greene, *Pursuits of Happiness*, 156.

84. Dunn, *Sugar and Slaves*, 87–88.

85. In the 1660s masters were supposed to obtain a Magistrate's permission before
flogging a servant. Rogozinski, *Brief History of the Caribbean*, 81.

86. The danger posed by an enslaved African majority was only one of a litany of reasons that whites left Barbados. By the mid-1660s deforestation, soil exhaustion, and
the lack of available land for settlers or servants who survived their indentures caused

As the blacks became an increasing majority, Barbadians took steps to maintain a sufficient number of whites for a competent militia; new legislation required planters to employ one white worker for every ten slaves they procured. Despite concerns for their own safety, many planters failed to comply with this law: the 1680 census revealed that Henry Drax owned 327 slaves but employed just seven white workers. At that point the island's militia consisted of only 5,588 men—a paltry force when compared to a slave population that outnumbered it sevenfold.[87] In 1683 reports of insolent behavior by blacks prompted white Barbadians to make examples of several "bold" slaves. Four or five were "whipped for terror to others" and one was burned alive for objecting to the spectacle.

Three years later another scare gave the Assembly reason to initiate a review of existing laws pertaining to the island's forty-seven thousand or so slaves (compared to a white population of twenty thousand at most).[88] The result was the 1688 *Act for the Governing of Negroes*, a law that repealed all previous slave laws only to repeat most of their verbiage and principal features. The new act included a frank admission that "the plantations and estates of these islands cannot be fully managed, and brought into use without the labor and service of great numbers of Negroes and other slaves." Barbadians were wholly dependent on blacks but given their "barbarous, wild and savage natures," they were "wholly unqualified" to be governed by the laws, customs, and practices of Great Britain, including such niceties as trial by a jury of one's peers. Slaves' natural inclination toward "disorders, rapines and inhumanities" meant they had to be "well-provided for" and "guarded from the cruelties and insolences of themselves, or other ill-tempered People or Owners."[89]

---

freemen to emigrate. In addition, during the 1660s wealthy planters and merchants were keen on establishing colonies in places such as Antigua, Surinam, Dominica, Nevis, St. Vincent, Grenada, and St. Lucia; some merely invested in these ventures, but others (or their sons and agents) emigrated to the new settlements. Major setbacks involving these colonizing ventures eventually contributed to the success of Carolina as disappointed investors and settlers looked to the American mainland as a safer and potentially profitable haven. Roberts and Beamish, "Venturing Out: The Barbadian Diaspora," in LeMaster and Wood, eds., *Creating and Contesting Carolina*, 49–55.

87. Dunn, *Sugar and Slaves*, 87.

88. Ibid.

89. *An Act for the Governing of Negroes*, August 8, 1688, in Richard Hall, comp., *Acts, Passed in the Island of Barbados. From 1643, to 1762 Inclusive* (London, 1764), 112–21, quoted in Christopher Tomlins, *Freedom Bound: Law, Labor, and Civic Identity in Colonizing English America, 1580–1865* (Cambridge: Cambridge University Press, 2010), 442

Once again the Assembly's language revealed their concern that unrestrained brutality by individual planters might instigate a widespread rebellion on the island.

The Assembly's fears would be realized just four years later when whites detected an elaborate conspiracy spearheaded by the island's Creole population. In October 1692 blacks born on Barbados intended to seize the fort, destroy of all the ships in the harbor, and then execute a bloody takeover of the island. After killing the governor and all of the planters, the Creoles intended to set up a government of their own: "They designed . . . to have enslaved all the black men and women to them, and to have taken the white women for their wives . . . no imported Negro was to have been admitted to partake of the freedom they intended to gain, till he had been made free by them, who should have been their masters. The old women (both black and white) were to have been their cooks, and servants in other capacities. And they had chosen a governor among themselves."[90]

Discovery of the plot and subsequent interrogations led to the arrest of several hundred slaves from more than twenty different plantations. "Many were hanged, and a great many burned" in a rash of public executions designed to intimidate the black population. An account published in London the following year stated that as the court martial drew to a close, seven of the accused remained on prominent display "for a terror to others . . . hanging in chains alive, and so starving to death."[91] Forty-two alleged conspirators were spared execution but as their punishment had to suffer castration at the hands of one Alice Mills (who received ten guineas for the grisly task).[92] One disturbing revelation that emerged during the interrogations was that many conspirators were "overseers, carpenters, brick layers, wheelwrights, sawyers,

---

fn. To address the racial imbalance on the island, the 1688 Assembly also revived a 1682 act "to encourage the importation of Christian servants, and for retaining them within the island," and drafted *An Act declaring the Negro-slaves of this Island to be Real Estates,* basically depriving Africans of their humanity in the eyes of the law.

90. *A Brief, but Most True Relation of the Late Barbarous and Bloody Plot of the Negro's in the Island of Barbados on Friday the 21 of October, 1692* (London: 1693) quoted in Handler, "Slave Revolts and Conspiracies," 26–27.

91. Ibid.

92. "Minutes of Council of Barbados: Order for sundry payments to officers, and for payment of ten guineas to Alice Mills for castrating forty-two negroes according to sentence of the Commissioners for trial of rebellious negroes." Great Britain Public Record Office, *Calendar of State Papers,* Col. Entry Bk., vol. 12 (London: Longman, 1908), 396–398.

blacksmiths, grooms and such others that have more favor shown them by their masters." Such ingratitude "adds abundantly to their crimes."[93]

Whites had long feared an uprising involving the thousands of Africans transported directly from African slave pens to Barbadian sugar fields; the 1692 conspiracy made it clear that all black people, regardless or origin or status, posed a threat to the people who enslaved and exploited them. Those on the "bottom rail" would constantly strive to place themselves on top.[94]

93. Tobias Frere, Richard Scott, Thomas Morris and John Duboys, "To His Excellency Collonel James Kendall ... [report of court martial], November 2 or 3, 1692." CO 28/1, 202–5, Public Records Office, quoted in Handler, "Slave Revolts and Conspiracies," 24.

94. In the wake of the conspiracy, Barbadian planters felt threatened from within and without. A 1693 "Petition of several persons interested in Barbados to the King" set forth the "dangerous condition of the Island from want of men; the late mortality, the expedition to Martinique and the burden of taxation having done much to dispeople it; and praying that a regiment may be quartered there during the war and frigates kept there constantly to secure the provision ships." Great Britain. Public Record Office, Nov. 30, 1693, 709, i. Read 6 Dec. 1698. *Board of Trade.* Barbados, 5. Nos. 32, 321, and 44, 44–46, in *Calendar of State Papers: Colonial Series, America and West Indies,* January 1693–May, 1696, vol. 14, ed. J. W. Fortescue (London: Mackie and Co., 1903), 214.

Two

Carolina

Even before slaves on Barbados harvested sugarcane, many colonists in British North America employed Native Americans and Africans in their fields, shops, and homes.[1] After the Restoration of the monarchy, the British seized or established additional colonies on the American mainland, all of which would import enslaved Africans.[2] The emergence of slavery in North America may have been inevitable, but its persistence was not. The first colonies to legalize slavery would also be the first to eradicate it, partly because of cultural imperatives, but largely because voluntary immigration and natural increase provided sufficient manpower. Slavery became most firmly entrenched in colonies where African laborers generated the greatest profits and where proprietors and administrators allowed or even encouraged their importation. In short, regardless of location, seventeenth-century British colonists made decisions based on their needs and opportunities, oftentimes ignoring the human cost, especially when other races were involved.

1. Virginia, founded in 1607, initially treated Africans as indentured servants, but by mid-century their status more closely approximated slavery than servitude; a 1662 act declared "Negro womens children to serve according to the condition of the mother." Maryland (founded 1634) proclaimed in 1639 that baptism would not free a slave, and in 1664 declared that all blacks in the colony—and those imported in the future—would be enslaved for life, as would their children. Following the Pequot War (1636–37), Puritans in New England enslaved Pequot women and children and exported male prisoners of war to Barbados; they also maintained a small number of African slaves. By virtue of its 1641 "Body of Liberties," Massachusetts Bay (founded 1630) became the first colony to codify slavery. Plymouth (1620), Connecticut (1636), and Rhode Island (1636) all legalized slavery by 1652. New Hampshire (founded 1623) did not impose a tariff on enslaved Africans, thereby becoming a base for the slave trade in New England—an ugly distinction later passed on to Newport, Rhode Island. Slavery was also present in Dutch New Amsterdam (1624) and in Delaware, which was founded by Swedes in 1638 and taken over by the Dutch in 1655.

2. New York, Delaware, and New Jersey were seized by force; Carolina and Pennsylvania were established as British possessions from the outset; Georgia, which initially banned slavery, was added to the list in 1733.

Nicolaes Visscher, *Insulæ Americanæ in Oceano Septentrionali ac regiones adiacentes : a C. de May usque ad LineamÆquinoctialem*, Amsterdam, c. 1692. Map from Norman B. Leventhal Map & Education Center at the Boston Public Library Digital Collections.

The prevalence and prominence of Barbadian immigrants in early South Carolina meant that the colony was likely to include enslaved Africans from the outset. But those Barbadian roots also meant that many colonists were familiar with the dangers posed by discontented whites as well as rebellious blacks; in the 1650s sugar barons had fortified their houses to repel attacks "by the Christian servants or negro slaves."[3] In 1675 news from Virginia and other colonies would only exacerbate those concerns. South Carolina's leading men realized that their prospects and the colony's very survival depended on the ability to combat external threats and to preserve internal order. Those capabilities hinged on the tenor of the colony's relationships with Native American neighbors and on its demographics—enslaved Africans provided crucial labor but a free white majority meant greater security. The wild card was profit, the scent of which seemed to render otherwise sane men insensible.

&

3. Ligon, in *A True History and Exact History*, ed. Kupperman, 22; Dunn, *Sugar and Slaves*, 69.

In 1661, the same year Barbadian lawmakers took steps to protect their lives and fortunes by passing *An Act for the better ordering and governing of Negroes*, the coronation of Charles II took place at England's Westminster Abbey.[4] Two years later, the new king named eight of his aristocratic supporters "Lords Proprietors" of the Province of Carolina, a massive tract that extended from Virginia to Florida and westward to the Pacific.[5] The grant encompassed thousands of square miles populated by indigenous groups who, in an era of European expansion, could be pushed aside, exterminated or, better yet, exploited in any number of ways. To the south, thinly manned Spanish Florida represented as much a target as a threat to potential English settlers.[6] To the west lay territory claimed by France, "unimproved" and poorly defended except by their Native American allies. In short, the land now called "South Carolina," as well as its inhabitants and neighbors, was ripe for the plucking. And then there were out-of-luck Englishmen, Scots, Irish, and downtrodden refugees from other European nations, all ripe for the plucking as well. The Province of Carolina would be of little value if the proprietors could not populate it with drones that were convinced that it was in *their* best interest to undertake the backbreaking work involved in establishing a profitable colony.

4. On May 8, 1660, the Convention Parliament proclaimed that King Charles II had been the lawful monarch since the execution of his father in 1649. After spending time in exile in France, the United Provinces, and Spanish Netherlands, Charles returned to England on May 25, 1660. The Parliament of Scotland had recognized him as the ruling monarch since February 1649, but his coronation as king of England and Ireland did not occur until April 23, 1661. A contemporary (John Evelyn) noted that the monarchy was restored "without one drop of bloud, & by that very Army, which rebell'd against him." Entry dated May 29, 1660, in John Evelyn, *Diary and Correspondence of John Evelyn, F.R.S.*, 4 vols., ed. William Bray (London: George Bell & Sons, 1906), I, 355.

5. The charter issued on March 24, 1663, gave the Lords Proprietors the land located between the 36th and 31st parallels. In order to include Albemarle Sound, where Virginians had already begun a settlement, a second charter was granted June 30, 1665, expanding the province to the area within 36°30′ and 29° and "so west, in a direct line, as far as the South-Seas." By virtue of the second charter, Carolina encompassed the land on which the Spanish settlement of St. Augustine stood, and another sixty-five miles of territory to its south. William L. Saunders, ed., *The Colonial Records of North Carolina, Vol. I-1662 to 1712* (Raleigh: P. M. Hale Printer to the state, 1886), 20–33, 102–14.

6. Sir Francis Drake razed St. Augustine in 1586; Spanish expeditions were sent out against Jamestown colony in 1609 and 1611. In 1668, two years before Charles Town, South Carolina was planted, Jamaica-based privateer Robert Searle (alias John Davis) raided St. Augustine in retaliation for the Spanish assault on Charles Town (modern-day Nassau), New Providence. In 1672 the Spanish began construction of a masonry fort, Castillo de San Marcos; South Carolinians would raid it in 1702.

Of course there were also "uncivilized" creatures, neither white nor Christian, who could be compelled to serve at the end of a whip, or worse.[7] All things considered, it was good to be a kingmaker.

The proprietor who engineered the massive Carolina grant was John Colleton, a royalist who fled to Barbados after the execution of Charles I. Upon his return to London, Colleton was knighted and appointed to the Council for Foreign Plantations. In that capacity, he became acquainted with a number of influential men who shaped England's colonial strategy and policies. They included Edward Hyde, 1st Earl of Clarendon and minister to Charles II; John Berkeley, 1st Baron Berkeley of Stratton, and his brother, Sir William Berkeley, governor of Virginia; Sir George Carteret, vice chamberlain of the royal household and treasurer of the navy; and Sir Anthony Ashley Cooper, the forward-thinking 1st Earl of Shaftesbury. To secure the Carolina charter, Colleton also reached out to his cousin, George Monck, 1st Duke of Albemarle, and to William Craven, 1st Earl of Craven. The assemblage was unmatched in terms of political acumen and experience in colonial affairs.[8] As Lords Proprietors of Carolina, they were granted powers normally reserved for the monarch. In *Leviathan* Thomas Hobbes reasoned that "men have no pleasure, (but on the contrary a great deal of grief) in keeping company, where there is no power able to over-awe them all." Charles II granted the proprietors sufficient authority to ensure that Carolina would proffer both "pleasure and profit."[9] Shaftesbury was so enamored of the possibilities that he came to refer to Carolina as his "Darling."[10]

7. Six years after Charles Town was established, Sir William Petty promoted a biological view of race in *The Scale of Creatures*. In 1684 European philosophers categorized humans into groups and posited that "distinct human species, each with their own physical, moral, and mental abilities, had evolved from separate origins." By 1754 David Hume could confidently assert that "the negroes ... [were] naturally inferior to the whites." Kirsten Fischer, *Suspect Relations: Sex, Race, and Resistance in Colonial North Carolina* (Ithaca: Cornell University Press, 2002), 2.

8. Six of the men were adventurers in the Royal African and Hudson's Bay Companies and five were members of the Council of Trade. M. Eugene Sirmans, *Colonial South Carolina: A Political History, 1663–1763* (Chapel Hill: University of North Carolina Press, 1966), 4–5.

9. Hobbes, *Leviathan*, 61; Robert Horne, *A Brief Description of the Province of Carolina* (1666), title page. Horne's *Brief Description* sets forth "The Healthfulness of the Air; the Fertility of the Earth, and Waters; and the great Pleasure and Profit will accrue to those that shall go thither to enjoy the same."

10. Shaftesbury to Sir Peter Colleton, November 27, 1672, in Langdon Cheves, ed., *The Shaftesbury Papers and Other Records Relating to Carolina. Prior to the Year 1676*, South Carolina Historical Society, Collections, vol. 5 (1897), 416–18.

Carolina Charter of 1663, first page. Courtesy of the State Archives
of North Carolina.

By 1663 colonies in North America and the West Indies had shown that
furs, tobacco, sugar, and other exports could generate considerable revenues
for planters, agents, merchants, and royal coffers. However, joint stock companies and other investment schemes that financed pathbreaking colonizing
ventures had met limited success: the Virginia Company of London, the Merchant Adventurers who sponsored Plymouth colony, Sir William Courteen's
syndicate to promote settlement on Barbados, and the Puritan backers of Providence Island were among the many English entrepreneurs who lost money
on transatlantic enterprises.[11] Not surprisingly, the Lords Proprietors' first
instinct was to encourage ventures in Carolina where colonists would bear

11. Edmund Morgan, *American Slavery, American Freedom* (New York: Norton, 2003),
79–123; Ruth A. McIntyre, *Debts Hopeful and Desperate: Financing the Plymouth Colony*
(Plymouth: Plymouth Plantation, 1963), passim; Karen Ordahl Kupperman, *Providence
Island, 1630–1641: The Other Puritan Colony* (Cambridge: Cambridge University Press,
1995), 1–3. The Dutch, on the other hand, showed how the role of middleman could
be extremely profitable. Lain Gately, *Tobacco: a Cultural History of How an Exotic Plant
Seduced Civilization* (New York: Grove Atlantic Press, 2007), 88–109.

the costs and risks of settlement, rewarding their distant landlords through a system of quitrents. However, false starts involving immigrants from Virginia and from New England (who found the Cape Fear area "scandalous") convinced the proprietors that a different, more proactive approach was required.[12] The planting of colonies was no undertaking for the faint of heart, the uninformed, the impatient, or investors with shallow pockets. But Carolina's proprietors were intimately familiar with colonial administration, trade networks, and the production of crops and commodities for export. They were confident that agricultural staples produced in the humid, subtropical climate of the American southeast would find ready markets elsewhere. The province promised riches enough for proprietors, as well as leading planters who would oversee the colony's servile workforce.[13] Smaller planters—"farmers" in the parlance of most settlements—also stood to benefit, but their path to prosperity would hinge on perseverance and emulation of their social and economic superiors.[14]

The marriage of interests that ultimately led to a transfer of Barbadian culture to the American mainland was the concurrence of the 1663 Carolina grant with increasing adversity in the West Indies. While Charles II was demonstrating his largesse in England, sugar barons were trying to cope with falling prices, restrictions imposed by the Navigation Acts of 1660 and 1663, soil exhaustion, deforestation, a declining supply of indentured servants, and dangers posed by the fast-growing population of enslaved Africans. Those problems, along with land shortages and high mortality rates, steered disgruntled planters and impoverished former servants toward other shores, most notably England, Jamaica, Virginia, and New England.[15] Unlike most

12. In 1661 a group of Massachusetts Puritans attempted a settlement on the Cape Fear River; after just a few months they returned to New England. This undoubtedly persuaded the Lords Proprietors to make liberal concessions and to favor colonists who had proven themselves in a colony focused on profit, not prayer.

13. The Lords Proprietors were "men of high rank and extensive experience at the leading edge of early modern commerce . . . a group of especially capable colonizers." Edelson, *Plantation Enterprise*, 15.

14. During this same period the governor of Jamaica was also actively recruiting wealthy planters and petitioning English authorities to deport poor and delinquent men to the island to bolster its workforce. Sir Thomas Modyford to Sir Henry Bennet (Lord Arlington), May 10, 1664, cited in Roberts and Beamish, "Venturing Out: The Barbadian Diaspora," in LeMaster and Wood, eds., *Creating and Contesting Carolina*, 56.

15. Russell Menard states that hard data regarding life expectancy on Barbados is unavailable, but "death rates on the island were high by mainland standards even in the seventeenth century." Menard, *Sweet Negotiations*, 26. The destinations of Barbadian

English farmers, Barbadian planters already knew what it took to succeed in a hardscrabble colonial setting. They had experience procuring workers, constructing buildings and "works," clearing fields, planting and harvesting crops for export, managing day to day operations, and using force, when necessary, to increase productivity and maintain control. Thus the Lords Proprietors welcomed and even solicited proposals from Barbadians regarding the establishment of a colony in Carolina.[16] The strategies and techniques the latter had perfected were already being replicated elsewhere in the Caribbean; perhaps they would work on the American mainland as well. Even Barbados's white underclass—those Irish servants "derided by the Negroes, and branded with the Epithite of 'white slaves'"—were familiar with the cycles and rigors of plantation life.[17]

In the summer of 1663, a group of Barbadian merchants and planters recruited William Hilton to explore eastern Carolina. His *Relation of a Discovery lately made on the Coast of Florida* provided the reassurance the eighty-five "Barbadian Adventurers" sought. After the Lords Proprietors made "concessions and agreements" that included self-government, freedom of religion,

---

emigrants is based on Gov. Jonathan Atkins's list of emigrants who departed in 1679, cited in April Lee Hatfield, *Atlantic Virginia: Intercolonial Relations in the Seventeenth Century* (Philadelphia: University of Pennsylvania Press, 2004), 143. Recent scholarship challenges the number and significance of Barbadians in South Carolina's founding and early development. According to Justin Roberts and Ian Beamish, Carolina nearly failed because colonial enterprises in St. Lucia, Surinam, and Jamaica attracted so many Barbadian emigrants. But although "only a few hundred" Barbadians came to Carolina before 1700, "there were many elite planters and merchants among them, as well as many influential Barbadians who were deeply investing in the Carolina colony, without ever becoming resident." Roberts and Beamish, "Venturing Out: The Barbadian Diaspora," in LeMaster and Wood, eds., *Creating and Contesting Carolina*, 49–50.

16. Sir John Yeamans, a Royalist, immigrated to Barbados in 1650 and became a major landowner and member of the Barbados Council. In 1663 his son, William, negotiated with the Lords Proprietors on behalf of more than eighty Barbadians. Robert M. Weir, "Yeamans, Sir John, first baronet (1611–1674)," *Oxford Dictionary of National Biography*, online, Oxford University Press, 2004.

17. Scott, "Some Observations on the Island of Barbados, c. 1667, C.O. 1/21, no. 170, quoted in Beckles, "A 'Riotous and Unruly Lot,'" *WMQ*, 3rd series, 47, no. 4 (October 1990): 511. The Portuguese and Dutch should be credited with the early development of the plantation system that came to fruition on Barbados. According to Kenneth Morgan, about a third of the servants attracted to South Carolina were migrants from the Caribbean. Kenneth Morgan, *Slavery and the British Empire: From Africa to America* (New York: Oxford University Press, 2007), 31.

and generous land grants, the islanders established a colony on the Cape Fear River.[18] Despite a promising start, poor relations with neighboring Native Americans and the failure of the proprietors to provide adequate support—an omen of future disappointments—eventually caused the settlers to abandon the colony.[19] One positive outcome of the enterprise was the Barbadians' impression that more suitable areas for settlement lay further south. In his 1666 *Relation*, Captain Robert Sandford reported that Carolina offered "ample Seats for many thousands of our Nation ... in a clime perfectly temperate to make the habitacon pleasant."[20] Opportunities in Carolina seemed boundless when viewed from distant and diminutive Barbados. Moreover, the peace concluded between England and Spain in 1667 seemed to open doors to new colonizing efforts, though territorial claims of the two nations did overlap in the Carolina grant—a minor point among diplomats but not so for colonists who would occupy the contested lands.[21]

It was at that point that the Lords Proprietors were stirred to action by Anthony Ashley Cooper, 1st Earl of Shaftesbury, who spearheaded an effort to acquire title to islands in the Caribbean that might be colonized in tandem with Carolina. In addition, the earl persuaded his fellow proprietors to contribute £500 to finance settlement on the mainland.[22] Profit was the group's primary goal, but their funds would also support an expansion of empire and an extension of Protestantism. The colonizing enterprise would enhance England's trade and provide a bulwark against Spanish and French papists

18. Hilton, "Relation of a Discovery," (1664) in Salley, ed., *Narratives*, 37–61. Hilton had visited the Carolina coast in 1662 in conjunction with a failed enterprise involving settlers from Massachusetts Bay. Walter Edgar, *South Carolina, A History* (Columbia: University of South Carolina Press, 1998), 40.

19. Robert M. Weir, *Colonial South Carolina—A History* (Columbia: University of South Carolina Press, 1997), 50–51. At its peak, the colony may have housed eight hundred settlers. The Lords Proprietors were "preoccupied with affairs of state"; in addition, Clarendon went into exile, Berkeley returned to Virginia, and Colleton died in 1666. Edgar, *South Carolina, A History*, 41. The Lords Proprietors' failure to support South Carolinians during the Yamasee War is discussed later in this work.

20. Sandford, "A Relation of a Voyage" (1666), reprinted in Salley, ed., *Narratives*, 107.

21. Edward McCrady, *The History of South Carolina Under the Proprietary Government, 1670–1719* (London: Macmillan Company, 1897), 129–30. In 1668 at the urging of Lord Ashley, six of the eight Lords Proprietors sought a grant for the Bahamas and other Caribbean islands yet to be colonized by the English. Though the expansion of sugar cultivation promised riches to planters in those locations, some entrepreneurs recognized the profit that could accrue by providing foodstuffs, timber, and other supplies to sugar growers.

22. Edgar, *South Carolina, A History*, 41.

Anthony Ashley-Cooper, 1st Earl of Shaftesbury after John Greenhill, oil on canvas, based on a work of circa 1672–1673. © National Portrait Gallery, London.

in North America. In Shaftesbury's view, the Province of Carolina presented settlers with an opportunity for economic and social improvement. But recent experience had shown that colonists could not simply be steered toward America and left to their own devices; they needed a contractual blueprint— one that served their interests as well as those of their landlords and their sovereign. Toward that end, Shaftesbury and John Locke and the other Lords Proprietors collaborated on a founding document—a "Grand Model"— consisting of 120 articles. In theory, it promised political stability, collective security, internal civility, and economic opportunities befitting one's station in life.

The *Fundamental Constitutions of Carolina* divided the province into counties, each of which contained eight signiories, eight baronies, and twenty-four colonies, each twelve thousand acres in size, spread across four precincts. The plan called for colonists to live and labor in a network of villages or towns located along navigable rivers. In those enclaves, agricultural experimentation and innovation would encourage the production of exotic commodities for export.[23] Carolina would thrive on commerce, complementing rather than competing with English agriculture and industry. One-fifth of the land would be "perpetually annexed" to the Lords Proprietors, an equal amount would be reserved for the province's "hereditary nobility," and the remaining three-fifths would be assigned to the various colonies so "the balance of the government may be preserved." By linking authority to land ownership, the *Fundamental Constitutions* would diffuse power and yet "avoid erecting a numerous democracy." The document also instituted a hierarchical administrative structure that included a Grand Council, a unicameral parliament, lesser officials, and a complex system of courts.[24]

While certain aspects of the *Fundamental Constitutions* harkened back to feudalism, the document did include progressive notions such as limited government and religious toleration, though it could be argued that these were not ideological markers, but merely concessions incorporated to entice colonists.[25] Dichotomies aside there was no attempt to conceal the fact that the whole enterprise was designed to make rich men even richer. Shaftesbury and Locke were at the forefront of political liberalism, but they were also pragmatists steeped in mercantile theory.[26] They knew that the welfare of the state

23. Shaftesbury and Locke wanted to establish "a variant form" of the traditional European manorial system, including manors, manorial courts, and "the equivalent of serfs." Sirmans, *Colonial South Carolina*, 9.

24. *The Fundamental Constitutions of Carolina*: March 1, 1669. The proprietors believed that dispersed settlement like that in the tobacco colonies would bring the Province to ruin. [Edelson, *Plantation Enterprise*, 15–16, 34–38.] Emma Hart regards the *Fundamental Constitutions* as "the first English colonial founding documents to make secular urban settlement an obligatory feature of a society." Shaftesbury believed towns were central to the economy and to society at large. In later years he wanted Charles Town "to serve both a social and an economic purpose in an otherwise 'uncivilized' New World." Hart, *Building Charleston*, 22–25.

25. Free land and religious toleration were Utopian ideals that motivated humble colonists, not the "great men" who ruled "in order to line their pockets, not serve the common good." Alan Gallay, *The Indian Slave Trade: The Rise of the English Empire in the American South* (New Haven: Yale University Press, 2002), 63.

26. In his *Second Treatise*, John Locke noted the futility of owning thousands of acres of cultivated land, well stocked with cattle, in the "in-land Parts of America" where a landowner had "no hope of Commerce with other Parts of the World." He ventured that "in the beginning all the World was *America* … for no such thing as *Money* was any

and its ruling elites depended on the laboring masses, both home and abroad. Colonial hives in particular needed an abundance of drones. Under the *Fundamental Constitutions*, the bulk of the labor in Carolina would be provided by indentured servants and by "leet-men" and "leet-women," perpetual tenants who toiled for their landlord's benefit. Unlike farmers who rented or leased landholdings in England, Carolina leet-men would have no right of appeal beyond their lord's court and no freedom of movement; they would be bought and sold with the land they occupied. Their offspring were destined to inherit their condition, "and so to all generations."[27] In medieval Europe, such people had been called "serfs," eking out a bare subsistence and bound to the land and will of the manorial lord.[28] The "Grand Model" that Shaftesbury and Locke developed was meant to exploit Carolina's natural resources, as well as its inhabitants; it hinged on a form and degree of individualism that countered traditional norms of reciprocity. New World realities would supersede Old World social contracts and antiquated notions about shared benefits.[29] For the colony (writ large) to prosper, people at the lower end of the socioeconomic ladder had to believe that their prospects were married to those of the planter elite . . . that distress of any kind at the top of society signified disaster at the bottom.

---

where known." [John Locke, *Two Treatises of Government*, ed. Peter Laslett, rev. ed. (Cambridge: Cambridge University Press, 1988), 48–49.] In 1674 the proprietors reminded Carolina's governor and Council that their intentions, embodied in the *Fundamental Constitutions*, were not "the profit of merchants" but the "incouragement of landlords." Proprietors to the Governor and Council, May 18, 1674, quoted in Edelson, *Plantation Enterprise*, 35.

27. *Fundamental Constitutions*, articles 22 and 23. Article 25 stipulated that anyone choosing to be a leet-man was to "voluntarily enter himself a leet-man in the registry of the county court."

28. The term "leet-men" in seventeenth-century England referred to individuals entitled to poor relief; not so in Carolina. Regarding the provisions in the *Fundamental Constitutions* concerning leet-men, David Wooton states plainly that "There is no question as to what this institution is: it is serfdom by another name." David Wooton, ed., *John Locke, Political Writings* (Indianapolis/Cambridge: Hackett Publishing Company, 2003), 43.

29. The right of an individual to his own labor set forth in John Locke's subsequent treatises "was not meant to be taken literally." Mercantilist theory endowed the government with the power to control the labor of certain groups; most common laborers were not masters of their own fates, but "servants enthralled to both a powerful minority and a powerful state." Seventeenth century political liberalism encouraged development of a "possessive form of individualism" that further diminished elites' sense of obligation to others, "especially to those in classes below." [Peter A. Coclanis, *The Shadow of a Dream:*

Though the *Fundamental Constitutions* may have deterred some likely immigrants, the prospect of representative government, trial by jury, religious tolerance, generous headrights, waiver of import and export duties, and a moratorium on quitrents proved attractive to many Englishmen and other Europeans. Despite the advantages reserved for the proprietors and the colony's propertied elite, ordinary men saw the possibility of upward mobility ... a chance to improve both economically and socially.[30] Freemen who settled in Carolina would be much better off than indentured colonists, but even the lowliest servant would not be in the worst of circumstances—that unwelcome distinction was reserved for the sons and daughters of Africa. Bowing to the demands of the Barbadian Adventurers, Article 110 of the *Fundamental Constitutions* guaranteed every freeman "absolute power and authority over his negro slaves."

When they opened the door to chattel slavery in Carolina, the proprietors were keenly aware of the profits that enslaved Africans could generate, as well as the risks that they posed. Three years before William Berkeley became Virginia's governor, an act passed by that colony's lawmakers mandated that "*all persons except Negroes*" be provided with arms and ammunition.[31] Just a few months after the Carolina grant, Berkeley and other tobacco barons narrowly averted an uprising involving discontented servants and African slaves.[32]

Economic Life and Death in the South Carolina Low Country 1670–1920 (New York: Oxford University Press, 1989), 23–26.] Thomas Wilson maintains that the hierarchical structure in the *Fundamental Constitutions* continued feudal ideas of class reciprocity, but they were undone by the expansion of slavery in Carolina. Thomas D. Wilson, *The Ashley Cooper Plan: The Founding of Carolina and the Origins of Southern Political Culture* (Chapel Hill: University of North Carolina Press, 2016), prologue.

30. Certainly some migrants would have balked at feudal nomenclatures such as "landgrave," "cazique," "signiory," and "leet-man"; one article stipulated, "All the children of leet-men shall be leet-men, and so to all generations." On the other hand, the *Constitutions* allowed that "seven or more persons agreeing in any religion, shall constitute a church or profession, to which they shall give some name, to distinguish it from others." [*Fundamental Constitutions*, articles 23, 97.] The requirement regarding belief in God, not Christ, opened the door to Jewish immigrants. Other provisions enabled Quakers and Huguenots to reside in the colony; the only religion not tolerated was Roman Catholicism. Edgar, *South Carolina, A History*, 43.

31. "1638. Act X.," in *Black Laws of Virginia: A Summary of the Legislative Acts of Virginia Concerning Negroes from Earliest Times to the Present*, ed. June Purcell Guild (Richmond: Whittet & Shepperson, 1936), 37.

32. Act CII, *Laws of Virginia*, March 1661–2 (Henning, *Statutes at Large*, 2:116–17) cited in Pamela Barnes Craig, *American Women: A Library of Congress Guide for the Study of*

Shaftesbury had invested in a sugar plantation on Barbados in the 1640s just as the transition from servitude to slavery began in earnest; forced labor had contributed to his coffers for decades. Similarly Edward Hyde had extensive landholdings in Jamaica. Clarendon, the county named in his honor, was precisely where a major slave uprising would erupt in 1690.³³ When Sir John Colleton was named a Carolina proprietor in 1663, he was one of Barbados' most prominent sugar planters and slave owners. His eldest son was destined to become one of the wealthiest land and slave owners in Carolina.³⁴ Four of the eight Lords Proprietors were members of the slave-trading operation known as the Company of Adventurers to Africa, and its successor, the Royal African Company, which established seventeen forts on the African coast and purchased 125,000 slaves between 1672 and 1713 (losing one-fifth of them on the notorious "Middle Passage").³⁵

The moral compass of these grandees not only allowed but also actively encouraged the use of slave labor. This did not make them distinctive; many other Englishmen including the Duke of York (the future King James II) and professed Christians from every corner of Europe accumulated wealth from the capture, sale, transport, or forced labor of men, women, and children from the African continent. Proceeds from the slave trade also enriched African kings, chiefs, and other members of ruling oligarchies who acted as commercial middlemen between European buyers on the coast and slave suppliers in the interior.³⁶ Moreover, the bondage, degradation, and abuse of others for

Women's History and Culture in the United States (Library of Congress, 2001), online version at American Memory website. In September 1663 servants and slaves in Gloucester County, Virginia, plotted to gain their freedom in what is considered the first organized rebellion involving Africans in British Colonial America. Exposed by an indentured servant, some of the conspirators were drawn and quartered and their heads placed on posts or chimney tops. Aptheker, *American Negro Slave Revolts*, 164–65.

33. Far larger than Barbados, Jamaica would become the premier English sugar colony; in 1754 the island's 467 largest planters owned more than one thousand acres each. Blackburn, *The Making of New World Slavery*, 406. The 1790 slave uprising became known as the known as the "First Maroon War."

34. Henry A. M. Smith, "The Baronies of South Carolina," II, *South Carolina Historical and Genealogical Magazine* 11, no. 4 (October 1910): 193–98. Colleton also had stakes in Virginia.

35. Blackburn, *The Making of New World Slavery*, 255.

36. Kristin Mann, *Slavery and the Birth of an African City: Lagos, 1760–1900* (Bloomington: Indiana University Press, 2007), 57, 313. The slave trade stimulated the commercial development of African kingdoms and capitals, enhancing their prestige nationally and internationally. Profits also enabled kings to expand the scope and prosperity of

financial gain did not always involve members of other races. As indentured servants, prisoners of European wars, kidnapped Irishmen, and convict laborers on Barbados could attest, their English cousins or conquerors did not hesitate to treat them as "merchandize" and sell them "uncondemned into slavery."[37] In the seventeenth century the ruthless exploitation of workers, red, black, or white, was considered business as usual, especially in colonies such as Barbados that depended on the production and export of a staple crop for financial success. In 1663 the Royal Adventurers into Africa had insisted that "the very being of the Plantations depends upon the supply of negro servants for their works." Charles II responded by prohibiting duties on all "Negro Slaves" shipped directly to England's colonies in America. Later that decade he encouraged colonial governors to favor English merchants who "shall bring Trade" to the colonies, particularly "ye Royal African Company of England."[38]

The *Fundamental Constitutions of Carolina* were adopted on March 1, 1669.[39] In a dispatch to his deputy, Maurice Mathews, the Earl of Shaftesbury, later described the *Constitutions* as "the compass you are to steer by" in Carolina, adding that "we have therein designed nothing but the quiet safety and prosperity of the people."[40] There was much in the document to contradict that assessment; it was, after all, a contractual blueprint intended to enrich the proprietors and the colony's landed aristocracy. But inducements such as a 150-acre headright for each freeman in the first fleet, *plus* an additional 150 acres for each adult male servant and slave, *plus* 100 acres for each adult female and male child he brought to Carolina, enabled a man to own a vast

---

constituencies and households with which they were "identified in the public imagination." [Ibid., 57.] By the turn of the century, Native Americans in the southeast would also supply captives to Europeans, conducting raids and waging war on neighboring tribes in order to acquire weapons and other goods and, in the process, garnering political or military advantage.

37. "England's Slavery, or Barbados Merchandize. Represented in a petition to the high and honourable court of Parliament, by Marcellus Rivers and Oxenbridge Foyle, Gentlemen, on behalf of themselves and three-score and ten more of freeborn Englishmen, sold uncondemned into slavery" (London, 1659), quoted in Schomburgk, *History of Barbados*, 284.

38. Marilyn C. Baseler, *"Asylum for Mankind": America, 1607–1800* (Ithaca: Cornell University Press, 1998), 75.

39. The *Fundamental Constitutions* would be revised in 1670, 1682 (twice), and 1698; they were suspended from 1693 to 1698.

40. Shaftesbury to Maurice Mathews, June 20, 1672 in Cheves, ed., *Shaftesbury Papers*, 398–99.

estate the moment he and his extended "family" stepped off the boat.[41] Barbados, at that moment, was a sickly, overpopulated, treeless speck of an island … one where deteriorating conditions had already compelled thousands of inhabitants to remove to larger islands or to the mainland. Shaftesbury was confident that he had found a way to tap that migratory stream of experienced planters, and indeed he had.[42] Consummate opportunists, the "Barbadian Adventurers" were eager to acquire estates in the New World (though some had no intention of abandoning their lucrative sugar plantations). The Lords Proprietors also recruited settlers and servants in England and Ireland; such prospects lacked the Barbadians' experience in a colonial setting, but they would provide much-needed labor. Whether the "Grand Model" for Carolina was practical—or enforceable—remained to be seen.

On September 6, 1669, the *London Gazette* reported that the "30 sail of ships" in the port of Falmouth included the *Carolina*, the *Albemarle*, and "one other ship bound with passengers for the Plantation of *Carolina*, a Colony in *America*."[43] The vessels put to sea "with a fair wind," stopped briefly in Ireland, and then proceeded to Barbados, where a November storm sank the *Albemarle*. After another vessel was leased (the *Three Brothers*), a sizeable Barbadian contingent joined the enterprise and the ships resumed their journey. In March 1670, following a seven-month ordeal that included an unplanned layover in Bermuda, the *Carolina* finally made landfall at Bull's Bay, north of present-day Charleston, her sister ships having been destroyed or delayed by storms.[44] Though setting foot on solid ground must have been immensely reassuring for the 148 or so *Carolina* passengers, they still sensed danger and quickly began construction of a defensive palisade on the west bank of the

41. *Warrants for Lands in South Carolina, 1672–1711* (Columbia: University of South Carolina Press, 1973), n.p., cited in "Granting of Land in Colonial South Carolina," *The South Carolina Historical Magazine* 77, no. 3 (1976): 209.

42. During the seventeenth century, roughly ten thousand Barbadians emigrated; most were recently freed indentured servants. In 1670 the island's one hundred thousand or less arable acres housed nearly sixty-three thousand people; more than four thousand of them were enslaved Africans. John J. McCusker and Russell R. Menard, *The Economy of British America, 1607–1789* (Chapel Hill: University of North Carolina Press, 1985), 150–55, 170–71.

43. *London Gazette*, September 6, 1669. The third ship was the *Port Royal*.

44. Arriving by way of Bermuda, the *Carolina* stopped briefly at Port Royal, but that area's proximity to Spanish Florida prompted the colonists to relocate to the banks of the Ashley River. The *Port Royal* was lost in the Bahamas, and storms drove *The Three Brothers* north to Virginia; many of the latter vessel's passengers eventually arrived at Charles Town.

Ashley River.[45] Their concern and that of the proprietors who attempted to manage the colony from afar was the ever-present threat of a land attack by Native Americans or Spaniards, or a sea-borne assault by French, Dutch, or Spanish marauders, or free-roaming pirates. Several months later, those trepidations were justified when the colony had to deal with hostile Westo Indians and a Spanish incursion at St. Helena Island. The appearance of three Spanish frigates at Stono Inlet in August 1670 only heightened the colonists' anxiety.[46]

Fortifications and organized militia served a purpose, but South Carolinians soon discovered that adversity assumed many forms, some of which were impervious to barricades. Having lost the bulk of their provisions at sea, the colonists faced starvation. The *Carolina* was dispatched to Virginia for provisions in May but was slow to return; by June the daily food ration was down to one pint of peas.[47] Joseph West informed the proprietors "wee cannot employ our servants as wee would because we have not victualls for them."[48] John Hash had become an indentured servant in order gain passage to America "to improve his fortune." Instead he found only "want and suffering...especially as regards [to] food."[49] Many immigrants were tradesmen, "poor and wholly ignorant of husbandry"; they simply wanted "to clear a little ground

45. Joseph West to Lord Ashley, March 1671, Cheves, ed., *Shaftesbury Papers*, 297, in Patrick Melvin, "Captain Florence O'Sullivan and the Origins of Carolina," *The South Carolina Historical Magazine* 76, no. 4 (October 1975): 246. Estimates of the number of passengers on the ship *Carolina* range from 92 to 150 people; among them were at least sixty-three servants. Some servants indentured to passengers aboard the *Carolina* traveled on her companion ships. [Smith, *White Servitude in Colonial South Carolina*, 4–6.] Florence O'Sullivan, deputy for Sir Peter Colleton, received nineteen hundred acres for himself and the twelve servants that arrived with him on the *Carolina*. Victoria Proctor, "South Carolina Ship's Lists," http://sciway3.net/proctor/ships/v1/Carolina1669.html.

46. Barbara Olexer, *The Enslavement of the American Indian in Colonial Times* (Columbia, MD: Joyous Publishing, 2005), 92–94.

47. Joseph West to Lord Ashley, June 27, 1670, Cheves, ed., *Shaftesbury Papers*, 173–74, cited in Converse D. Clowse, *Economic Beginnings in Colonial South Carolina 1670–1730* (Columbia: University of South Carolina Press, 1971), 57.

48. "Letter of Joseph West, June 27, 1670," in Salley, ed., *Narratives*, 120–21. The colonists bound for Carolina originally set out with "eighteen Moneths Victuals, with Clothes, Tools, Ammunition, and what else was thought necessary for a new Settlement"; the loss of two ships deprived the colony of many of those supplies. Samuel Wilson, "An Account of the Province of Carolina" (London, 1682), in Salley, ed., *Narratives*, 166–7.

49. Edelson, *Plantation Enterprise*, 70.

to get Bread for their Familyes."[50] But even subsistence farming required nature's cooperation and the mainland's climate proved unpredictable: a "great
blast" of frost "kill[e]d all things" in the first winter, and crops withered in a
"great drought" the following summer.[51] The colony's leaders beseeched the
Lords Proprietors to send food, clothing, cattle, hogs, and other aid until a
successful harvest could solve the crisis.

In the autumn of 1671 the governor and Council concluded that "Indians
are endeavouring and contriving the distruction of this settlement and his
Majesties subjects therein." South Carolinians had to neglect their crops in
order to battle "Southerne Indians" who planned to join forces with the Spanish and "cutt off the English people in this place."[52] Alarmed settlers looked
to their leaders for reassurance, but instead of calming their fears, Governor
William Sayle enacted laws to discipline troublemakers and to prevent colonists from leaving South Carolina.[53] In Sayle's view, the best way to combat
external threats was to increase the number of able-bodied men in the colony.
The arrival of more settlers increased the population to nearly five hundred,
but that meant more mouths to feed at a time when the colony was already
rationing provisions.[54] For the next few years, prospective immigrants were

50. "Letter of Thomas Newe, May 29, 1682 by way of Barbados," reprinted in Salley,
ed., *Narratives*, 184.

51. The only edibles that survived the onslaught were maize, beans, cattle, and hogs—
the staples of the emerging economy. Edelson, *Plantation Enterprise*, 32–41.

52. Council Meeting, Sept. 27, 1671, in Alexander S. Salley, ed., *Journal of the Grand
Council of South Carolina: August 25, 1671-June 24, 1680* (Columbia: South Carolina Historical Commission, 1907), 8. A decade later Thomas Ashe wrote that "Natives of the
Country . . . hath hitherto lived in good Correspondence and Amity with the English,
who by their just and equitable Cariage have extremely winn'd and obliged them; Justice
being exactly and impartially administered, prevents Jealousies, and maintains between
them a good Understanding." Ashe, *Carolina*, in Salley, ed., *Narratives*, 156–57.

53. In 1670 the Lords Proprietors appointed Sayle as governor of Carolina and established a ten-member council to advise him. When it met with the governor to make
decisions or discuss executive orders, the council was designated the *Grand Council*. The
proprietors also appointed a lower legislative body consisting of twenty influential merchants or property owners who ratified legislative proposals introduced by the council;
that body was known as the *Commons House of Assembly*. The proprietary government
remained in place for twenty-eight years until it was overthrown in 1719. Luther F. Carter and Richard D. Young, "The Governor: Powers, Practices, Roles and the South Carolina Experience," South Carolina Governance Project website, Center for Governmental
Services, Institute for Public Service and Policy Research, University of South Carolina.

54. In January 1672 Joseph Dalton reported to the proprietors that there were 470
people in the colony; John Locke calculated that 396 colonists—268 men, sixty-nine

advised to bring eight months' supply of food for themselves and their families.[55] In 1671 interim governor Joseph West ordered that all tradesmen suspend their normal work routines and plant crops, blacksmiths and carpenters being the only exceptions. No colonist would be issued food from the public supply unless he planted two acres of corn and peas for every member of his family.[56] One colonist later wrote, "The first 5 or 6 years I cannot readily say wee liked, for wee wer in continuall want, few in number, few Cattle, and what is worst of all, ignorant what to doe."[57]

The population swelled once again in April 1672 with the arrival of Sir John Yeamans and his entourage, including two hundred slaves. A "landgrave" and the most prominent man in Carolina, Yeamans had long behaved like the unprincipled protagonist in a Hobbesian drama—ambitious, acquisitive, and enormously selfish. A decade earlier, when he was a prominent planter, judge, and council member in Barbados, Yeamans was accused of conspiring to poison his business partner, Benjamin Berringer "for noe other reason but that he had a mind to the other gentleman[']s wife."[58] Exonerated by his close colleagues, Yeamans married widow Berringer ten weeks after her husband's death. In 1665 he helped plant the Barbadian settlement at Cape Fear, serving as its first governor, but soon abandoned the short-lived colony to pursue his own interests. In 1670 Yeamans accompanied South Carolina's founders

---

women, and fifty-nine children—were in Carolina at that time. [Joseph Dalton to Lord Ashley, January 20, 1672, Cheves, ed., *Shaftesbury Papers*, 376–83, cited in Clowse, *Economic Beginnings*, 50–51.] In 1671 a number of Dutch immigrants arrived from Holland and New York.

55. Captain Halsted to Lord Ashley, March 1672, Cheves, ed., *Shaftesbury Papers*, 389, cited in Clowse, *Economic Beginnings*, 57.

56. McCrady, *History of South Carolina*, 147.

57. Maurice Mathews, "A Contemporary View of Carolina in 1680," *The South Carolina Historical Magazine* 55, no. 3 (July 1954): 157. Though conditions were difficult, Carolina's first settlers at least avoided the privation and sickness that devastated colonies such as Jamestown and Plymouth. Until subsistence farming enabled South Carolinians to feed themselves, relief ships and food acquired through trade with Native Americans prevented any catastrophic "starving time" or excessive first-year mortality. Spanish reports indicated that the colony was being assisted by English colonies in the Caribbean and on the American mainland. "Report of the War Board of the Indies to the Queen," February 12, 1674, A.G.I. 58–2–14. Lowery Transcripts, VIII, reprinted in Jose Miguel Gallardo, "The Spaniards and the English Settlement in Charles Town," *The South Carolina Historical and Genealogical Magazine* 37, no. 2 (April 1936): 49–64.

58. *Colonial Records of North Carolina*, vol. 1, 177, quoted in McCrady, *History of South Carolina*, 173.

only as far as Bermuda before he decided to return to Barbados. Because the *Fundamental Constitutions* were initially vague regarding headrights, Yeamans did not settle in South Carolina until he received assurances that he would be granted 150 acres for each slave he transported to the colony. Somewhat perplexed by Yeamans's capriciousness, the proprietors responded: "We find that you are mistaken in our Concessions that wee have not made provision of Land for negroes by saying that we grant 150 acres of land for every able man servant in that we mean negroes as well as Christians."[59]

Joseph West, the colony's interim governor, warned the proprietors that Yeamans's arrival would destroy any chance for "a hopeful settlement." The Executive Council in Charles Town notified the proprietors that Yeamans's appointment as governor would breed "a very great dissatisfaction to the people."[60] When Yeamans did arrive with his family and slaves, he quickly wrenched the governorship from Joseph West. Realizing that the colonists were still pinched by hunger, Yeamans used his connections to import food from Barbados, which he then sold at exorbitant prices. As if profiteering was not sufficiently damning, a contemporary accused Yeamans of complicity in the death of an Indian. The Lords Proprietors found Yeamans "extravagant and indifferent to their interests." One remarked, "If to convert all things to his private profit be the marke of able parts Sir John is without a doubt a very judicious man."[61]

In 1672 the proprietors promised liberal concessions to freemen and servants from Ireland—a tactic undoubtedly frowned on by planters from Barbados who had denounced Irish servants in the past.[62] Many leading men worried that their lives and property were endangered not just by Indians and Spaniards but also by threats emanating from within the colony. Indentured

59. *South Carolina Historical Society Collections*, vol. 5, 164, quoted in Wood, *Black Majority*, 19–20.

60. *Calendar of State Papers, Colonial*, Sainsbury, ed. (London, 1889), 428, in McCrady, *History of South Carolina*, 151.

61. Lord Ashley to Colleton, November 27, 1672, Cheves, ed., *Shaftesbury Papers*, 416, in Sirmans, *Colonial South Carolina*, 404. According to Robert Weir, Yeamans and other Barbadians "resembled pirates ashore" who spawned factionalism and "both promoted and retarded the development of the colony." Weir, "Yeamans, Sir John," *Oxford Dictionary of National Biography* (2004). In November 1671 Captain Thomas Gray accused Yeamans of stealing timber from his land. Salley, ed., *Journal of the Grand Council*, November 27, 1671.

62. The concessions tendered to the Irish included their own settlement in Carolina and freedom to practice their Catholic faith. McCrady, *History of South Carolina*, 180.

servants outnumbered freemen in the new settlement; they soon discovered that their interests and those of poorer planters were routinely compromised or ignored by their social betters.[63] A breach between rich and poor, or between free and unfree, might lead to rebellion, pitting colonist against colonist, or prompting servants to run away and join the enemy. These concerns intensified in 1672 when Brian Fitzpatrick, one of twelve servants from Kinsale, killed a Native American and fled to St. Augustine. Two colonists were sent to bring him back or, if he resisted, to "maim, destroy or kill him."[64] Fitzpatrick eluded his pursuers and gave the Spanish information about Charles Town's "discontented and miserable condition."[65] He revealed that the colony had no "paid soldiers," but it had "about eight hundred English and three hundred Negroes, all of whom bear arms."[66]

The Spanish welcomed any reliable information about Charles Town. In 1674 the War Board of the Indies sent a report to the Spanish queen, noting that the new English settlement "has been strengthened with men, arms and artillery, and several Indian nations have become its allies." The colony was receiving assistance from England, Virginia, Bermuda, Barbados, and "other settlements of English nationality on that coast." These developments caused the Board members "a great deal of concern and anxiety." They feared that, with the ports the English held "on the sea and on the Mexican gulf," they could "cause irreparable damage to our commerce in America." The War Board's "greatest sorrow and grief" stemmed from "the thought of the diminution of the Catholic faith resulting from the intercourse between the Indians

---

63. Regarding the number of servants in the colony, see St. Julien R. Childs, "The First South Carolinians," *The South Carolina Historical Magazine* 71, no. 2 (April 1970): 107–8. Servants would have constituted an even greater majority if Joseph West had not been stymied in his recruiting efforts at Kinsale. There the Irish had become terrified by "the ill practice of sending them to the Caribbee islands, where they were sold as slaves." Some of the few servants that West did manage to procure soon ran away, as would others once they reached the American mainland. *Calendar of State Papers, Colonial: America and West Indies 1669–1674*, 19, in Melvin, "Captain Florence O'Sullivan …," 237–38. In the first decade of settlement, 22 of the 117 known immigrants from Barbados were indentured servants. Richard Waterhouse, *A New World Gentry: The Making of a Merchant Planter Class in South Carolina* (Charleston, SC: The History Press, 2005), 31.

64. The Council Journals, August 24, 1672, in Cheves, ed., *Shaftesbury Papers*, 411.

65. Arthur Mitchell, *South Carolina Irish* (Charleston, SC: The History Press, 2011), 16.

66. "Brian Fitzpatrick's Deposition," in South, *Archaeological Pathways*, 281. Fitzpatrick also described Charles Town's palisade, saying it was stocked with weapons and that it housed about twenty families.

and the English." The report noted that the Spanish Windward Fleet "may be of some help in remedying such serious dangers."[67]

Brian Fitzpatrick was not the only discontent servant in South Carolina; the same summer he took flight, the colony's Grand Council sentenced Philip O'Neill (Orrill) to twenty lashes for threatening to overturn his mistress's boat, throw the servants' meager provisions "to the Doggs," and run away to the Indians. It also warned O'Neill's fellow servants that all "gross abuses and destructive practices" would be similarly punished. Shortly thereafter, authorities considered measures to regulate servants' activities and sentenced two servants to death for running away, though they suspended the verdict when the defendants begged for clemency.[68] The gross inequities that riled poorer planters, laborers, seamen, servants, and paupers could not be eliminated, so the colony's leaders turned to coercion, legislation, and severe punishments to maintain order.

Because the colony's black population grew slowly during the 1670s, enslaved Africans were not viewed as a significant threat.[69] Some used firearms to hunt on the frontier and, when necessary, whites equipped slaves with guns to defend Charles Town (as Brian Fitzpatrick informed the Spanish). In 1672 several dozen "well-armed" Africans at the governor's plantation in Carolina were charged with defending it from attack by Spaniards and Indians.[70] However in 1675 news from other colonies reminded South Carolinians that virtually any oppressed group might suddenly lash out against men who exploited them. Travelers from Barbados reported that a massive slave uprising had been narrowly averted.[71] That same year, vessels from New England brought news of devastating attacks on outlying settlements by Indians who were considered allies of the English. In neighboring Virginia, "Poore Endebted Discontented and Armed" colonists, many of them former

67. "Report of the War Board," in Gallardo, "The Spaniards and the English Settlement in Charles Town," 49–64.

68. Salley, ed., *Journal of the Grand Council*, June 13, 1672, and December 9, 1671; Cheves, ed., *Shaftesbury Papers*, 357–59; Ibid., March 10, 1673, 421, cited in Clowse, *Economic Beginnings*, 52–53.

69. In 1680 Maurice Mathews reported that "Wee are now about 500 fighting Inglish men beside many trusty negros. I think wee are in all, men, women, and children about 1000 and doe daily increase from all parts." Mathews, "Contemporary View of Carolina," 158.

70. Wood, *Black Majority*, 23. In 1708 and 1715, South Carolina slaves were armed to defend the colony.

71. *Great Newes From the Barbados* (London 1676), 9–12, quoted in Handler, "Slave Revolts and Conspiracies," 14–16.

servants, went on a rampage, killing inoffensive Native Americans, destroying the estates of wealthy tobacco planters, and burning Jamestown to the
ground.[72]

In none of those places—Barbados, New England, Virginia—did mounted
cannon or defensive ramparts offer adequate protection. In a world of "haves"
and "have nots," of oppressors and oppressed, the real face of danger was
likely one you saw every day. Not just one face, perhaps, but a multitude, and
their complexion—black, red, or white—depended on the uneven course
of human affairs. By the time those crises occurred in other colonies, South
Carolinians had already done battle with Spaniards, the Kussoe (twice), the
Westo, and the Stono. The *cacique*, or leader, of the latter group sought a
pan-Indian alliance "to murder some of the English Nation, and to rise in
Rebellion against this settlement."[73] As an incentive to fight the Stono, Governor West offered a bounty for every hostile Indian that was captured and
brought to Charles Town. The prisoners would be transported to the West
Indies where they met their doom on sugar plantations.[74] The bounties stimulated the growth of the Indian slave trade in Carolina—a vile business that
eventually endangered every person in the province, regardless of race, age,
or gender.

In the first decade of settlement, about half of the South Carolina immigrants whose origins can be identified came from Barbados. Several dozen
hailed from other Caribbean islands, one-fifth sailed directly from Great
Britain, and a handful came from colonies on the American mainland.[75]
The immigrants from Barbados included a fair number of middling artisans,
small planters, enslaved Africans, and indentured servants. Shocked by the

72. Edmund S. Morgan, "Slavery and Freedom: The American Paradox," *Journal of
American History* 59, no. 1 (1972): 5–29. Governor Berkeley estimated that the malcontents may have comprised six-sevenths of the population.

73. Salley, ed., *Journal of the Grand Council*, July 25, 1674. In a tract promoting settlement in Carolina, Maurice Mathews reported in 1680 that "Wee have lived in a continuall peace since the first of our Setlement which was in March elevin years ago. Wee have
ever afforded the Indians Justice making them give satisfaction for any injury they have
done to any of us, And in like maner giving them satisfaction for the wrongs our people
have at any time done unto them." Mathews, "Contemporary View of Carolina," 158.

74. Alexander Hewatt, *An Historical Account of the Rise and Progress of the Colonies of
South Carolina and Georgia*, vol. 1 (London: Printed for Alexander Donaldson, 1779), 78.

75. This tally is based on 683 immigrants of known origins; these estimates include
servants but not enslaved Africans. [Waterhouse, *New World Gentry*, 28–30.] Jack Greene
states that "almost half of the whites and considerably more than half of the blacks"
who settled in Carolina in 1670–71 hailed from Barbados. A study involving 1,343

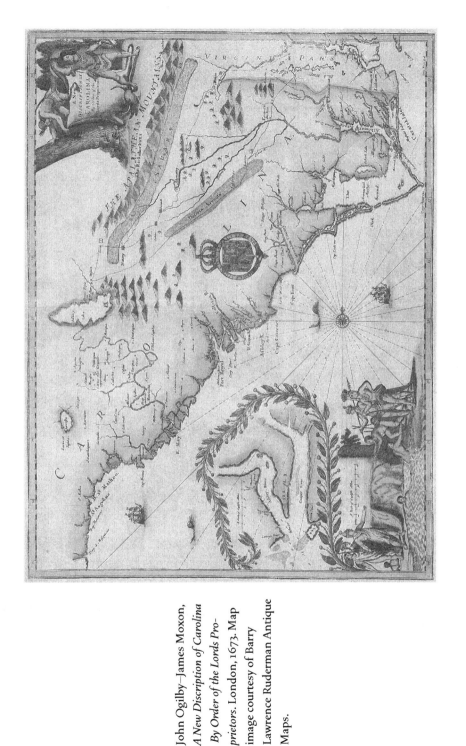

John Ogilby–James Moxon, *A New Discription of Carolina By Order of the Lords Proprietors*. London, 1673. Map image courtesy of Barry Lawrence Ruderman Antique Maps.

deficiencies of the latter group, Governor West informed Shaftesbury that "one of our Servants wee brought out of England is worth 2 of ye Barbadians, for they are soe much addicted to Rum, that they will doe little whilst the bottle is at their nose." Some prominent Barbadians obtained land grants, dispatched agents and servants to their mainland plantations, and then stayed on the island, managing the trade between South Carolina and Barbados.[76] A number of affluent Barbadian immigrants flaunted the township scheme integral to the proprietors' "Grand Model" and settled fifteen miles northwest of Charles Town on a tributary of the Cooper River. These "Goose Creek men," former sugar barons who held religious dissenters and small planters in contempt, thrived in the competitive milieu envisioned by Hobbes.[77] It was not long before they made it clear that they had no intention of abiding

---

whites who immigrated between 1670 and 1690 revealed that "more than 54 percent were probably from Barbados." [Jack S. Greene, "Colonial South Carolina and the Caribbean Connection," *The South Carolina Historical Magazine* 88, no. 4 (October, 1987): 197.] There were approximately one thousand whites in Carolina in 1680, three hundred to four hundred of whom migrated from Barbados. The bulk came from England, "accompanied by streams of Scottish, Irish, and French Huguenot settlers." [Edelson, *Plantation Enterprise*, 42.] Drawing on Barbadian archives and Agnes Leland Baldwin's list of migrants to South Carolina, Justin Roberts and Ian Beamish conclude that fewer than 120 of the 2,541 migrants entering the colony between 1670 and 1700 owned land in Barbados. They concede that some landless men probably travelled from Barbados to Carolina during this period, as did many enslaved Africans, but the notion that Carolina was settled by wealthy Barbadian sugar planters is erroneous. [Roberts and Beamish, "Venturing Out: The Barbadian Diaspora and the Carolina Colony, 1650–1685," in LeMaster and Wood, eds., *Creating and Contesting Carolina*, 58–59.] Walter Edgar considers efforts to minimize the Barbadian connection with South Carolina using surviving documentation in Barbados to be "a weak reed upon which to base a case." [Edgar, *South Carolina, A History*, 596, fn 2.] Peter Coclanis estimates that between 1670 and 1680, 88 percent of settlers whose origin is known came from England or Barbados, and that the latter "supplied almost as many 'settlers' to Carolina as did England over the course of that decade." Some were English gentry and Barbadian planters and merchants, but most were from groups "at the bottom of the seventeenth-century social hierarchy" ... servants, men "out of their time," (former servants), and enslaved Africans. Coclanis, *Shadow of a Dream*, 22.

76. The wealth that sugar planters generated on Barbados was "a catalyst for the settlement of Carolina." Roberts and Beamish, "Venturing Out: The Barbadian Diaspora," in LeMaster and Wood, ed., *Creating and Contesting Carolina*, 54, 59.

77. Thomas Hobbes maintains that in a state of nature, the lack of restraints make it impossible to distinguish between lawful and lawless conduct. John Locke, by contrast, "presumes a firm demarcation" between law-abiding and criminal individuals. Hobbes

by the *Fundamental Constitutions* and would readily ignore any provisions of that document that interfered with their enrichment.[78] Authorities worried that their speeches against the government might foment "seditions and mutinies" and lead to "the ruin of the settlement."[79] Joseph West, who temporarily succeeded Sayles as governor, found it easier to cooperate with the former Barbadians rather than oppose them. Despite his amenable attitude, Sir John Yeamans, a former sugar planter, directly challenged West's authority and claimed the office for himself.

In the years to come, incessant squabbling between political and religious factions did nothing to advance the interests of the average colonist; rather, the obstacles and hazards that a small planter and his family faced were exacerbated by wealthy, contentious, and highly ambitious planters and merchants who placed their interests above those of everyone else. Throughout the founding period, the Goose Creek men used protest, dissent, and duplicity to manipulate affairs to their advantage. The Lords Proprietors warned one newly appointed governor, "Beware of the Goose Creek men . . . don't expect to carry on the government with all parties."[80]

---

believes that justice requires that contracts be honored, but contracts are generally invalid in a state of nature. Whereas Hobbes uses natural law to defend absolutism, Locke uses it to promote limited government. Patrick Coby, "The Law of Nature in Locke's Second Treatise: Is Locke a Hobbesian?," *The Review of Politics* 49, no. 1 (1987): 5.

78. Michael James Heitzler, *Goose Creek, South Carolina, A Definitive History 1670–2003*, Volume 1 (Charleston, SC: The History Press, 2005), 64–65. The Goose Creek men were also known as the Anglican Party, the Church Party, the Barbadians, and the Anti-Proprietary party. Some of these groups involved colonists from places other than Barbados, but the Barbadians clearly took the leadership role. [Edgar, *South Carolina, A History*, 84–85.] L. M. Roper challenges the distinctions of proprietary and anti-proprietary factions; he argues that political activity of the Goose Creek men "revolved around their enslavement of Indians." Their intransigence regarding the lucrative Indian slave trade disrupted the colony's political scene, inhibited white immigration, and provoked the Yamasee War. It was the avariciousness of the Goose Creek men—not the actions of the proprietors—that led to the latter's overthrow. [Roper, *Conceiving Carolina*, 7–8.] Alan Gallay notes that even where only a "small portion of the colonists" disregarded colonial and imperial laws in the pursuit of wealth, "that group had a dramatic impact because neither fellow colonists nor government officials would or could stop them." Gallay, *Indian Slave Trade*, 64.

79. Cheves, ed., *Shaftesbury Papers*, 291.

80. Heitzler, *Goose Creek*, I, 69. Regarding the influence of Barbadian investors who did not migrate, see Roberts and Beamish, "Venturing Out: The Barbadian Diaspora," in LeMaster and Wood, ed., *Creating and Contesting Carolina*, 49–72. L. M. Roper maintains

Despite the controversy that surrounded them, former Barbadians were the most powerful and financially successful group to immigrate to South Carolina. In the colony's first decade, Sir John Yeamans, Thomas Drayton, Robert Daniel, Stephen Fox, Richard Quintyne, Christopher Portman, and John Ladson were among those who brought slaves from Barbados and established sprawling plantations near Charles Town.[81] Edward and Arthur Middleton emigrated from Barbados in 1678 and settled in Goose Creek; through shrewd acquisitions, business enterprises, and political manipulation, they established a colonial dynasty that would operate at the highest levels of government.[82] Another Barbadian emigrant, James Moore, became an Assembly leader, then provisional governor from 1700 to 1703 and led several slave raids into Spanish Florida and west toward the Mississippi. Moore used his political influence to advance his commercial interests, defying any laws that impinged on his moneymaking schemes. Though merchants and planters from Barbados generally fared well in the new colony, many members of the Corporation of Barbadian Adventurers regarded Carolina merely as one of many investment opportunities; instead of migrating, they opted to remain on the island, monitoring their other Caribbean and mainland enterprises from afar. Passenger lists for 1679 shed light on this trend. That year, thirty-eight individuals are known to have sailed from Barbados to Carolina; fifteen acquired land in the colony but an even greater number—most likely sugar planters interested in diversification (and/or their agents)—soon returned to Barbados.[83]

After the first few years, the pace of immigration into South Carolina slowed to a trickle despite generous headrights and a policy of religious toleration. By 1680 the proprietors fretted not only about recovering their invest-

---

that the connection between Barbados and South Carolina has been overstated. He acknowledges that Barbadians "did comprise a sizeable element in the colony's population" and Carolina did adopt the "Barbadian approach to 'managing' slave labor," but most of the leading Goose Creek men came from England and had "no direct experience with slavery or slaves." [Roper, *Conceiving Carolina*, 6.] The presence of English immigrants in Goose Creek did not necessarily compromise the influence of the Barbadians, or in any way negate their experience with plantation slavery and their intention to replicate it in South Carolina.

81. Kay Wright Lewis, *A Curse Upon the Nation: Race, Freedom, and Extermination in America and the Atlantic World* (Athens: University of Georgia Press, 2017), 41.

82. George W. Lane, "The Middletons of Eighteenth-Century South Carolina: A Colonial Dynasty, 1678–1787." Ph.D. diss., Emory University, 1990.

83. Roberts and Beamish, "Venturing Out: The Barbadian Diaspora," in LeMaster and Wood, ed., *Creating and Contesting Carolina*, 61–62.

ment in the colony but also about regaining political control. Ten years had passed since the *Carolina* made landfall, yet many colonists, particularly those from Barbados, still had not endorsed the *Fundamental Constitutions*. That was not the only cause for distress among the proprietors; it had become clear that they and the Barbadian immigrants had a basic disagreement regarding the economic function of the colony. Shaftesbury and his associates wanted colonists to live in orderly villages and concentrate on the production of exotic commodities that would be exported to England for resale. But early experiments with silk, tobacco, cotton, wine, linen, ginger, indigo, fruits, and medicinal plants had lackluster outcomes. Some failed due to unfavorable growing conditions; others required too much in terms of labor and capital.[84] Barbadian immigrants, many of whom had relatives and business associates on the island they formerly inhabited, knew that there was a ready market for wood, meat, and naval stores in the West Indies. Even more profitable than these was the trade in deerskins and captive Native Americans. These exports generated income, but Goose Creek men, energized by the windfalls that sugar plantations produced for Barbados planters, continued to search for a cash crop—one with unlimited demand in Europe. Such a find would enable them to replicate the plantation system honed on Barbados, but with Carolina's enormous advantage of limitless land reserves.

Although prosperous immigrants from Barbados posed the most flagrant challenges to the *Fundamental Constitutions*, ignoring any provision that stood in the way of profits, lesser planters were also eager to capitalize on their landholdings—tracts that would have astounded the average farmer in England. In the first few years of settlement, many colonists barely grew enough food to meet their own needs, but by the 1680s most families had a garden and "a stock of Hogs and Cows" which they sold to newcomers or exported to Barbados.[85] Although they were excluded from the Indian trade, "middling" planters eagerly pursued obvious economic opportunities, rather than the fanciful delusions of distant proprietors. Many farmers joined the colony's elite in opposing the land policies laid out in the *Fundamental Constitutions*. The Goose Creek men welcomed the support of these underlings, confident that their own interests would have top priority in any future negotiations with the proprietors.

84. Coclanis, *Shadow of a Dream*, 60–61.
85. Clowse, *Economic Beginnings*, 68; "Letter of Thomas Newe," in Salley, ed., *Narratives*, 183. South Carolinians exported four tons of beef and pork to Barbados in 1679. Three years later Samuel Wilson wrote from Carolina that cattle "thrive and increase here exceedingly." Wilson, "An Account" (1682), reprinted in Salley, ed., *Narratives*, 171.

As the colony moved into its second decade, it became clear that a shared mentalité had emerged. Most South Carolinians had developed an external orientation—an unwavering focus on long-distance trade. Men at all levels of society expended their energies (or those of their indentured and enslaved laborers) in response to the "stimuli and signals of the market."[86] Success hinged on supply and demand. Carolinians had become suppliers intent on delivering items that would garner the greatest profit. In a setting where land was abundant but labor and capital in short supply, exports such as hogs, cattle, timber, and deerskins took precedence until some staple crop emerged. When they conceived and financed Carolina, the Lords Proprietors envisioned an export-based economy, but one that involved cargoes in high demand in England and on the Continent, not shingles or barrels of meat bound for the West Indies. Shaftesbury and his associates viewed the sugar islands as recruiting grounds for experienced colonists, not the primary destination for commodities produced in their slice of the North American pie. But the imperatives of commerce shaped the colony and its changing role in a transatlantic economy.[87] In fact, some Barbadians invested in South Carolina on the premise that the colony's main function was to respond to the needs of Caribbean sugar planters.

In 1682 hoping to bolster South Carolina's population and undermine the power of the Goose Creek men—most of whom were Anglicans—the Lords Proprietors initiated a promotional campaign to attract Presbyterians, Baptists, Congregationalists, Quakers, German and Swiss Lutherans, and French Huguenots to the province.[88] The proprietors' agents, appointees, and admin-

---

86. Coclanis, *Shadow of a Dream*, 50. In the absence of a staple crop, colonists made a "gradual adjustment to factoral realities." Barbadians who "hoped to make Carolina the colony of a colony" supported that adjustment. Ibid., 61.

87. Edelson, *Plantation Enterprise*, 5. In 1665 proprietor John Colleton attempted to purchase sows for the settlement at Albemarle "whereby we may have a quantity of Hoggs flesh, wch will soonest come to bare to send to Barabados wch will pduce [produce] us Neagroes & Sarvts: to rayse a plantacon." William S. Powell, ed., *Ye Countie of Albemarle in Carolina: A Collection of Documents, 1664–1675* (Raleigh: North Carolina State Department of Archives and History, 1958), 7.

88. Edgar, *South Carolina, A History*, 88. The proprietors attempted to revise the *Fundamental Constitutions* in 1682 but the Goose Creek men contended that the 1669 document could not be amended without the consent of the South Carolina parliament. Governor Joseph Morton was unsuccessful in an attempt to force the Assembly (controlled by the Goose Creek men) to ratify the document. The stalemate led to the dissolution of the Carolina parliament. L. H. Roper, "Morton, Joseph, Sr.," Walter Edgar, ed., *South Carolina Encyclopedia* (Columbia: University of South Carolina Press, 2006), 1015.

istrators touted the colony in conversation, publications, and correspondence, reminding them of its abundance and its policy of religious toleration. Assuring readers that he had written "nothing but the truth," Samuel Wilson described South Carolina as "a pleasant and fertile Country, abounding in health and pleasure."[89] In another 1682 publication Thomas Ashe praised "the Healthfulness of the Air [and] Pleasantness of the Place."[90] *The True Protestant Mercury* offered advice to prospective immigrants and announced when Carolina-bound ships would depart from European ports. Joel Gascoyne's *New map of the country of Carolina* was issued to accompany these glowing descriptions of the province; it depicted thirty-three established plantations, available lands, and a network of rivers that ensured easy access to Charles Town.[91] These promotional efforts, coupled with worrisome developments in Europe—particularly on the religious front—steered hundreds of Protestant dissenters toward South Carolina.[92]

This second wave of immigration came shortly after the relocation of the colony's main settlement from Albemarle Point to Oyster Point, a site on the peninsula between the Ashley and Cooper rivers. About twenty houses already stood at the new location; within a year, Charles Town boasted one hundred wooden structures. In 1680 Maurice Mathews penned a description of the colony. He said Charles Town's new location was "convenient for public Commerce . . . Ships ride safe in all weathers under the Towne in both Rivers." Cannon in the newly constructed fort commanded both rivers and

---

89. Wilson, "An Account," in Salley, ed., *Narratives*, 174. Wilson was secretary to the Earl of Craven, one of the Lords Proprietors.

90. Ashe, *Carolina*, in Salley, ed., *Narratives*, 138.

91. Rowland, Lawrence Sanders and Alexander Moore and George C. Rogers, Jr., *A History of Beaufort County, South Carolina: Vol. 1, 1514–1861* (Columbia: University of South Carolina Press, 1996), 68; Edelson, "Defining Carolina" in LeMaster and Wood, *Creating and Contesting Carolina*, 31.

92. French Huguenots began arriving in 1679; the largest influx came in 1687 when six hundred arrived. Some settled at French Santee north of Charles Town, but most Huguenot merchants and tradesmen remained in the town. [Hart, *Building Charleston*, 26; Bertrand Van Ruymbeke, "The Huguenots of Proprietary South Carolina: Patterns of Migration and Integration," in Jack P. Greene, Rosemary Brana-Shute, and Randy J. Sparks, eds., *Money, Trade, and Power: The Evolution of Colonial South Carolina's Plantation Society* (Columbia: University of South Carolina Press, 2001), 26–36.] In 1684, Charles II authorized the transportation to Carolina of prisoners who refused to take the test that ensured the commitment of all officeholders to the Protestant faith, but who otherwise appeared penitent. Tim Harris, *Restoration: Charles II and His Kingdoms, 1660–1685* (London: Penguin Books, 2006), 369.

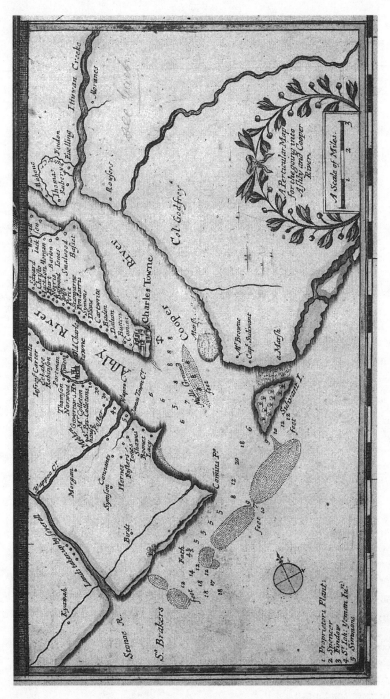

Detail from Joel Gascoyne, *A new map of the country of Carolina*. S.I., 1682. Oriented with north toward the right. Library of Congress, Geography and Map Division.

the future addition of "great guns" would enable defenders to "deale with the greatest force of ane [sic] enemy that can on a sudden come up upon us from Sea." Indians who formerly resided at Oyster Point had removed from "their old habitations" and were given a place where they "might plant and live comfortablie." Mathews stated that few colonists, "except some new comers," lacked cattle, and that during the past four years, most settlers had "such plenty of provisions that it is to be admired rather than beleeved."[93] Two years later, Thomas Ashe reported that Charles Town was inhabited by "1[,]000 or 1[,]200 Souls" and "great Numbers of Families from England, Ireland, Berbadoes [sic], Jamaica, and the Caribees . . . daily Transport themselves thither."[94] In its second decade, the colony appeared to be on the verge of modest prosperity. It was perhaps at that point in the mid-1680s that the visions of John Locke and Thomas Hobbes collided and the glint of optimism became tarnished by the grim pallor of reality.

Promoters depicted South Carolina as a place in which production and consumption were linked—where pleasure and profit existed in tandem. On Charles Town's busy wharves, New World exports and Old World imports regularly crossed paths. However, newly arrived immigrants often felt misled; one noted that promotional tracts embellished conditions instead of describing "the difficulties that one endures in establishing oneself."[95] Judith Giton, a Huguenot who fled from La Voulte-sur-Rhône, lost her mother to "spotted fever" en route to America. Upon her arrival in Charles Town in 1686, she encountered only "maladies, famine, poverty, and hard work." Giton wrote that "we suffered every kind of evil." She went six months without tasting

93. Mathews, "Contemporary View of Carolina," 153–57. Mathews voiced little confidence in the colony's tobacco crop, but he said that "the great and easie product of our Cattle, hogs, and other stock gives us ane happier life then all the tedious Thousands of tobacco plants the slavery of our Northern Nighbour [sic] can afford." Ibid., 156.

94. Ashe, *Carolina* [1682] in Salley, ed., *Narratives*, 158; Michael Patrick Hendrix, *Down and Dirty: Archaeology of the South Carolina Lowcountry* (Charleston, SC: The History Press, 2006), 38. Ashe noted that Charles Town was "regularly laid out in large and capacious Streets," but Gideon Johnston was unimpressed when he arrived decades later. Johnston wrote: "The same fine appearance dos Charles Town make in the Maps . . . yet many of those fine and regular Buildings which are represented in it, are not to be met with when we come upon the Spot to look for them; and we find our Selves more deceived & disappointed in the other particulars, than we do in this." "Comy Johnston to the Secry, S. Carolina Charles Town," July 5, 1710, in Frank J. Klingberg, ed., *Carolina Chronicle: the Papers of Commissary Gideon Johnston, 1707–1716* (Berkeley: University of California Press, 1946), 61.

95. Edelson, *Plantation Enterprise*, 22–23; McClain and Ellefson, "A Letter from Carolina, 1688," 390.

bread "whilst I worked the ground like a slave." Her eldest brother soon died, "not being fitted to the harsh work to which we were exposed." Just eight months after Giton arrived, Spanish troops invaded South Carolina and a massive hurricane turned the "whole country" into "one entire map of devastation."[96] Giton married Noé Royer, a Huguenot weaver who immigrated in 1685. The couple had three sons and was living in Charles Town in 1698 when Royer died, leaving his widow in debt. Judith's youngest son died shortly thereafter. Giton remarried, bore two more children, and helped her second husband, Pierre Manigault—who had been raising cattle—establish a distillery and cooperage. Judith died in 1711; Manigault eventually struck it rich in the warehouse-and-mercantile business.[97]

Two male immigrants reported that they had never seen "so miserable a country, nor an atmosphere so unhealthy." The pair fled to Boston and reported that, in South Carolina, "fevers prevail all the year, from which those who are attacked seldom recover."[98] A Huguenot who arrived in 1686 wrote: "The country is not at all like it was depicted ... the place is new and so little peopled." He added: "One needs determination to surmount the first difficulties and not everyone has that ... a considerable number of our newly arrived French abandoned us." South Carolina was "neither as beautiful as they told us nor as advanced ... life here is without refinements."[99]

The author of the letter was one of fifty French refugees living in a makeshift shelter fashioned from a sail, "and the earth our bed." Using palmetto logs, they built "a cabin like that of savages." For five months the group endured "a great deal of discomfort." Their first summer was "rather severe with

96. "Paper to the Lords Proprietors c. 1686, quoted in J. G. Dunlop, *South Carolina Historical & Genealogical Magazine*, 1929, 83–84, in Tom Rubillo, *Hurricane Destruction in South Carolina: Hell and High Water* (Charleston, SC: The History Press, 2006), 34.

97. Pierre Manigault spent several years in the Caribbean before moving to South Carolina in the early 1690s. His brother and business partner died in 1704 when he fell off a roof. The Manigaults had two children by 1704; Judith died at the age of forty-six. Her husband outlived her by eighteen years and bequeathed property and slaves to their offspring. Slann Legare Clement Simmons, ed., "Early Manigault Records," *Transactions of the Huguenot Society of South Carolina*, no. 59 (1954): 2; Baird, *History of the Huguenot Emigration*, 2:393, in McClain and Ellefson, "A Letter from Carolina, 1688," 381–82; Bertrand Van Ruymbeke, "Judith Giton: From Southern France to the Carolina Lowcountry," in *South Carolina Women: Their Lives and Times*, vol. 1, Marjorie Julian Spruill, Joan Marie Johnson, Valinda W. Littlefield, eds. (Athens: University of Georgia Press, 2009), 30–37.

98. Charles W. Baird, *History of the Huguenot Emigration in America*, 2 vols. (1885: repr., Baltimore, 1973), 2:393.

99. McClain and Ellefson, "A Letter from Carolina, 1688," 390–93.

almost continuous rains and fevers." Noting that he and his companions had set out from Europe with "heads full of great lands and other extravagances," the writer speculated that "God . . . has deprived us of our goods and of the pleasures of life because we had abused them." The Almighty "does not want wealth to expose us again to the same abuses and to the same effects of his wrath." But many other colonists were far worse off and the uprooted Huguenot strove "to be of help to the miserable ones." He concluded with this observation: "This country is neither for those who have many goods, nor for those who want to lead an easy life, nor for those who have nothing. It is good only for those who still have some belongings, who want to work, who are resolved to suffer and who prefer peace to anything else."[100]

In South Carolina's second decade, few planters were genuinely prosperous. Despite much experimentation, the colony remained in need of a staple crop. A herd of cattle and a field of Indian corn were considered "the Basis and Props of all New Plantations and Settlements," though planters increasingly engaged in mixed farming.[101] Like their predecessors, freemen recruited in the 1680s received headrights for themselves and for each person they brought to Carolina.[102] This enabled immigrants with large families or, more likely, with numerous servants or slaves, to acquire large estates, even though their headrights were less generous than those given to some firstcomers.[103] Of course land was only valuable if it was well timbered, tilled, converted to

---

100. Ibid., 387–94.

101. Ashe, *Carolina, or a Description*, in Salley, *Narratives*, 145. Rich Barbadians were exceptions in Carolina; the great majority arrived as indentured servants; even some freemen were unable to pay their own passage to America and depended on the proprietors to extend credit until a cash crop was harvested. [Smith, *Colonists in Bondage*, 285–86; Clowse, *Economic Beginnings*, 51.] Many enslaved Africans were familiar with the open-grazing style of farming practiced in South Carolina's Lowcountry. Hart, *Building Carolina*, 29.

102. In 1894 Shirley Carter Hughson speculated that "In Carolina . . . It was easy enough for a new-comer to attach to himself any number of low characters, enter them as servants, receive the broad domain to which he was entitled, and then either turn the people loose on the country, or else attempt to settle them as "leetman" in accordance with the terms of the laws of the colony." She added, ". . . these rogues knew well enough what their freedom would be in a new, wild country like America." Shirley C. Hughson, *The Carolina Pirates and Colonial Commerce, 1670–1740*, Johns Hopkins University Studies in Historical and Political Science, 12th series (Baltimore: Johns Hopkins University Press, 1894), 11–12.

103. In Carolina and many other colonies, headrights declined in value over time. Carolina's first freemen (those who arrived in March 1670) were entitled to up to 150 acres for each adult male (including servants and slaves) they brought to the colony and

pasture, or sold at a profit.[104] Besides raising cattle and hogs for export to the West Indies, South Carolinians produced pitch and tar for English ships and exported pipe-staves, barrels, shingles, and other lumber products.[105]

When Thomas Newe migrated to South Carolina in 1682, he intended to develop vineyards that would cause the colony to "flourish exceedingly." Those plans were soon dashed and Newe became one more settler trying to eke out a living by raising hogs and cows for export to "the Islands." Wealthy planters charged neophytes like Newe a premium for a breeding pair of cattle that might, with luck, eventually produce a small herd. Provisions were "so dear" in Charles Town that Newe envied people in the interior who "are fu-nisht with Venison, fish, and fowle by the Indians for trifles." Like so many firstcomers, Newe did not survive the seasoning process and died during his first year in South Carolina.[106] But many immigrants did survive, and some

---

100 acres for each male child and female. Settlers who arrived later that year received one hundred acres and seventy acres, respectively, for each person in those categories. Later arrivals were entitled to sixty to seventy acres per family member, servant, or slave. Anon., "Granting of Land in Colonial South Carolina," *The South Carolina Historical Magazine* 77, no. 3 (July 1976): 209.

104. Even before Carolina was settled, yeomen farmers in England had already become commercial farmers pursuing every opportunity to increase their profits; market opportunities were "the first factor to consider in their husbandry." It was a "fiercely competitive climate" in which property was increasingly concentrated in fewer hands, and economic inequality "proceeded at a rapid pace." [Greene, *Pursuits of Happiness*, 31.] In 1688 England's landless laborers, paupers, and vagrants made up about half of the population and subsisted on only one-fifth of the national income. [Ibid., 104.] This "ever widening gap" between the elite and those who lived below the poverty line would be replicated to some degree in South Carolina, but not until the second half-century of its existence.

105. In 1712 John Norris listed many goods produced for export in early Carolina. [*Profitable Advice for Rich and Poor in a Dialogue, or Discourse between James Freeman, a Carolina Planter, AND Simon Question, a West-Country Farmer* (London, 1712), in Jack P. Greene, ed., *Selling in a New World: Two Colonial South Carolina Promotional Pamphlets* (Columbia: University of South Carolina Press, 1989), 77–147.] The Earl of Shaftesbury envisioned Carolina as a place well suited to the production of raw silk and wine. Huguenot immigrants made repeated but unsuccessful attempts to make wines that might resemble those produced by vineyards in Languedoc. Owen Stanwood, "Imperial Vineyards: Wine and Politics in the Early American South," in Patrick Griffin, *Experiencing Empire: Power, People, and Revolution in Early America* (Charlottesville: University of Virginia Press, 2017), 50–70.

106. "Letter of Thomas Newe," in Salley, ed., *Narratives*, 181–82; Edelson, *Plantation Enterprise*, 49. In 1680 Maurice Mathews stated, "Venison is no rarity with us unless about

eventually prospered. A 1712 promotional tract claimed that some men in Carolina who were practically destitute when they arrived or completed their indentures purchased a few cows or swine and "hath by their stocks of cattle and hogs, in few years, become rich." One former servant reportedly owned one hundred horses, three thousand cattle, "and three hundred calves yearly" when he died.[107]

In early South Carolina, adaptability and resourcefulness often made the difference between prosperity and mere subsistence. In 1679 the proprietors enabled several prominent Huguenots to transport about eighty families "skilled in ye manufacture of silks, oyles, wines &c." to the colony.[108] Efforts to produce those commodities failed, but men like John Guerard, Sr., made the best of it. Guerard worked as a planter and weaver, but in 1691, he applied for a patent for a "Pendulum Engine, which doth much better, and in lesse time and labour huske rice."[109] After that scheme failed, Guerard entered a partnership in the deerskin trade ... an enterprise that soon included the purchase and sale of enslaved Africans and Indians. Guerard also sold dry goods on commission from London. When he died in 1714, Guerard left his widow and four children a substantial estate that included property in Charles Town and 750 acres on the Cooper River. His son and namesake would become one of the colony's leading merchants and slave traders.[110]

---

the Towne. Those who live toward the Indian parts of the settlements have brought them by ane [any] Indian in one year 100 sometimes 200 deer." Mathews, "Contemporary View of Carolina," 157.

107. Norris, *Profitable Advice* (London: 1712), in H. Roy Merrens, ed., *The Colonial South Carolina Scene: Contemporary Views, 1697–1774* (Columbia: University of South Carolina Press, 1977), 48. According to Norris, few former servants would hire themselves out "by reason they can employ themselves very advantageously in their own business, and on their own land, by planting of corn and rice." Ibid., 51.

108. Owen Stanwood describes the high expectations regarding the wine and silk industries in Carolina. In 1683 a Huguenot colonist wrote that he had planted "vines which do wonderfully well," but he may have suffered an outcome like that of a Swiss settler whose wine and silk experiments failed by 1690. Owen Stanwood, "Between Eden and Empire: Huguenot Refugees and the Promise of New Worlds, in *The American Historical Review* 118, no. 5 (December 2013): 1319–44.

109. Horne, "A Brief Description," in Salley, *Narratives*, 69 fn.

110. R. C. Nash, "Trade and Business in Eighteenth-Century South Carolina: The Career of John Guerard, Merchant and Planter," in *South Carolina Historical Magazine* 96, no. 1 (January 1995): 8–9. John Guerard, Jr. left an estate worth approximately £25,000 when he died in 1764.

Profit often dictated the course of a man's activities in South Carolina. A group of Huguenot weavers who migrated together soon found that their craft had limited potential in the colony, so most turned to farming or raising livestock. When he died in 1722, former weaver Jean Petineau owned one hundred acres, six slaves, fourteen cattle, two geldings, eleven sheep, and his "old weaver loom."[111] Another Huguenot, Nicholas de Longuemare, repaired clocks and watches, crafted jewelry and cutlery, imported silks, and finally raised cattle just outside Charles Town. Many other "middling" tradesmen discovered that the limited demand for their services would eventually leave them impoverished. Some abandoned the town and became small planters; others moved on to more promising situations in Boston, Philadelphia, or New York.[112]

Huguenots in South Carolina proved the value of familial, communal, and religious connections. As their numbers grew, these French immigrants provided essential support to newer refugees. Isaac Mazyck arrived in the colony around 1689. After marrying the daughter of a well-to-do merchant, Mazyck capitalized on his Huguenot connections to establish a thriving mercantile operation. When he died in 1736, Mazyck owned a house, a shop, house lots in Charles Town, several plantations, and a four-thousand-acre island. He bequeathed nearly £32,000 in Carolina currency to relatives and several Charles Town congregations.[113] When he arrived in 1707, Huguenot Benjamin Godin joined an established mercantile enterprise and entered politics. Godin eventually acquired an estate of over eleven thousand acres, a house in Charles Town, a Goose Creek plantation, £30,000 in Carolina currency, and several hundred slaves.[114] Mazyck and Godin prospered in South Carolina, but most immigrants became modest farmers or tradesmen. Some men who arrived as indentured servants never acquired lands of their own. With no

111. Van Ruymbeke, "Huguenots of Proprietary South Carolina," in Greene et al., *Money, Trade, and Power*, 33.

112. Hart, *Building Charleston*, 26–31. Not until the 1740s did Charles Town become a mecca for tradesmen, many of whom built prosperous careers as the city expanded around them. In earlier years, small merchants were caught in the same bind as artisans. Hart describes the very limited offerings—stockings, gloves, tea, rum, sugar, and groceries—sold by a Charles Town partnership in the late 1720s and contrasts it with the extensive wares offered by merchants like Thomas Corker, who left an inventory valued at £13,000 (£1,860 sterling) when he died in 1771. Ibid., 41.

113. Van Ruymbeke, "Huguenots of Proprietary South Carolina," in Greene et al., *Money, Trade, and Power*, 26–36.

114. Ibid., 34–35. Based on Godin's will, dated December 26, 1747. Charleston County Wills, WPA Transcripts, vol. 6 (1747–1752), 85–88.

support group akin to the Huguenot community, poorer men from England and Barbados often found themselves isolated and impoverished. In early South Carolina, neither economic nor physical survival was assured. Diseases would invariably take their toll, but so would competition with immigrants who were more ambitious, better funded, and better connected. Virtually every freeman cherished his liberty, but some discovered that the colony's market ethos simply gave them to the liberty to fail.

South Carolinians experimented with different crops in the 1670s and 1680s, but farming did not seem to hold as much promise as the export of deerskins, livestock, and naval stores. Most men were not allowed to barter with Native Americans for pelts because the proprietors believed that the best way to control the deerskin trade—and to reap a goodly portion of its profits—was to maintain a monopoly on that business. They planned to use agents and hirelings to do the actual work involved in procuring hides. As it turned out, the "Indian trade" in deerskins did operate as a virtual monopoly, but some of the colony's leading men reaped the lion's share of the profits. They operated with few restraints and their greed led to catastrophe. The deerskin trade was compromised almost from the start when, just four years after the founding of Charles Town, Henry Woodward informed the Lords Proprietors that Indians in South Carolina were "well provided with arms, ammunition, tradeing cloath and other trade [items] from the northward [Virginia] for which at set times of the year they truck drest deare skins[,] furrs and young Indian Slaves."[115] At the time, the Spanish and the Virginians were engaged in the Indian trade, but South Carolinians had an advantage in terms of geography and, when competing with Spanish agents, trading goods.

The proprietors were keen on entering the deerskin trade, but Shaftesbury and the others were resolved that South Carolina would not engage in the Indian slave trade. They were already worried about threats posed by the Spanish and French; it would be foolish to let the colonists antagonize their Native American neighbors by treating them as commodities to be bought and sold. Moreover, the Indian slave trade would disrupt the highly profitable deerskin trade and distract planters from the business of agriculture. But spurning the proprietors' wishes, enterprising colonists—particularly the Goose Creek men—recognized a lucrative opportunity and seized on it in true

115. "Henry Woodward to the Early of Shaftesbury, December 31, 1674," Cheves, ed., *Shaftesbury Papers*, 634; "Henry Woodward's Westoe Voyage," in Salley, ed., *Narratives*, 133. Even before the colony was planted, Sir John Yeamans and other Barbadians may have envisioned the North American mainland as a new source for slaves for sugar planters. Roper, *Conceiving Carolina*, 45.

Hobbesian fashion. As far as the Indian slave trade was concerned, South Carolina was indeed a place where every man had "a Right to every thing: even to one another's body."[116] Former Barbadians realized that Native Americans could be sold to that island's sugar planters for half the cost of captive Africans. Transportation costs from Charles Town were less (Africa being twice as far away), fewer captives would die in passage, and enslaved Indians were not subject to Imperial taxes.[117]

Thanks to an unholy alliance brokered by Henry Woodward, Westo Indians, armed by South Carolinians, began to conduct slave raids against other tribes. They delivered their captives to men with close ties to Barbados planters and merchants. The proprietors were outraged, but in December 1675, the colony's Grand Council informed Shaftesbury that their Native American allies wanted to sell "Indian prisoners" taken in intertribal wars. Addressing the proprietors' mandate that "no Indian upon any occasion or pretense whatsoever is to be made a Slave, or without his own consent be carried out of Carolina," the councilors brashly claimed that "the said Indian prisoners are willing to work in this country, or to be transported from hence."[118] The profits from the trade fostered intense competition at the colony's highest levels. As Hobbes had warned, "Where no law, no injustice," so factions formed and jockeyed for power, trying to corner the market on the sale of Native Americans to South Carolinians, Barbadians, and anyone else with the necessary lucre.[119]

Advertisements in the *Boston News-Letter*, 1707–1716

March 24, 1707—A Pretty Carolina Indian Boy aged about 12 years, to be Sold; Enquire of John Campbell, Port-master of Boston and know further.

---

116. Hobbes, *Leviathan*, 64. In 1675 Shaftesbury commented that until colonists put the "Excellent Modell" for Carolina into practice, a virtual "state of Warr" existed in the colony. Shaftesbury to Governor and Council, June 10, 1675, in Cheves, ed., *Shaftesbury Papers*, 468.

117. Gallay, *Indian Slave Trade*, 299–301. Barbados is 1,865 miles from South Carolina, 4,231 miles from Nigeria.

118. "Agrarian Laws or Instructions from the Lords Proprietors to the Governor and Council of Carolina, June 21, 1672," in William James Rivers, *A Sketch of the History of South Carolina: To the Close of the Proprietary Government by the Revolution of 1719* (Charleston: McCarter & Co., 1856), 358; Council meeting, December 10, 1675, in A. S. Salley, ed., *Journal of the Grand Council*, 80.

119. Hobbes, *Leviathan*, 64; Gallay, *Indian Slave Trade*, 50.

September 29, 1707—Ran-away from her Master, Nathaniel Baker of Boston, Baker ... a Tall Lusty Carolina Indian Woman named Sarah, aged about five or six and twenty years ...

March 29, 1708—To be Sold at the Sign of the blew Anchor in Boston five Carolina Indians, viz. a Man, a Boy and 3 Women.

August 27, 1711—A Carolina Indian Woman Aged about 25 years, to be Sold, by Mrs. Grace Rankin; and to be seen at her House in Mackeril Lane Boston[.]

September 10, 1711—Ran away from their Masters at Boston ... the following Indians, viz. From the Reverend Mr. Samuel Myles, a Carolina Indian Man nam'd Toby, Aged about 20 years of a middle stature ... From the Hon. Col. Thomas Savage, a Carolina Indian Woman nam'd Jenny aged about 40 years, a pretty thick set Woman ... From Mr. John Staniford Taylour, a Carolina Indian Woman name[d] Phillis, well set[,] Aged about [ ] years[.]

October 29, 1711—A Carolina Indian Boy Aged about Ten years, to be Sold, Inquire at the Post Office.

December 10, 1711—A Carolina Indian Woman of a Middle Stature, Speaks very little English, Aged about 40 years. [T]aken up as a Runaway; Inquire at the Post-Office in Boston, and know further.

January 12, 1712—A Carolina Indian Woman aged about 24 Years a very good Servant to be Sold by Capt William Clark, and to be seen at his House in Clark's-Square, near the North Meeting-House in Boston.

March 16, 1712—A Carolina Indian Man aged about 22 years, to be Sold Inquire at the Post Office in Boston.

June 9, 1712—A Carolina Indian Boy aged about fourteen years to be sold, Inquire at the Post-Office in Boston and know further.

March 2, 1713—A Carolina Indian Boy about eleven years old, to be Sold, Inquire at the Post Office in Boston.

September 17, 1716—Ran away from their Masters in Boston ... Three Carolina Indians, viz. Two Men-Servants and One Woman, they speak

but broken English, about 30 Years of Age or above; one from Mr. Samuel
Adams[,] Malter, named James, well sett, he hath a Leather Jacket, black
Stockings. Another of them Servant to Mr. Nehemia Yeals, Ship-Carpenter,
named Robin, with double Breasted Jacket, Leather Breeches; they both have
other Cloaths with them. The Indian Woman Servant to Mr. Thomas Salter
[,] Cordwainer, named Amareta, pretty Lusty, she hath a strip'd home-spun
Jacket, blue Petticoat.

For four decades, South Carolinians would conduct a thriving business in the
purchase and sale of Native Americans. Without the profits generated by the
Indian slave trade, the colony might have been unable to develop many of
the plantations that exploited African laborers. Spurred on by traders, Westo
Indians may have penetrated as far as Natchez territory along the Mississippi
in their quest for prisoners.[120] But the Westo raiders soon learned what Englishmen bent on profit would do. Accusing the Westo of attacks on friendly
tribes and the murders of two whites, the colony went to war against their
former partners in the slave trade. Seemingly unaffected by any ethical concerns, South Carolinians persuaded Savannah and Creek Indians to wage war
against the Westo in order to bring captives to Charles Town so they could
be sold or shipped off in exchange for African slaves from Barbados.

The colony's propensity for shifting alliances accelerated the arms race
that was already underway among Native Americans in the southeast.
Thomas Newe wrote that Woodward and his associates had "armed the next
most potent tribe of the Indians to fight the former," whom they had also
armed. According to Newe, many settlers were "mightily dissatisfied" because
"3 or 4 of the great ones" had monopolized the trade in furs and deerskins
since 1677.[121] Whether or not the average colonist wanted to trade just for
pelts, or also for captive Indians, is a matter of conjecture. Though most

---

120. Alan Gallay, ed., *Indian Slavery in Colonial America* (Lincoln: University of Nebraska
Press, 2009), 8; Gallay, *Indian Slave Trade*, 56.

121. "Letter of Thomas Newe," in Salley, ed., *Narratives*, 183. Native Americans' seemingly insatiable appetite for firearms and other European goods quickly led tribes into
dependency and a "vicious cycle of debt-inspired violence" that placed the Indian slave
trade at the center of intertribal and Euro-Indian conflicts in the southeast. [LeMaster
and Wood, eds., *Creating and Contesting Carolina*, 10.] Native Americans also sought allies to assist in their battles with long-standing enemies; South Carolinians relied on
different tribes for the same reason. Such collaborations were "crucial to the establishment of the Carolina colonies." Michelle LeMaster, "War, Masculinity, and Alliances on
the Carolina Frontiers," in LeMaster and Wood, ed., *Creating and Contesting Carolina*,
166.

South Carolinians were not directly involved in the Indian slave trade, a great number were complicit by virtue of their purchase and exploitation of Native Americans. For much of the colony's first half-century, enslaved Africans and Indians worked side by side on lowcountry plantations. But many captive Indians were doomed to toil in fields of sugarcane on Barbados. At Charles Town's docks, some newly arrived Africans probably crossed paths with Native Americans being loaded on vessels headed for the West Indies.

In 1691 South Carolina authorities attempted to restrict the number of traders by placing a tax on deerskins; that and other measures proved ineffective.[122] Between 1699 and 1715, the colony shipped an average of fifty-four thousand deerskins annually. The resulting decline in the deer population caused Native American hunters to encroach on the lands of other groups, fostering additional intertribal conflict. The average colonist lacked the capital (for goods, labor, and transportation), lines of credit, and partnerships that successful Indian traders had or quickly developed.[123] Men who became "Master Traders" lived among Native Americans, far beyond the line of English settlement; they had the money and connections to purchase large quantities of trade goods. Such men had great earning potential, but not so much the packhorse men, servants, and slaves that they employed on the frontier.[124]

122. Eirlys M. Barker has analyzed the inner workings of the Indian trade and the essential role of Master Traders who served as go-betweens, consulting and advising colonial authorities and tribal leaders. [Eirlys M. Barker, "Indian Traders, Charles Town and London's Vital Link to the Interior of North America, 1717–1755," in Greene et al., *Money, Trade, and Power*, 141–65.] Traders were necessary for building and maintaining alliances with Native American groups and keeping them armed against Indian allies of the French and Spanish, but those efforts were often compromised by the traders' reckless conduct. Gary L. Hewitt, "The State in the Planters' Service: Politics and the Emergence of a Plantation Economy in South Carolina," in Greene et al., *Money, Trade, and Power*, 53.

123. Verner Crane, *The Southern Frontier, 1670–1732* (Tuscaloosa: University of Alabama Press, 2004), 111–12. Traders' attitudes toward different Indian groups "were based on their perception of relative profitability." This made Indians who moved closer to Charles Town to engage in trade preferable to groups like the Cherokee who "did not actively pursue trade." Jon Bernard Marcoux, *Pox, Empire, Shackles, and Hides: The Townsend Site, 1670–1715* (Tuscaloosa: University of Alabama Press, 2010), 42.

124. The three hundred men known as Indian traders were the agents of merchants. The principal or "Master" traders were often educated men, some of whom were compelled to enter the trade to settle financial debts. Hundreds of pack-horsemen were also called "Indian traders"; their status was "nearer that of outcast than exile." Robert Meriwether describes them as, "Illiterate, irresponsible, often fugitives from justice, and as a

Over time, some Master Traders became so prosperous that they joined the ranks of the colony's elite, but many failed to strike it rich or died in the wilderness. Few "Middling" and "Lesser" traders would ever achieve the financial success that they coveted.[125]

South Carolina traders became notorious for their abusive conduct and the intertribal wars they initiated, but many colonists tolerated such behavior because they perceived certain benefits to the colony at large. By instigating wars and exporting the Native American prisoners, slave traders reduced the indigenous population in the southeast and made a pan-Indian alliance less likely.[126] The identification of all Indians and Africans as "inferior and deserving of enslavement" constituted a brand of racism that was still on its way to becoming a shared ideology in British America.[127] One remarkable aspect of South Carolina's entry into the Indian slave trade was that it occurred during the very years that New England colonists were engaged in a brutal war against a pan-Indian alliance led by Metacomet (King Philip), their former ally.

It should be noted that not all interactions between whites and Indians in colonial South Carolina were violent or predatory. In addition to the deerskin trade, Native Americans also assisted in the procurement of naval stores; some even contributed to the colonists' food supply. Samuel Wilson wrote that for less than twenty shillings a year, planters could hire Indian hunters who would feed a family of thirty people "with as much Venison and Foul [sic], as they can well eat."[128] In addition, the colony occasionally called on its Native American allies for defensive purposes and offered bounties to Indians who tracked down runaway servants, slaves, and criminals. The prospect of hiring (rather than enslaving) Native Americans for fieldwork proved a will-o'-the-wisp. In 1690 Scotsman John Stewart approached Governor James Colleton with a plan to employ Yamasee Indians as paid laborers. He proposed to hire three hundred Yamasee "to work for me in silk and cotton" and to pay his workers with trade goods. The governor gave his approval and even agreed to be a partner in the enterprise, but then struck his own seven-year

---

class lacking in any sense of decency or morality, they were ... objects of scorn and wrath to the orderly members of society." Robert L. Meriwether, "The expansion of South Carolina, 1729–1765," Ph.D. diss., Columbia University, 1940, 15.

125. Lesser traders operated at the fine edges of prosperity and ruin; one shipment of deerskins could bring a much-needed payoff or, if lost, financial disaster. Barker, "Indian Traders," in Greene et al, *Money, Trade, and Power*, 141–65.

126. Clowse, *Economic Beginnings*, 84.

127. Gallay, ed., *Indian Slavery in Colonial America*, 5.

128. Wilson, "An Account" (1682), reprinted in Salley, ed., *Narratives*, 171.

agreement with Altamaha, the Yamasee chief. Colleton, however, was banished in 1690, putting an end to the venture.[129]

The 1680s proved that, even in the direst circumstances, Carolinians were anxious to seize any opportunity to make money. In 1682 the governor was informed that eight hundred Spaniards from St. Augustine were headed for Charles Town "to fall upon the English." Rather than panic, South Carolinians "mightily rejoiced at the news of it, wishing that they might have some just cause of War with the Spaniards, that they might grant Commissions to Privateers, and themselves fall on them at St. Augustine."[130] Four years later, Scots Covenanters who had established an independent settlement south of Charles Town raided Spanish settlements near St. Augustine, killing fifty Timucuan Indians, capturing twenty-two slaves, and burning several towns.[131] In retaliation, the Spanish sent "3 Spanish halfe Gallies with 155 men" to destroy Stuart's Town. After completing that task Spaniards moved up the coast and "plundered Mr Grimballs & two of the Govrs plantations" and carried away "17 negroes & whyt servants" before they destroyed a plantation belonging to Daniel Axtell. Charles Town was not attacked only because a "dreadful hurry cane" destroyed one Spanish ship and grounded another, whereupon it was burned.[132] Goose Creek men, eager to pillage St. Augustine and enslave any blacks or Indians they captured in the process, forged an alliance with interim Governor Joseph Morton to carry out a retaliatory attack but the new governor, James Colleton, arrived in time to declare martial law and prevent the raid.[133]

129. John Stewart to William Dunlop, June 23, 1690, "Letters from John Stewart to William Dunlop," *South Carolina Historical Magazine* 32 (April 1931), 83–84, quoted in Gallay, *Indian Slave Trade*, 89–90. Gallay maintains that "there was nothing inherently impossible about using free Indian labor. The difficulty lay not with the Indians … but with the Europeans, who wanted a labor force they could sharply discipline: free Indians would have none of it." Ibid., 90.

130. "Letter of Thomas Newe, August the 23, 1682," in Salley, ed., *Narratives*, 186.

131. Rubillo, *Hurricane Destruction*, 33–34. The Lords Proprietors approved the planting of Stuart's Town near present-day Beaufort, in hopes that the Scots Covenanters would counter the Goose Creek men and prove more amenable to the goals and instructions of their landlords in England.

132. "Letter of Edward Randolph to the Board of Trade," March 16, 1699, reprinted in Salley, ed., *Narratives*, 205; J. G. Dunlop and Mabel L. Webber, eds., "Paul Grimball's Losses by the Spanish Invasion," *South Carolina Historical Magazine*, 29 (1928), 231–37, cited in Roper, *Conceiving Carolina*, 91. Governor Joseph Morton's brother-in-law was taken captive and later murdered.

133. L. H. Roper, "Morton, Joseph, Sr." Walter Edgar, ed., *Encyclopedia*, 1015.

At times it seemed that the entire colony was so hell-bent on making money that no scheme was too immodest or immoral. Shortly after its settlement, Charles Town developed a thriving trade with pirates who provided hard coin and various goods in return for food and medicine. In the past, these seagoing raiders used the province's harbors and inlets as places of refuge while they refitted and repaired their ships. As groups of immigrants planted along the southeast coast, pirates viewed developing seaports as a place to trade and to recruit new crewmates. During the seventeenth century, much of the specie in circulation in Charles Town consisted of gold and silver furnished by brigands who preyed on vessels in the Caribbean. London officials instructed the Lords Proprietors to "use your utmost endeavour to seize any Pyrates that Shall come to Carolina" and to prosecute "all such as shall presume to trade with them, or have any Comerce with them contrary to Law."[134]

Such mandates had little effect; pirates appeared regularly in Charles Town and the hard coin they brought was a boon to the economy. The Goose Creek men led the way in the illicit trade (as they did in the Indian slave trade), but even appointed officials had to be chastised or replaced by the proprietors for their dealings with pirates. Only when the colony began to lose valuable cargoes of rice to bandits lurking off the coast did this nefarious alliance crumble. As more and more shipments were taken, Charles Town merchants began to view men who sailed under the black flag as their enemies, not their partners in trade.[135]

In the 1680s South Carolina remained a predominately white settlement.[136] On Barbados, the growing dependence on African slaves fostered a

134. "Instructions for Collonell Phillipp Ludwell, [sic] Governor of Carolina, May 20, 1692," in A. S. Salley, Jr., ed., *Commissions and Instructions from the Lords Proprietors of Carolina to Public Officials of South Carolina, 1685–1715* (Columbia: The State Co., 1916), 16. The Earl of Shaftesbury was so certain that the discovery of gold would cause South Carolinians, "covetous of present booty," to abandon agriculture and begin prospecting, that he developed a secret code to mask any such news. Edelson, *Plantation Enterprise,* 30–31, 46–47.

135. William E. Nelson, *The Common Law in Colonial America: Volume II: The Middle Colonies and the Carolinas, 1660–1730* (New York: Oxford University Press, 2012), 74; Hughson, *The Carolina Pirates,* 9–48; "Earl of Craven to Lords of Trade, May 27, 1684," *BPRO-SC,* II, 284–85, in Clowse, *Economic Beginnings,* 87–89; Heitzler, *Goose Creek,* I, 63. In 1699 pirates seized three vessels from the colony; nine of the raiders were captured and tried, and seven condemned to death. After 1700 South Carolina officials seemed eager to set an example by quickly prosecuting and executing men charged with piracy.

136. Based on Shaftesbury's correspondence, Converse Clowse figures that South Carolina had one to two thousand settlers by 1680. ["Lord Ashley to the Governor and

black majority a full decade before Charles Town was founded. The possibility of a slave uprising troubled the colony's leaders; they responded by drafting the notorious "Barbados Slave Act" of 1661. They regarded indentured servants and men "out of their time" as safeguards and made significant concessions to win their support. In 1670, when some Barbadians departed for Carolina, the black-white ratio on the island was nearly two to one. Those migrants brought their paranoia and prejudices to South Carolina; few envisioned a black majority in their new setting. But in both colonies, the scent of profit often dictated the course of men's actions. The same year that sugar planters set out for Charles Town, the governor of Barbados noted that "since people have found out the convenience and cheapness of slave labour they no longer keep white men, who formerly did all the work on the plantations."[137]

In South Carolina the proximity of potentially hostile Native Americans and the Spanish presence in nearby Florida argued for the ongoing recruitment of white males, free and unfree, rather than the importation of Africans who might revolt or combine with the colony's enemies. But since the 1650s, the demand for indentured servants in the colonies far outstripped the supply.[138] Moreover, Africans could be transported from Barbados (where there was a thriving market in enslaved blacks) for less than it cost to bring servants from England or the Continent. Planters found other reasons to use slave labor: servants' terms of service were limited, they were more prone to illness

---

Council, June 10, 1675," Cheves, ed., *Shaftesbury Papers*, 466–68, cited in Clowse, *Economic Beginnings*, 73.] Peter Coclanis estimates the colony housed eight hundred whites and four hundred blacks in 1680. The white population soon would be bolstered by the arrival of French Huguenots, English Dissenters, and Scots, but the growth of the black population outpaced that of the whites. In 1690, after two decades of settlement, Carolina's 1,500 African slaves accounted for 38 percent of the population. Coclanis, *Shadow of a Dream*, 64.

137. Harlow, *A History of Barbados*, 309, 308n, quoted in Wood, *Black Majority*, 46. In Carolina, enslaved Africans would perform a great many labors other than fieldwork. During the colony's first few decades they were expert keepers of livestock, and "essential hands in the production of naval stores such as tar, pitch, and staves." Hart, *Building Charleston*, 19.

138. Historian L. H. Roper attributes the shortage of servants not only to demographic changes in Britain and competition from other colonies, but also to "explosive politics" in Carolina and "frequent epidemics of malaria and yellow fever." However, the first outbreak of yellow fever was in 1699 and many Carolina planters had already opted for slave labor by that date. L. H. Roper, "The 1701 'Act for the better ordering of Slaves': Reconsidering the History of Slavery in Proprietary South Carolina," *William and Mary Quarterly*, 3rd series, 64, no. 2 (April 2007): 397.

in the summer, and they often proved lazy.[139] In 1688 Edmund White of London assured Governor Joseph Morton of South Carolina that "you need not trouble your friends for servants from hence: you still fill up your letters with the bad conditions of the Milkmayd I sent." He advised Morton: "Let your negroes be taught to be smiths shoemakers & carpenters & bricklayers: they are capable of learning anything & I find when they are kindly used & have their belly full of victuals and [given] clothes, they are the truest servants."[140] Having been informed that "negroes were more desirable than English servants" in the colony, White was organizing a slaving voyage to the Guinea Coast.

Lowcountry planters found other reasons to use slave labor. They were reluctant to send white female servants into the fields, but they did not hesitate to make African and Native American women plant, tend, and harvest crops. Also, when servants completed their indentures, masters had to provide "freedom dues," typically clothing, corn, and farming tools.[141] No such recompense was due to slaves. Another reason to use slaves was the sweet nectar of unchecked power. Like sugar planters on Barbados, South Carolina planters knew they could not treat servants the same way they treated slaves. Subjects of the king could not be worked as hard, punished as severely, or deprived of basic necessities. In his "profitable advice" about South Carolina, John Norris made a point of saying that "as for Servants receiving from their Masters undeserved Correction, the Laws of the Country doth protect them."[142] In choosing between servants who had those protections and enslaved Africans or Indians whose only allies shared their wretched condition, more and more planters opted for unchecked power.

139. David J. McCord, ed., *The Statutes of South Carolina, Volume Second, Containing the Acts from 1682 to 1716,* (Columbia: A. S. Johnston, 1837), 30–31; Wood, *Black Majority,* 43.

140. "Letter from Edmund White to Joseph Morton, London, February 29, 1687," *South Carolina Historical and Genealogical Magazine* 30, no. 1 (January 1929): 3–4. Slaves who became skilled in certain crafts gained "leverage to extend their autonomy and expand their freedom of action." Though at a disadvantage, they sometimes "exacted contractual obligations they expected to be upheld." Daniel C. Littlefield, *Rice and Slaves: Ethnicity and the Slave Trade in Colonial South Carolina* (Baton Rouge: Louisiana State University Press, 1981), 166.

141. Freedom dues varied by time, place, and gender. In the seventeenth century, most male servants in Carolina received apparel, tools and land when they completed their indentures, while female servants received clothing and money or a supply of corn. Herbert A. Applebaum, *Colonial Americans at Work* (Lanham, MD: University Press of America, 1996), 98; R. Douglas Hurt, ed., *American Agriculture: A Brief History* (West Lafayette: Purdue University Press, 2002), 55.

142. Norris, *Profitable Advice* (London: 1712) in Greene, ed., *Selling a New World,* 94.

If ever there were a moment of historical contingency for South Carolina, a time when African slavery was an alternative, not a certainty, it would
have been before the introduction of rice when the deerskin trade, cattle and
hog farming, and the production of naval stores formed the colony's economic backbone.[143] Massachusetts's farm families augmented their own efforts with servants and hired hands; some owned slaves, but bondage proved
to be a short-lived phenomenon in most of New England. In early Virginia,
small planters tended to their own crops and wealthy landowners relied on
indentured servants; the tobacco boom that enriched many founders was not
dependent on slave labor. Like South Carolina, Restoration colonies such as
Pennsylvania and New Jersey experienced labor shortages, but they found
a middle ground where slavery never became a permanent fixture. Seventeenth-century landowners dealt with labor shortages in various ways, but
only South Carolina included a hegemonic group of former sugar planters—
immigrants who measured a man's worth in land and slaves—and only South
Carolina had proprietors who fashioned a "Grand Model" that prioritized
commercial agriculture and encouraged the use of slave labor.[144]

143. There is no historical consensus regarding race and slavery, or the inevitability
(or lack thereof) of African slavery in North America. David Brion Davis attributes the
"Africanization of large parts of the New World" to "innumerable local and pragmatic
choices" rather than "concerted planning, racial destiny, or immanent historical design." [David Brion Davis, *Slavery and Human Progress* (New York: Oxford University
Press, 1984), 52.] Russell Menard states plainly, "There was nothing inevitable about
the Africanization of slavery or its entrenchment in the Americas." He points out that
the notion that Carolina "was not capable of being cultivated by white men" emerged
"only after the lowcountry had become a thoroughly Africanized slave society." Earlier
on there is little evidence that planters preferred enslaved Africans to Native American
or indentured white laborers; they took whatever workers they could get. [Russell R.
Menard, "Transitions to African Slavery in British America, 1630–1730: Barbados, Virginia and South Carolina," *Indian Historical Review* 15 (1988–89), reprinted in Kenneth
Morgan, ed., *Slavery in America: A Reader and Guide* (Athens: University of Georgia Press,
2005), 33.] Edward Countryman also maintains that the institution of African slavery
was not inevitable in colonial America. Edward Countryman, *How Did American Slavery
Begin?* (Boston: Bedford/St. Martin's Press, 1999), 3–10.
144. The Lords Proprietors ensured prospective settlers that headrights would be given
for the importation of slaves as well as servants, and that freemen would wield "absolute
power and authority" over any Africans they imported. In 1674 Lord Ashley instructed
Andrew Percival, owner of a plantation south of the Charles Town settlement and Ashley's principal agent in Carolina, to "endeavor to begin a trade with the Spaniards for
Negroes, cloathes, or other commodities." William S. Pollitzer, *The Gullah People and
Their African Heritage* (Athens: University of Georgia Press, 2005), 40; Steven C. Hahn,

Barbados had nearly completed the transition to slave labor before Charles Town was planted.[145] South Carolina's ongoing trade with the West Indies, coupled with absentee landlordism and further immigration, ensured Barbados's continuing influence on the colony. Former sugar planters demanded headrights for African slaves they imported, and some figured prominently in the rise of the Indian slave trade.[146] But the Goose Creek men and the Lords Proprietors were not wholly responsible for the emergence of slavery in South Carolina. Colonists from England, the Continent, and other mainland colonies displayed willingness—indeed eagerness at times—to profit from the toil of slaves. In his 1682 *Account of the Province of Carolina*, Samuel Wilson stated that many planters who were "single and have never a Servant" had profited handsomely by raising and selling hogs in order to "get wherewithal to build them more convenient Houses, and to purchase Servants, and Negro-slaves."[147] In a rhetorical question posed for his readers, Wilson provided a telling glimpse into the mentalité of South Carolina planters then and in the future: "But a rational man will certainly inquire, When I have Land, what shall I doe with it? What Comoditys shall I be able to produce that will yield me mony in other Countrys, that I may be inabled to buy Negro slaves (without which a Planter can never do any great matter)?"[148]

"The Mother of Necessity: Carolina, the Creek Indians, and the Making of a New Order in the American Southeast, 1670–1763," in Robie Ethridge, Charles M. Hudson, ed., *The Transformation of the Southeastern Indians, 1540–1760* (Jackson: University Press of Mississippi, 2002), 86.

145. Menard, *Sweet Negotiations*, 31.

146. Heitzler, *Goose Creek*, I, 39–49. Of the sixty or so grantees who arrived between 1670 and 1675, most had at least one or two servants to tend their several hundred acres. But the only mentions of slaves or "negroes" in the land grant records occur beside the names of Simon Berringer (who received three thousand acres), Lady Margaret Yeamans (1,950 acres), William Sayle (2,350 acres), Mrs. Dorcas Smith (610 acres), Francis Boult (600 acres), and a handful of lesser planters such as William Thomas (270 acres), Mrs. Joan Carner (270 acres), and Captain Richard Conant (150 acres). See Table II, "Land-Grant Records of Early Carolina—with servants noted" in Smith, *White Servitude in Colonial South Carolina*, 12–16.

147. Wilson, "An Account" (1682), in Salley, ed., *Narratives*, 167. Because of the "mildness of the winter," according to Wilson, enslaved Africans could "thrive and stand much better, than in any of the more Northern Collonys, and require less clothes." Ibid., 172.

148. Ibid., 174. The transition from pioneer to plantation in South Carolina did not signal moral declension or a shift in mentalité; it represented "an economically rational, indeed quite predicable response by market-oriented whites to changing factor proportions and changing market possibilities." Coclanis, *Shadow of a Dream*, 57.

In 1688 a French immigrant noted that a fellow Huguenot was "a little more advanced than we are" because he had acquired a plantation and "three Negroes and a Negress." The envious planter regarded the enslaved Africans as "a considerable possession," and lamented that "We do not have any and I do not even know whether we will ever have some."[149] Even though they still lacked a staple crop, many planters—including men who had never owned slaves—insisted that Africans were indispensable for any type of rigorous work. That mind-set became even more entrenched over time. In 1702 Edward Hyrne estimated that his six-to-seven-hundred-acre estate contained "above £10,000 worth of cypress-timber," but he lacked "a competent number of hands." The demand for African slaves outstripped the supply and Hyrne could "make little advantage" of his land and lumber "[']till I can compass a good gang of Negroes; but God knows when that will be."[150]

The colony's generous headright system also played a major role in the emergence of slavery in South Carolina. Unlike early Massachusetts colonists, whose landholdings were geared to subsistence farming or small surpluses, South Carolina's founders received enough land to engage in commercial agriculture from the outset.[151] The Lords Proprietors anticipated burgeoning exports of wheat and exotic commodities such as silk, almonds, olives, ginger, indigo, sugarcane, grapes, tobacco, and cotton that were "fit for the market of England." When cattle and hogs became the colony's principal exports in the opening decades, Lord Ashley noted that it was the proprietors' design to "have Planters there and not Graziers."[152]

149. McClain and Ellefson, "A Letter from Carolina, 1688," 392. The implied link between rice cultivation and African slavery at this early juncture should be noted.

150. "Edward Hyrne to his brother," Charles-Town, January 19, 1701, in Merrens, *Colonial South Carolina Scene*, 18.

151. The initial land grants in Watertown (founded 1630) average twelve acres. [Roger Thompson, *Divided We Stand: Watertown, Massachusetts, 1630–1680* (Amherst: University of Massachusetts Press, 2001), 51–52.] In Billerica, Massachusetts, the median holding in 1651 was sixty acres, and the mean, ninety-six acres. In Springfield, landholdings ranged from six to 237 acres, but the median was only sixty acres. David Hackett Fischer, *Albion's Seed: Four British Folkways in America* (New York: Oxford University Press, 1989), 167.

152. W. Noel Sainsbury, ed., *Calendar of State Papers, Colonial* (London: 1889), 1277, cited in McCrady, *History of South Carolina*, 175. Carolina's subtropical climate was not suited to the growth of wheat, which produced "dirty-colored flour." Many smaller planters emulated Native Americans and switched to maize and bean agriculture; they also fenced their cornfields and let their cattle and hogs roam wild until they harvested them for meat and tallow to export and for their own consumption. Edelson, *Plantation Enterprise*, 38–39, 47, 69.

In South Carolina wealth determined a man's status. To exploit their lands to the fullest extent, planters needed all the workers they could afford. In the absence of servants, they turned to slave labor. As more and more Africans were transported to the colony, concerned Assemblymen drafted legislation to control slaves, to establish a Town Watch, to regulate the militia, and to encourage the importation of white servants.[153] But in agricultural communities, prosperity and production were inextricably linked. Planters envisioned thriving plantations where slaves toiled for scant food, clothing, and shelter. Overwork and abuse would undoubtedly foster resentment, but a stern hand would keep slaves on task. So, the colony lurched forward, grabbing at the golden ring wherever it appeared, regardless of the cost to present or future generations of South Carolinians, Native Americans, or Africans.

153. See Acts 157, 162, 167, and 168 in *The Statutes of South Carolina*, vol. 7, 135–56.

Three

Paradise Lost

Early promoters of South Carolina described a sort of Eden in which an ideal climate and abundant resources provided a life free from sickness, want, or worry. Explorer William Hilton commented on the health and longevity of the Native Americans that he encountered; pamphleteer Robert Horne said that Carolina had the best environment for "English Constitutions"; colonist Thomas Ashe hailed the province's salubrious air, fertile soil, and "luxuriant and indulgent blessings of nature."[1] Of course, immigrants familiar with the Book of Genesis knew that Adam and Eve dwelled in Paradise until their mutual sin led to their expulsion. "Cursed is the ground for thy sake," their Creator said as he drove them out of Eden and into a world of evil and sorrow.[2] Had South Carolinians reflected on that bit of Scripture, they might have thought twice about trafficking in Indian and African slaves. Early in the eighteenth century, Dr. Francis Le Jau, a missionary for the Society for the Propagation of the Gospel, saw signs of God's wrath all around him. In his eyes the "great Hurricane" of 1713 that pummeled Charles Town, drowning seventy people and destroying fortifications, shops, houses, and plantations,

---

1. Hilton, "Relation of a Discovery," in Salley, ed., *Narratives*, 45; Horne, "A Brief Description," Ibid., 70; Ashe, *Carolina, or a Description*, Ibid., 139. Max Edelson notes, "Given the unspoken realities of early deaths from infectious diseases, hostile Indians, and a climate liable to hurricanes and droughts," the early publications promoting South Carolina "can seem like deceptions designed to lure the gullible to a false paradise." Edelson, *Plantation Enterprise*. 17.

2. *King James Bible* (New York: American Bible Society, 1999), Genesis 2: 9, 3: 16–17. Carolina reflected its Barbadian heritage even in religious matters. Thanks to the influence of the Goose Creek men, who were overwhelmingly Anglican, in 1706 the Assembly passed the Church Act, establishing the Church of England as the official church of South Carolina, as it had been in Barbados. The names of six of South Carolina's ten parishes established by the act duplicated those on the island. Until 1778 taxes paid for the construction and upkeep of Anglican churches and for the salaries of Anglican clergy. Edgar, *South Carolina, A History*, 96.

Pieter Mortier, *Carte Particuliere De La Caroline Dresse sur les Memoires le plus Nouveaux Par Le Sieur S[anson]*. Amsterdam, 1696. Map Collection, South Carolina Department of Archives and History.

was divine retribution. He wrote, "I wish I could prevail upon the Inhabitants of this Place to make serious Reflexions upon the judgments wch our Sins ... bring down upon our heads from time to time."[3]

As the colony's slave population soared and traders lured Native Americans into a state of perpetual warfare, South Carolinians counted on racial solidarity, strategic alliances, and legislative measures to protect their lives and property. The choices they made transformed their American Eden into a place of violence and suffering; it would only be a matter of time before the people they exploited sought vengeance. But that prospect failed to deter many colonists, especially those who had lived on Barbados where appalling exploitation went hand in hand with profits. And so South Carolinians proceeded earnestly and often recklessly in pursuit of mammon.

৶

South Carolina's first twenty-five years were shaped by the "Grand Model" of the proprietors, the ambitions of the settlers, the power of the market ethos, imperial policies, interactions with Native Americans, Africans, and Spaniards, and the colony's physical and biological environment.[4] The second twenty-five years—1695 to 1720—proved to be even more tumultuous, bringing unexpected crises and unprecedented opportunities. Perhaps the most significant development was the "discovery" and gradual proliferation of rice. It was the missing piece of the puzzle ... the long-awaited staple crop that became the lowcountry's economic engine. Rice would eventually turn South Carolina—an insignificant colonial outpost—into one of England's most prized possessions in North America. But that success was hardbought; many who paid the price would not share in the rewards.

In the 1680s South Carolinians experimented with rice and deemed it a failure. One colonist wrote, "For the rice, one cannot succeed ... it is a thing that can only be done at great expense and only rich people could under take it."[5] In the 1690s Scottish agriculturalist John Stewart conducted trials with rice on Governor James Colleton's Wadboo Barony, eventually producing "glorious and hopefull" crops in two different locations.[6] In 1695 a small quantity of rice was shipped from Charles Town; four years later, Edward

---

3. Dr. Francis Le Jau to the Secretary, January 22, 1714, in *The Carolina Chronicle*, 137.

4. Regarding the dominance of the market ethos in South Carolina, see Coclanis, *Shadow of a Dream*, 49–59.

5. McClain and Ellefson, "A Letter from Carolina, 1688," 392.

6. John Stewart, "Letters from John Stewart to William Dunlop," *South Carolina Historical Magazine* 32 (1931): 29, in Edelson, *Plantation Enterprise*, 72.

Randolph reported that local planters had grown "more rice ... then we have Ships to Transport."[7]

Rice cultivation initially developed in areas where the crop had to compete with ranching, mixed farming, and production of naval stores. In 1702 Elizabeth Hyrne wrote that she and her husband were "goeing to make tar, which is the readiest mony of any thing in this country."[8] Rice was simply too new, costly, and labor-intensive to deter colonists from commodities in high demand in the West Indies. But the crop gradually made inroads at all levels of agricultural enterprise. In 1707 Martha Armory bequeathed four plantations in South Carolina; one was a 420-acre rice plantation maintained by an overseer and twenty-four slaves.[9] After Daniel Axtell's slaves constructed a reservoir dam and carved embankments that conducted water from a creek onto his seven-acre field, he sold an average of ten thousand pounds of rice annually between 1701 and 1707.[10] Even poorer planters gave the new crop a try: a 1712 promotional tract stated that few former servants would hire themselves out, "by reason they can employ themselves very advantageously in their own business, and on their own land, by planting of corn and rice."[11]

Early rice harvests mainly fed South Carolinians and their slaves, but as the crop's commercial potential became evident, men with significant finan-

7. "Letter of Edward Randolph to the Board of Trade, 1699," in Salley, ed., *Narratives*, 204–10. Randolph informed members of the Board that "[i]f this Place were duly encouraged, it would be the most useful to the Crown of all the Plantations upon the continent of America." [Ibid., 209.] An isolated shipment of rice occurred in 1674 and the crop was planted experimentally in 1689 and 1690, but the "first significant crop for export" (330 tons) was produced in 1699. [Edelson, *Plantation Enterprise*, 63.] Carolinians initially grew white rice; the famous "Carolina gold rice" was introduced after the American Revolution.

8. "Elizabeth Hyrne to her brother," c. 1702, in Merrens, ed., *The Colonial South Carolina Scene*, 22. In 1705 Parliament offered substantial bounties for naval stores produced in the colonies; exports of pitch and tar were insignificant before 1705, but they surpassed fifty thousand barrels by 1718. McCusker and Menard, *Economy of British America*, 180.

9. *The Descendants of Hugh Armory, 1605–1805* (London, 1901), 38–39, in Alexander Samuel Salley, Jr., *The Introduction of Rice Culture into South Carolina*, Bulletins of the Historical Commission of South Carolina, No. 6 (Columbia: The State Company, 1919), 7.

10. Alexander Moore, "Daniel Axtell's Account Book and the Economy of Early South Carolina," *South Carolina Historical Magazine* 95 (October 1994): 299.

11. The same publication described the production of tar and pitch as "very profitable" to country planters with a good supply of "that wood of which it is made." Norris, *Profitable Advice* (London: 1712), in Merrens, ed., *Colonial South Carolina Scene*, 48–51.

cial resources and extensive landholdings invested heavily in the new staple. Some individuals involved in the lucrative deerskin and slave trades used proceeds from those enterprises to grow rice in areas once spurned as wastelands. As rain-fed rice production gave way to more labor-intensive wetlands production, it became even more apparent that rice was destined to be a rich man's crop. Land prices soared, forcing humbler men and their families into frontier settlements where contact with Native Americans became more frequent and sometimes violent.[12]

Major planters eventually resorted to the tidal system, using thousands of Africans to carve out and maintain lowcountry plantations that produced enormous quantities of high-quality rice.[13] It would take several decades for South Carolinians to develop a plantation system similar to that on Barbados, but even in those formative years, rice culture fostered a more severe labor regime. Persuaded that Africans were accustomed to extreme temperatures, planters forced their slaves to work in appalling circumstances.[14] Several decades later, Benjamin Martyn of Georgia made a distinction between "Works rather of Nicety than Labour." He noted, "Sugar, Rice, and Tobacco are Works of Hardship and Fatigue; and perhaps it would be impossible to get white People from any Parts of Europe, who would sustain the Labour of them." Growing rice was difficult and dangerous, whereas the cultivation of

12. Hewitt, "The State in the Planters' Service," in Greene et al., *Money, Trade, and Power*, 51. Hewitt points out that rice production stimulated subsidiary enterprises like provision farming, barrel making, and house building.

13. The techniques used for inland swamp production were similar in principle to those employed in West Africa, making slaves from that region the preferred workforce on many plantations. Judith Carney, "Out of Africa: Colonial Rice History in the Black Atlantic," in *Colonial Botany: Science, Commerce and Politics in the Early Modern World*, ed. Londa Schiebinger and Claudia Swan (Philadelphia: University of Pennsylvania Press, 2005), 216. Daniel Littlefield believes the colonists were "always aware of individual and ethnic distinctiveness among slaves," and they came to value characteristics of certain regional types. [Littlefield, *Rice and Slaves*, 9, 173.] One of the earliest references to tidal rice production appeared on January 19, 1738, in an advertisement in the *South Carolina Gazette* for riverfront land. In the heyday of rice cultivation, over 80 percent of slaves in South Carolina lived on plantations of twenty or more slaves; only 7 percent lived on plantations with fewer than ten slaves. Two-thirds of the plantations in South Carolina exceeded five hundred acres. The need to alternately flood and drain rice fields with tidewater meant that lowcountry plantations were located near estuaries. Gordon S. Wood, *Empire of Liberty: A History of the Early Republic, 1789–1815* (New York: Oxford University Press, 2009), 510.

14. Edelson, *Plantation Enterprise*, 62.

silk, cotton, and cochineal stood "only in Need of a careful and tender Management," the type that whites could offer.[15]

In 1680 South Carolinians held four hundred Africans in captivity; ten years later that total had nearly quadrupled.[16] Many planters also owned Native American slaves, adding to the number of unfree people in the colony. Legislative proposals reflected the schizophrenic nature of colonists' relations with their slaves. In 1691 the Assembly passed *An Act for the Better Ordering of Slaves*, requiring tickets for slaves on legitimate errands, regular searches of slave quarters, and brutal punishments such as whipping, nose slitting, branding, and execution for striking a white person.[17] The act, which also stipulated that "no slave shall become free by becoming a [C]hristian" was based on the most recent iteration of the notorious Barbadian slave code.[18] The Lords Proprietors disallowed the act, along with all other laws passed during Seth Sothel's self-proclaimed governorship, but it revealed the concerns of South Carolinians, particularly those from the West Indies who

15. Benjamin Martyn, *An Impartial Enquiry into the State and Utility of the Province of Georgia*, 2nd edition (London: Printed for W. Meadows at the Angel in Cornhill, 1741), 31. The rationale that whites were not fit for certain work—particularly arduous labor in hot climates—was a convenient and oft-voiced excuse for the use of slaves. In 1739 Thomas Stephens wrote that the "sultry Heat of the Sun" was "in no way disagreeable or hurtful" to enslaved Africans, but malarial conditions in Georgia incapacitated white laborers from March to October. ["Patrick Talifer and Others to the Trustees, Mills Lane," [undated], *General Oglethorpe's Georgia* (Savannah: Beehive Press, 1975), 225–27.] In 1744, when Carolina's rice prices were at historic lows, a planter writing under the pseudonym "Patricola" maintained that indigo "may be carried on with a great deal of Ease by white People only, without Blacks, which Rice cannot be." Joyce E. Chapin, *An Anxious Pursuit: Agricultural Innovation and Modernity in the Lower South* (Chapel Hill: University of North Carolina Press, 2012), 192.

16. Russell Menard estimated South Carolina's four thousand residents in 1690 included 2,400 whites, 1,500 blacks, and one hundred Indian slaves. In 1710 the colony's ten thousand residents included 4,200 whites, 4,300 blacks, and 1,500 Indian slaves. Russell Menard, "Financing the Lowcountry Export Boom: Capital and Growth in Early South Carolina," *The William and Mary Quarterly* 51, no. 4 (Oct. 1994): 660.

17. *An Act for the Better Ordering of Slaves*, Feb. 7, 1691, *The Statutes of South Carolina, Volume Seventh, Containing the Acts relating to Charleston, courts, slaves, and rivers*, David J. McCord, ed. (Columbia: A. S. Johnston, 1840), 343–47.

18. *An Act for the Governing of Negroes*, August 8, 1688, in Hall, comp., *Acts Passed in the Island of Barbados. From 1643 to 1762 Inclusive* (London, 1764), 112–21, quoted in Tomlins, *Freedom Bound*, 442 fn. The Barbados Assembly also addressed the racial imbalance on the island by reviving a 1682 act to encourage the importation of servants, and by drafting an act that declared African slaves to be real estate.

pushed the legislation.[19] In 1696 a revised version of the act passed in the Assembly; one significant innovation was a provision that rewarded whites, blacks, and Indians who captured escaped slaves. Another change was a declaration of who were slaves; it provided the first legal foundation for slavery as an institution in South Carolina: "[A]ll Negroes and Mollatoes and Indians which at any time heretofore have been bought and sold or now are held and taken to be or hereafter shall be Bought and sold for slaves are hereby made and declared that they and their children slaves to all Intents and Purposes."[20]

In 1696 and 1698, hoping to maintain a white majority, the South Carolina Assembly passed acts to encourage the immigration of whites.[21] Among the new measures was legislation requiring owners of six or more slaves to employ a white overseer. Discontented servants had proved troublesome in the past but the specter of a general slave uprising prompted lawmakers to welcome all whites, no matter what their status; they offered ship captains £13 for each indentured servant brought to the colony.[22] Despite these new

19. Peter Wood, "Black Labor, White Rice," in Gad J. Heuman, *The Slavery Reader* (New York: Routledge, 2003), 232. Like Sir John Yeamans, Seth Sothel truly flourished in an unfettered Hobbesian environment. He has been described as "one of the dirtiest knaves that ever held office in America" . . . a "beastly and detestable man" who attempted to monopolize North Carolina's Indian trade, who seized ships and their cargoes without cause, who appropriated livestock, slaves, and even whole plantations, and who accepted bribes from convicted felons. Sothel became governor of South Carolina in 1690, but was removed from power by the Lords Proprietors. John Fiske, *Old Virginia and Her Neighbors*, vol. 2 (Boston: Houghton Mifflin, 1897), 286–87.

20. *An Act for the Better Ordering of Slaves, Records of the General Assembly: Acts, Bills and Joint Resolutions—Act of the General Assembly*, March 2–16, 1696, 60–66, cited in Tomlins, *Freedom Bound*, 439. The 1691 act had been slightly revised on September 11, 1693, and then renewed on July 16, 1695. The 1696 act was entirely new and superseded the act originally passed in 1691. Roper, "The 1701 'Act'," 396–97 fn.

21. In 1696 the Assembly passed *An Act for the encouragement of the better settlement of South Carolina* and *An Act for making aliens free of this part of this Province, and for granting liberty of conscience to all Protestants*. The 1698 measure was *An Act for the encouragement of the importation of white settlers*. Emberson Edward Proper, "Colonial Immigration Laws: A Study of the Regulation of Immigration by the English Colonies in America," *Studies in History, Economics and Public Law* 12, no. 2 (1900): 69.

22. Ironically following Bacon's Rebellion (1675), tobacco planters in Virginia began purchasing slaves rather than servants to avoid future uprisings. [Morgan, *American Slavery, American Freedom*, 295–307.] The colony did attempt to prevent interaction between slaves and servants by drafting an "Act Inhibiting the Trading between Servants and Slaves," but it was never well enforced. As in Barbados, large planters feared that unfree laborers might unite against them. Heitzler, *Goose Creek*, I, 66.

provisions and recruiting efforts, the colony's black population continued to grow at a faster pace than the white population. Lowcountry planters may have slept restlessly, but come dawn they resumed business with slave traders.[23] Writing to the Board of Trade in March 1699, Edward Randolph estimated that South Carolina housed "4 Negroes to 1 White man, and not above 1,100 families, English and French."[24] Randolph's calculations were askew but his observations demonstrated the prominence of Africans in the colony.

In 1701 concerns about the growing black presence, the defection of whites, and the threat posed by the Spanish at St. Augustine prompted legislators to pass *An Act for the Prevention of Runaways Diserting this Government*. Any person who departed the province without written permission was decreed a "runaway." Colonists and Indians would be rewarded for the capture of fugitives and were legally empowered to beat, maim, assault, or kill those who resisted.[25] The recruitment of Native Americans to capture runaway slaves was a routine practice, but reliance on Indians to seize whites attempting to flee the colony—using deadly force if necessary—must have startled South Carolinians. Other legislation enacted in 1701 targeted the "great number of slaves" who traveled to Charles Town "to drink, quarrel, curse, swear & profane the Sabbath." Because blacks might contrive "dangerous plots & designs," constables were ordered to "go through all the streets & round Charlestown" and apprehend slaves from the countryside. Offenders would be "publicly and severely whipped" and then held until their owners paid a fine and reclaimed them. The act also declared that conversion to Christianity would not qualify a slave for manumission, and owners would be compensated for slaves who were gelded or executed by authorities.[26]

As the eighteenth century dawned, armed conflict continued to test the colony (and its Spanish and Native American neighbors). Edward Randolph

23. Based on a study of South Carolina wills, only 13 percent of households owned African slaves between 1690 and 1694, but that percentage doubled by the end of the decade. Ramsey, *Yamasee War*, 36.

24. "Letter of Edward Randolph to the Board of Trade, 1699," in Salley, ed., *Narratives*, 204–6.

25. *An Act for the Prevention of Runaways Diserting this Government*, March 1, 1700–1, *The Statutes of South Carolina*, vol. 7, 180. Colonists apprehending a runaway received up to £5; Indians were to receive any arms and ammunition the runaway carried, plus a monetary reward not to exceed twenty shillings.

26. Roper, "The 1701 'Act'," 415–18. Roper posits that the political strife in Carolina gave slaves "greater opportunity to rebel or otherwise resist their enslavement," hence more repressive laws were necessary. Ibid., 400.

noted in 1699 that the prospect of French plans to settle along the lower Mississippi River "greatly alarmed" South Carolinians.[27] The proximity of Spanish and French forces became more worrisome in 1702 when England went to war against Spain and France. Both sides dragged colonists and their Indian allies into the eleven-year conflict, though settlers in Florida and South Carolina had been trading blows for decades.[28] Prior to the official declaration of war in Europe, Creek Indians helped the colony repel Spanish and Apalachee invaders. Shortly thereafter, Governor James Moore overcame stiff political opposition to secure funding for an invasion of Florida.[29] Enticed by the prospect of "free plunder and a share of all slaves," five hundred militiamen, three hundred Native American allies, and an unknown number of slaves under Moore's command assaulted St. Augustine in the autumn of 1702, torching the settlement and taking 350 Indian captives.

The unexpectedly high costs of Moore's expedition created a political firestorm; one colonist complained, "Two Thousand Pounds were raised to equip his Honour and his Comrades out for their beloved Exercise of Plundering, and Slave Catching."[30] The following year, in an effort to slow the growth of the slave population and to defray the expenses of the St. Augustine raid, the Assembly imposed a duty of twenty shillings for each slave, nine and older, imported from the West Indies or from elsewhere in America, and half that amount for slaves imported directly from Africa.[31] The higher duty on slaves from other British colonies reflected a growing concern that

27. "Letter of Edward Randolph to the Board of Trade, 1699," in Salley, ed., *Narratives*, 204–6.

28. Queen Anne's War, also known as the War of the Spanish Succession, lasted from 1702 to 1713. Holland, England, and Austria declared war upon France and Spain in May 1702.

29. Rivers, *A Sketch of the History of South Carolina*, 197. The Flint River is in present-day Georgia; the Carolina Assembly contributed £2,000 toward the subsequent expedition against St. Augustine. The 1665 Carolina charter allowed the proprietors "to make war, and pursue the enemies aforesaid, as well by sea, as by land; yea, even without the limits of said province, and . . . to put them to death, by the law of war, and to save them at their pleasure." "The Second Charter Granted by King Charles the Second, to the Proprietors of Carolina," in *The Colonial Records of North Carolina*, I: 112.

30. John Ash, "The Present State of Affairs in Carolina, by John Ash, 1706," in Salley, *Narratives*, 272.

31. *The Statutes of South Carolina*, vol. 2, 201, cited in McCrady, *History of South Carolina*, 383. At that time the colony housed approximately 3,800 whites, three thousand enslaved Africans, and 350 enslaved Native Americans. Wood, *Black Majority*, 25–26.

outsiders considered South Carolina the best place to dispose of sick and unruly slaves.[32] Despite periodic increases in those fees, the black population
continued to grow faster than that of whites. In 1704 Governor Moore returned to Spanish Florida with fifty Englishmen and over 1,500 Creeks; they
destroyed twenty-nine missions and effectively exterminated the Apalachee
and Timucua peoples.[33] Thomas Nairne wrote, "Our Forces intirely broke
and ruin'd the Strength of the Spaniards in Florid, destroy'd the whole Country, burnt the Towns, brought all the Indians, who were not kill'd or made
Slaves, into our own Territories ... nor have they any Houses or Cattle left."[34]
Concerned about retaliatory raids, the Assembly funded the repair of existing fortifications and construction of new defensive works. Soon enough,
Charles Town was walled on three sides and bounded by creeks and marshes
on the fourth.[35]

In late 1704 the Assembly drafted legislation intended "to make the assistance of our said and trusty slaves more certain and regular" in case of
invasion. Any "negroes, mulattoes and Indian slaves" who were judged serviceable were to be armed with a lance, hatchet, or gun and ammunition;

32. William Roy Smith, *South Carolina as a Royal Province, 1710–1776* (New York: Mc-
Millan, 1903), 285n.

33. The South Carolinians compelled the Yamasee to exchange their captive Apalachee
Indians for powder and shot. When Spanish vessels from Havana "bottled up" the
harbor, Moore burned his eight ships and marched forty miles overland to reach relief
ships. Moore claimed to have seized 325 Apalachee men and four thousand women and
children in the 1704 raid. [John H. Hann, *The Land Between the Rivers* (Gainesville: University Presses of Florida, 1988), 279.] According to Jean-Baptiste Le Moyne Bienville,
six thousand to seven thousand Apalachee were killed or taken prisoner, and seventeen of thirty-two Spanish captives were burned alive, included three Franciscans. Alan
Gallay estimates the number of Indians taken in the 1702 and 1704 expeditions was
1,500 to 2,000, with the high end being more likely. [Gallay, *Indian Slave Trade*, 148.]
For a description of the political chaos in Charles Town, see the 1703 petition in Daniel Defoe, *Party-Tyranny* (1701), reprinted in Salley, ed., *Narratives*, 239–44. L. H. Roper
believes the Goose Creek men involved in the Indian trade wrecked Carolina's economy
when they issued worthless paper money to finance the failed assault on St. Augustine.
[Roper, *Conceiving Carolina*, 8–10.] The currency provided the underpinning for "an
expansionist system of conquest, Indian trade, and plantation development." Hewitt,
"The State in the Planters' Service," in Greene et al., *Money, Trade, and Power*, 62.

34. Thomas Nairne, *A letter from South Carolina: giving an account of the soil, air, product,
trade, government, laws, religion, people, military strength, &c. of that province; together with
the manner and necessary charges of settling a plantation there, and the annual profit it will
produce* (London: printed for A. Baldwin, 1710), 34.

35. Hendrix, *Down & Dirty*, 38.

should any be killed while defending the colony, their masters would be compensated.[36] The act provided little incentive for slaves to fight on behalf of their white overlords—a shortcoming that became evident in 1706 when a seaborne force of French and Spanish troops launched an unsuccessful attack on Charles Town.[37] Two years later, when the colony's militia consisted of just 950 whites, each company commander was obliged to enlist and train "one able-bodied slave armed with a gun or lance for each man in his company."[38] New legislation rewarded "trusty slaves" for "good service" in any future emergency and manumitted any slave who killed or captured enemy invaders or who suffered disabling wounds.[39] Ironically the same act that offered slaves this path to freedom placed "an imbargo to confine all persons not to depart this Province" and restricted free males above the age of sixteen to the area wherein "the signals of alarm can be heard." Violators would be fined £50 or suffer one year's imprisonment; the same punishment awaited any freeman who refused to "appear under their respective colours" in time of alarm.[40]

South Carolinians were willing to put weapons in the hands of trusted slaves when the enemy was at the gates, but they still worried about the growing number of Africans in their midst. A census compiled by Governor Johnson in 1708 revealed that the colony's 4,100 African slaves outnumbered the 4,080 white inhabitants. South Carolina had become the first and only British colony in North America where blacks constituted a majority. Upon closer inspection, the numbers were even more troubling—planters also owned

36. *An Act for raising and enlisting such Slaves as shall be thought serviceable to this Province in time of alarms*, Nov. 4, 1704, *The Statutes of South Carolina*, vol. 7, 347–49.

37. In the assault more than 320 French and Spanish were captured and approximately thirty were killed; their Indian allies were sold as slaves. Gallay, *Indian Slave Trade*, 152–53.

38. "Official Report on the State of the Province, 1708," in Yates Snowden and Harry Gardner Cutler, *History of South Carolina*, vol. 1 (Chicago and New York: Lewis Publishing Company, 1928), 149.

39. *An Act for enlisting such trusty Slaves as shall be thought serviceable to this Province in time of alarms*, April 4, 1708. *The Statutes of South Carolina*, vol. 7, 349–51. Owners would still be compensated if their slaves were killed, maimed, or captured. In 1710 Thomas Nairne wrote, "There are likewise enrolled in our Militia, a considerable Number of active, able, Negro Slaves: and the Law gives every one of those his Freedom, who in the Time of an Invasion, kills and Enemy." Nairne, *Letter from South Carolina*, 31.

40. *The Statutes of South Carolina*, vol. 7, 351. The area to which men were restricted was that enclosed by the Santee River on the north, the Savannah River on the south, and William Follingsbey's plantation to the west. This was basically a renewal of geographic constraints established in the 1700 "Act for the Prevention of Runaways Diserting this Government."

1,400 Native American slaves.[41] Between 1700 and 1710, the colony imported approximately three thousand Africans; that total would double in the next decade.[42] When they drafted the *Fundamental Constitutions*, John Locke and the proprietors anticipated a *society with slaves*, but not a *slave society*. Shaftesbury's "Darling" was descending into an abyss from which there would be no escape.[43]

In terms of racial composition, South Carolina had become more an extension of the Caribbean than a typical mainland colony. But Barbadian plantations were wholly devoted to sugarcane, whereas the capital required to establish a rice plantation meant that most South Carolinians had to depend on other sources of income. Some grew rain-fed rice, but their returns paled in comparison to those of wealthy landowners who, after years of investment, employed the tidal system.[44] Francis Le Jau, an Anglican missionary, reported in 1707 that the colony had "fruitfull Soil where anything grows without much trouble," but colonists "all aim at riches which are hard to be got."[45]

41. "Report of Governor N. Johnson," in Rivers, *A Sketch of the History of South Carolina*, 232.

42. Between 1700 and 1710, the black population rose from 2,444 to 5,768; it climbed to 11,868 by 1720. Coclanis, *Shadow of a Dream*, 64.

43. In a slave society, "slavery is *the* determinative institution." When a significant proportion of its population is enslaved, "a slaveowning society may become a slave society." But even more important than sheer numbers of slaves in determining the transition is "when slavery becomes central to the economic functioning of that society." Philip D. Morgan, "British Encounters with Africans and African-Americans, circa 1600–1780," in Bernard Bailyn and Philip D. Morgan, *Strangers within the Realm: Cultural Margins of the First British Empire* (Chapel Hill: University of North Carolina Press, 1991), 163. Allan Gallay expands on the distinction between "societies with slaves" and "slave societies," noting that slaves were defined not as laborers but as people without kin in "non-slaveholding societies," whereas slaves were viewed as laborers, often acquired through warfare, in "slaving societies" (Gallay, *Indian Slavery*, 8.)

44. Plantations using the tidal system required years of backbreaking labor before they became fully operational. Charles Joyner maintains that slaves were "not merely property . . . A slave was also a human being who had an immense investment in the plantation." By perceived inheritance (based on the labor of their ancestors) and personal contribution, slaves "developed a strong sense of ownership of those plantations" Charles Joyner, *Down by the Riverside: A South Carolina Slave Community* (Urbana: University of Illinois Press, 1984), 43.

45. Le Jau to Philip Stubs, July 3, 1707, St. James Goosecreek, S. Carolina, in *The Carolina Chronicle*, 29. That same year, Governor Archdale wrote a tract promoting the colony. John Archdale, *A New Description of that Fertile and Pleasant Province of Carolina* (London, 1707), reprinted in Salley, ed., *Narratives*, 288.

Many smaller planters purchased just one or two Africans or Indians and worked alongside them in the fields. Landowners who could not afford slaves sometimes tried to rent them during peak planting and harvest times, but John Norris observed that it was "very seldom that any Man will hire out his Slaves to others, but will employ them in following Plantation Business for himself, their Labor being well paid for in their Crops."[46]

During South Carolina's first half-century, the intense prejudice and fixed social and legal boundaries that characterized race relations in later years were still in a developmental stage. Thomas Graves and his slave both worked in Daniel Axtell's lumber mill, the slave garnering half wages for his owner. Joseph Griffin trained several slaves as weavers, basically making them life-long apprentices.[47] In the colony's interior, frontier conditions and the mobility inherent in herding livestock, cutting lumber, and securing tar and pitch tended to foster a tenuous equality of blacks and whites.[48] This blurring of color lines even reached into political and religious circles. In 1703 colonists in Colleton County sent a petition to the proprietors complaining that in the last election not only did strangers, servants and "indigent persons" vote, but also "several free Negroes were receiv'd, & taken for as good Electors as the best Freeholders in the Province."[49] Francis Le Jau informed his superiors that he planned to reserve time each week "for instructing the poor and ignorant from among the white[s], black[s] & Indians." He reported that masters and parents were "well satisfied that their Children and Slaves may be taught how to become Christians" and "several Negroes" came to his church in Goose Creek.[50] The biracial composition of Le Jau's Goose Creek congregation was notable because mainly former Barbadians populated that settlement. Whether conversion to Christianity made slaves more manageable or more likely to resist their enslavement was an issue that would be hotly debated in later years.

46. Norris, *Profitable Advice* (London: 1712) in Greene, ed., *Selling a New World*, 107.

47. "Daniel Axtell's Account Book and the Economy of Early South Carolina," *The South Carolina Historical Magazine* 95, no. 4 (October 1994), 296–98.

48. Wood, *Black Majority*, 109–16, 196.

49. "The Representation and Address of several of the Members of this present Assembly return'd for Colleton County, and other the Inhabitants of this Province . . . ," June 26, 1703, in Rivers, *Sketch of the History of South Carolina*, 453–60.

50. Le Jau to the Secretary, April 15, 1707, in *The Carolina Chronicle*, 22; Le Jau to the Secretary, December 2, 1706, in Ibid., 19. Le Jau found the Native Americans "very quiet, sweet humour'd and patient, content with little which are great Dispositions to be true Christians."

Despite shifting racial dynamics, colonists continued to view the ownership of slaves as a symbol of status and their best path to prosperity. In 1710
Thomas Nairne wrote that to live comfortably in South Carolina, a colonist
needed "2 Negro Slaves, £40 each," plus four cows and calves, four sows, two
hundred acres of land, and an assortment of tools and foodstuffs. With £150
worth of provisions, plus moderate industry and the "Blessing of Heaven," a
man could "get a competent Estate, and live very handsomely." Nairne also
provided an expanded list for the prospective colonist who had £1500 to invest. Eighty percent of that money should be spent on "30 Negroes, 15 Men
and 15 Women, £40 each," and £27 allocated to purchase one thousand acres
of land. Any group that intended to settle in the colony should stock their
lands with "20 Negroes, Cows, Hogs, etc." several years prior to their arrival.
Nairne also called on the English government to transport one hundred families "of the poorer Sort of People" to South Carolina, with each household
consisting of three whites and four slaves. He estimated that, in two decades,
those families and their slaves would generate over £36,562 in capital, and
£67,500 in "real Estate settled."[51] Nairne clearly envisioned a future that included a black majority in South Carolina.

John Norris's tract, *Profitable Advice for Rich and Poor . . . Containing a Description or true Relation of South Carolina*, also informed prospective colonists
that slaves were a sound investment, especially if they hailed from Africa: "An
Indian Man or Woman may cost 18 or 20 Pound, but a good Negro is worth
twice that Sum . . . we have greater Encouragement to buy Slaves, for with
good Management and Success, a Man's Slave will, by his Labor, pay for his
first cost in about four Years at most... the Remainder of his Life, you have his
Labor as free Gain." When employed chiefly on planting rice, a slave's work
could be worth "25 or 30 Pounds a Year of the Crops of Rice," according to
Norris.[52]

In South Carolina it took money to make money, and that was a problem for many colonists. In 1708 Minister Gideon Johnston wrote that things
were so "extravagantly dear" in Charles Town that "£100 in London will go
as far at least as £300 here and very often as far as 4 or £500." In a letter to
his superiors, Johnston confessed, "I have never repented so much of any
thing, my Sins only excepted, as my coming to this Place." Not only did he

51. Nairne, *Letter from South Carolina*, 52–63.
52. Norris, *Profitable Advice* (London: 1712) in Greene, ed., *Selling a New World*, 107.
Norris noted that "there is a Necessity for these Slaves, because very few Servants are
there to be procured to perform the Business of the Country." In 1712, the same year that
Norris's *Profitable Advice* was published, the Province of Carolina was divided into two
colonies, North Carolina and South Carolina.

think he would be unable to support his large family on a minister's paltry salary, Johnston was not fond of "staying in such a place and amongst such a strange sort of people." He described South Carolina's white population in less than flattering terms: "The People here, generally speaking, are the Vilest race of Men upon the Earth they have neither honour, nor honesty nor Religion enough to entitle them to any tolerable Character, being a perfect Medley or Hotch potch made up of Bank[r]upts, pirates, decayed Libertines, Sectaries and Enthusiasts of all sorts ... and are the most factious and Seditious people in the whole World."[53]

Johnston told his superiors that he would be "extremely well pleased I shou'd be to return to the meanest thing [appointment] in South Brittain." Three years later, when Mary Stafford and her family arrived at Charles Town with "noe Money & not known to any body," they encountered "a Country that looked so little inhabited ... I will leave you to judge whether any thing upon Earth could be more dismall." But her husband's baggage included lancets and he soon established a thriving practice in "Physick & Surgery." Once the couple bought or rented a house, they took in boarders. Writing to a friend in England, Stafford lamented her fate but observed that South Carolina was "a good Country for many things and has good com[m]odities [sic] in it." It appears she quickly embraced the prevailing mentality, endorsing ruthless exploitation of enslaved Africans and professing there was really no other option. She wrote: "Here is good [e]ncouragement for handy crafts men or for husband men that can manage the Land and get a few slaves and can beat them well to make them work hard, here is no living here without." Although Stafford described herself and her family as "miserable unhappy poor wretches," a postscript suggested her circumstances had improved. She stated, "Our business goes on with Courage." Stafford boasted seventeen "lodgers," half a dozen cows, and "a Negroe man which cost me 55 pound[s]."[54] For better or worse, she was fast becoming a representative South Carolinian.

In 1712 the South Carolina Assembly created the first public land bank in the colonies and ordered that £52,000 in currency be printed and issued.

53. "Mr Johnston to Ld Bp of Sarum, Charles Town, Septr 20th 1708," in Klingberg, ed., *Carolina Chronicle: the Papers of Commissary Gideon Johnston*, 19–22.

54. Mary Stafford to Mrs. Randall, August 23, 1711, in Mary Stafford and St. Julien R. Childs, "A Letter Written in 1711 by Mary Stafford to her Kinswoman in England," *South Carolina Historical Magazine*, 81 (1980): 2–6. Gideon Johnston remarked that "there is little help to be had from any of the Doctors of this place ... the best of them, having originally been no more than Barbers." "Comy Johnston to the Secry, S. Carolina Charles Town," July 5, 1710, in Klingberg, ed., *Carolina Chronicle: Papers of Commissary Gideon Johnston*, 55.

Loans were the basis of the new currency, but only land and enslaved Africans could be used as collateral. In effect, politically powerful planters had outflanked politically powerful merchants and crafted legislation on the principle that what was good for plantation owners was good for the colony at large.[55] Colonists unable to obtain credit were put at an even greater disadvantage; the value of their currency (both old and new) declined about 50 percent in the next four years.[56] The big losers, of course, were Africans and Indians whose enslavement was facilitated by the land bank. That same year, the colony exported 12,727 barrels of rice worth some £40,000.[57] The largest planters, many of whom were wealthy when they stepped off the boat, grew richer with every successful rice harvest. By reinvesting in land and slaves, some would build the greatest fortunes in British America.[58]

Slavery and profits were clearly linked in the lowcountry, but with each cargo of slaves that arrived at Charles Town, colonists had more cause for alarm. At any moment, hundreds, or even thousands, of Africans might seek

55. Hewitt, "The State in the Planters' Service," in Greene et al., *Money, Trade, and Power*, 63–64. The rivalry between planters and merchants should not be overstated, since Charles Town merchants invested heavily in plantations from 1700 onward. This diversification into planting was a prudent response to the surging rice trade and it linked merchant and planter interests based on return on investment. Nash, "The Organization of Trade and Finance in the Atlantic Economy," in Greene et al., *Money, Trade, and Power*, 97.

56. Weir, *Colonial South Carolina*, 95–96. In addition the "Publick" was "greatly in debt on the Accot of ffortifying and defending this Town agst the Fr[ench] and Spaniards." "Comy Johnston to the Secry, S. Carolina Charles Town," July 5, 1710, in Klingberg, ed., *Carolina Chronicle: Papers of Commissary Gideon Johnston*, 36.

57. John Solomon Otto, "Livestock-Raising in Early South Carolina, 1670–1700: Prelude to the Rice Plantation Economy," *Agricultural History* 61, no. 4 (1987): 23. John Norris's 1712 tract stated: "Our chiefest Commodities sent here to England is our most excellent Rice, of which comes great Quantities; and great Numbers of Deers-Skins . . . also great Quantities of Pitch and Tar; some Rosin and Turpentine and Hatters' Furs: To the West-India Islands and other Places is sent Beef, Pork, Tallow, Hides, Leather, Candles, Myrtle and Bees-Wax, Corn, Peas, Barrel, Hogshead, and Pipe-Staves, Cyprus, Shingles, Cedar, and many other Commodities." [Norris, *Profitable Advice* (London: 1712), in Jack P. Greene, ed., *Selling a New World*, 95.] The deforestation of Barbados created a market for all kinds of wood products, including planks and shingles that were produced in great quantity for planters who devoted all of their land to the production of sugar. Edelson, *Plantation Enterprise*, 81.

58. Creation of the land bank paved the way for increased importations of enslaved Africans and transformed the colony's paper money from "an expedient for financing military adventures" into a "vehicle for plantation development." Hewitt, "The State in the Planters' Service," in Greene et al., *Money, Trade, and Power*, 63–64.

revenge for the loss of their freedom, for separation from their families and homeland, and for the abuse they endured on a routine basis.[59] Even settlers who owned no slaves knew that they too could fall victim to enraged blacks. Though they often proved false, rumors of slave conspiracies frequently circulated. When they did occur, acts of rebellion tended to be limited in scope— individual slaves were prone to resist abusive masters or overseers, or to run away.[60] Over time, fugitive slaves became wilier and troublesome maroon communities started to spring up in the wilderness.

In May 1711 Governor Robert Gibbes asked the Assembly to "consider the great quantities of negroes that are daily brought into this government and the small number of whites that come amongst us, and how many are lately dead or gone off."[61] The fact that blacks outnumbered whites was only part of the problem; Gibbes noted, "How insolent and mischievous the negroes are become" and that prevailing laws did not "reach up to some of the crimes they have lately been guilty of." The solution he proposed was "some more exemplary punishment, by gibbet or otherwise," along with an effort to reduce cruelties that caused slaves to resist or flee. The governor recommended that slave masters be required "to furnish their slaves sufficient food and clothing, and to treat them humanely." Gibbes also suggested that the colony "advance the transportation charges for bringing in more white inhabitants."[62]

One month later South Carolinians were put in "great fear and terrour" by runaway slaves who were "robbing & plundering houses & Plantations." The Assembly called on Governor Gibbes to "prepare p[er]sons to apprehend,

---

59. In March 1708/9 Francis Le Jau wrote about the "unjust, profane & Inhumane practices" he witnessed in South Carolina, including the burning of "a poor Slave-woman" who was accused of arson and executed despite "any positive proof of the Crime." Le Jau to the Secretary, March 22, 1709, in *The Carolina Chronicle*, 55.

60. Charles Joyner maintains that "[a] common condition of servitude did not necessarily produce a common response or a conformity in work attitudes." Slaveholders used a flexible system of rewards and punishments to control and motivate their slaves, but the master's power, "however omnipotent in theory," was never absolute. Despite their abject legal status, slaves "were never completely powerless" and they employed a variety of types of resistance, including running away. Joyner, *Down by the Riverside*, 50–51.

61. Months earlier the Assembly passed *An Act to encourage Strangers to come to this Port, by making Sullivan's Island more remarkable by building a new Look-Out, repairing the old house, and buoying the Channel*, March 1, 1710–11, *The Statutes of South Carolina*, vol. 2, 361.

62. "Governor Gibbes' Speech to the Assembly, May 15, 1711," reprinted in David Duncan Wallace, *The History of South Carolina*, vol. 1 (New York: American Historical Society, 1934), 368.

hunt & take the runaway Negroes & to employ a number of Indians to assist them." The renegades were armed, and led by a "Spanish Negroe" named Sebastian; for months they remained at large, committing "Barbarities, Fellonies & abuses." Responding to "constant complaints," the governor offered substantial rewards to anyone who could bring in Sebastian or "any other Negro runaway . . . dead or live." Gibbes also called for new laws "that effectively prevent those fears and jealousies wee now lye under from the Insolence of the Negroes we have already in this province & the numbers that are daily brought unto us." He noted that "scarce a day passes without some robbery or insolence committed by them in one part or other of this Province." That autumn, the Assembly recompensed Elizabeth Dutch, a widow whose house and possessions had been burned by "Sebastian, the Spanish Negroe who was Lately Executed." Widow Sarah Perry received £10 as compensation for "her Indian, who was killed by Bastian," and £50 was paid out of the public treasury to "the Indians who took & killed Bastian" as a reward for their "Publick Service."[63]

The following spring, news of a deadly slave insurrection in New York did nothing to allay the fears of South Carolinians.[64] The Assembly passed a new *Act for the Better Ordering and Governing of Negroes and Slaves* that included provisions struck down by the proprietors in previous legislation. The act borrowed language from the 1688 Barbados slave code. It acknowledged that South Carolinians were dependent on the "labor and service of negroes and other slaves," but blacks' "barbarous, wild, savage natures" meant laws and customs that applied to whites could not govern them. New regulations were needed to "restrain the disorders, rapines and inhumanity" to which slaves were "naturally prone and inclined." Slaves who traveled without a ticket or

63. J. Harold Easterby, ed., *The Colonial Records of South Carolina: The Journal of the Commons House of Assembly* (Columbia: South Carolina Archives Department, 1914), reprinted in Timothy James Lockley, *Maroon Communities in South Carolina: A Documentary Record* (Columbia: University of South Carolina Press, 2009), 8–10; Edwin C. Holland, *A refutation of the calumnies circulated against the southern & western states, respecting the institution and existence of slavery among them . . . by a South-Carolinian* (Charleston: A. K. Miller, 1822), 63.

64. On April 6, 1712, several dozen African slaves and two enslaved Native Americans set a fire in New York City and attacked the whites that responded. The conspirators killed about nine men and wounded five or six others; twenty-seven slaves were condemned, but some were pardoned and others committed suicide. Massachusetts and Pennsylvania authorities reacted to the New York uprising by passing legislation to discourage or prevent the importation of slaves into their colonies. Aptheker, *American Negro Slave Revolts*, 172–73.

note from their master would be whipped; whites who demanded such proof could use brutal and even deadly force against any slave who resisted. Slave quarters would be searched biweekly for runaways and contraband. Prior legislation encouraged the arming of blacks for the colony's defense; the new law forbade them to own guns, swords, clubs, or other "mischievous" weapons. In trials for "heinous or grievous" crimes, a justice and three freeholders could call for immediate execution of convicted slaves—"the kind of death to be inflicted to be left to their judgment." Capital crimes included "mutiny, insurrection or rebellion." Because such crimes involved multiple slaves, one offender could be singled out for "exemplary" execution and the rest returned to their owners. Lesser crimes would be punished by whipping or, in the case of repeat offenders, branding, mutilation, or even execution.[65]

Men who regarded slaves as personal property drafted the 1712 legislation, so the consequences for repeated flight were incredibly harsh. A male slave who ran away a fourth time would be castrated; if that led to his death, the owner would be compensated from the public treasury.[66] A female slave would be whipped, branded, and lose an ear for the same crime. Any slave who risked a fifth attempt would suffer the loss of a leg or be executed.[67] Not everyone condoned such brutality; Minister Francis Le Jau wrote, "I have taken the Liberty to say Mutilation and Death are too Great punishments."[68] Parts of the new act addressed the behavior of slave owners. The law required masters to administer punishments for certain crimes, but because some whites suffered from "violent passions," lawmakers included this provision: "If any person shall, of wantonness, or only of bloody-mindedness, or cruel

65. *An Act for the Better Ordering and Governing* . . . , *The Statutes of South Carolina*, vol. 7, 352–65.

66. In 1697 the South Carolina Assembly ordered the castration of three slaves who had attempted to flee to St. Augustine. Stephen J. Oatis, *A Colonial Complex: South Carolina's Frontiers in the Era of the Yamasee War, 1680–1730* (Lincoln: University of Nebraska Press, 2004), 35.

67. *An Act for the Better Ordering and Governing* . . . , *The Statutes of South Carolina*, vol. 7, 352–65.

68. Le Jau to the Secretary, August 30, 1712, in *The Carolina Chronicle*, 121. As South Carolina's slave population increased, fearful whites prepared for massive retaliation, if such a response was needed. Kay Wright Lewis maintains that African Americans deliberately sought strategies of nonviolence to win their freedom, but whites believed they needed to be prepared for total warfare, "making the threat of extermination an essential tool for maintaining the institution of enslavement and white supremacy." [Lewis, *A Curse Upon the Nation*, 3.] Many of the punishments called for in the 1712 legislation were already the custom of the country.

intention, violently kill a negro or other slave of his own, he shall pay into the public treasury fifty pounds, current money; but if he shall so kill the slave of another man, he shall pay the owner . . . the full value, and into the public treasury, twenty-five pounds, but not be liable to any other punishment or forfeiture for the same."[69]

The act explicitly stated that "any negro or Indian slave" could be baptized, but "he or they shall not thereby be manumitted or set free" as a result. Anyone who had been sold was a slave, as were his or her children, born and unborn.[70] South Carolinians hoped that, even though the act's main provisions had been in force since 1696, the new legislation would reduce the likelihood of a widespread slave uprising. But blacks continued to congregate whenever they had the opportunity, and whites were left to imagine what secrets they shared and what desperation or vengeance might one day cause them to do.

Around Christmas of 1713, rumors spread that slaves in Goose Creek were involved in a conspiracy "like that of New York." Authorities seized a dozen or more suspects and determined that a slave from Martinique "had Inticed some Slaves to joyn with him that they might get their liberty by force." He was put to death and two others were "severely chastis'd for hearkening to him" but a lack of evidence prevented their executions.[71] It appears that crimes involving slaves were so numerous and enforcement so rigorous after the passage of the 1712 *Act for the Better Ordering and Governing of Negroes and Slaves* that the law had to be amended to make transportation outside the colony an alternative to execution. The revision limited compensation to slave owners because "the public treasury hath been very much exhausted" by executions of blacks for minor felonies.[72] Subsequent legislation stipulated that reimbursement for executed slaves would be provided by slave owners "where the fact [crime] was committed."[73] Also, because lawmakers

69. *An Act for the Better Ordering and Governing . . .* , *The Statutes of South Carolina*, vol. 7, 363–64. A servant who wantonly killed a slave would receive thirty-nine lashes and three months' imprisonment; he or she also had to serve the owner of the deceased slave for four years after completing his or her current term of service.

70. Ibid., 352, 365.

71. Le Jau to the Secretary, January 22, 1714, in *The Carolina Chronicle*, 136. The plot was betrayed by a slave belonging to Captain David Davis; the informant "was promised a reward" for his actions according to the *House Journal of the Colony* for May 11, 1715.

72. *An additional Act to an Act entitled An Act for the Better Ordering and Governing . . .* , *The Statutes of South Carolina*, vol. 7, 366.

73. Charles Town residents sometimes had to bear the charges for executions of slaves from the countryside. On November, 1725, William Miles requested £80 from the

concluded that deportation gave blacks "encouragement to pursue their villa-nies," the provision that called for transportation outside the colony was later voided.[74]

As it turned out, whites in South Carolina had good reason to fear for their lives, but they were mistaken about the direction from which the threat would come. Nine months before the 1712 *Act for the Better Ordering and Governing of Negroes and Slaves* was enacted, Tuscarora Indians launched coordinated raids on frontier settlements in North Carolina. Enraged by encroachment on their lands, the enslavement of their women and children, and a devastating out-break of smallpox that they blamed on white settlers, the Tuscarora killed 130 colonists.[75] South Carolina sent hundreds of militia and Native American allies to assist their northern neighbors; the force killed more than three hun-dred Tuscarora and captured one hundred others.[76] Francis Le Jau reported, "Our Traders have promoted Bloody Warrs this last Year to get slaves and one of them brought lately 100 of those poor Soules."[77] North Carolina's gov-ernor requested assistance again in 1713, noting that "hundreds of [Native American] women and children . . . perhaps 3 or 4 thousand" could be en-slaved. In response, several dozen colonists and approximately 900 Yamasee

---

Precinct of Charles Town "for a Negroe of his Executed for killing another Negroe"; the Committee responded favorably, noting that "there is Sufficient Provision made by Law . . . for the payment of all such Negroes as should be condemned and Executed Accord-ing to Law, by an assessment to be made on the Inhabitants of the Precints [*sic*] where such Negroe is executed." "Petition of William Miles," November 17, 1725, *The Journal of the Commons House of Assembly of South Carolina, November 1, 1725—April 30, 1726*, A. S. Salley, ed., (Columbia: Printed for the Historical Commission of South Carolina by the State Co., 1808; reprinted in Columbia: General Assembly of South Carolina, 1945), 21–22.

74. *A further additional Act . . .*, *The Statutes at Large of South Carolina*, vol. 7, 368–70.

75. Anthony Wallace, *Tuscarora, A History* (Albany: State University of New York Press, 2012), 67–68; Arwin Smallwood, *Bertie County: An Eastern Carolina History* (Charleston, SC: Arcadia Publishing, 2002), 40–42.

76. Legislative records indicate that Colonel John Barnwell had "six hundred militia and three hundred and sixty Indians," but Barnwell's correspondence states he started with about 528 men and desertions reduced that total to 400 by the time they reached the Cape Fear River. Barnwell to [Governor Craven?], Feb. 4, 1711/12, 30, in Gallay, *Indian Slave Trade*, 267.

77. Dr. Francis Le Jau described the South Carolina contingent as "a Generall Called Barnewell and 16 White men, whome 6 or 700 Indians have Joined." Le Jau to the Sec-retary, February 20, 1712, 107, in *The Carolina Chronicle*, 107–9.

and Cherokee Indians under the leadership of Colonel James Moore Jr. went north and killed or captured 950 Tuscarora Indians.[78]

Provoking wars to procure Indian captives was hardly new to South Carolina traders; they had been shipping Native Americans to Barbados since the mid-1670s. The colony did not hesitate to switch alliances when it worked to the traders' advantage; the raids they instigated reached west to the Mississippi. In 1700 a Muklasa Indian noted that "the greatest traffic between the English and the savages is the trade of slaves ... the [Indian] men take the women and children away and sell them to the English."[79] Decades earlier, the proprietors had berated colonists for persuading Native Americans "to make war upon their neighbors, to ravish the wife from the Husband, kill the father to get to the Child, and to burn and Destroy the habitations of these poor people." They were appalled that "poor Innocent women and children [were] Barbarously murdered, taken and sent to be sold as slaves."[80] French explorer Bénard de La Harpe reported that South Carolinians and their Chickasaw allies took three hundred women and children captive in just one of three devastating raids on Choctaw settlements between 1706 and 1711.[81]

During Queen Anne's War (1702–12), sugar planters in Barbados faced major increases in the price of African slaves, so an even greater number purchased Indians captured in South Carolina (who were not subject to

78. *Journal of the Commons House of Assembly*, 21 vols., Alexander S. Salley, Jr., ed., (Columbia: Historical Commission of South Carolina, 1907–1946), August 5, 1712–August 8, 1712, in Gallay, *Indian Slave Trade*, 267–74, 298. The Yamasee and Cherokee wanted captives to exchange for guns, ammunition, and other goods proffered by South Carolina traders. Moore's expedition burned several hundred Tuscaroras to death in Fort Neoheroka. Tuscaroras who managed to survive fled from North Carolina. LeMaster and Wood, eds., *Creating and Contesting Carolina*, 1.

79. Vernon J. Knight and Sheree L. Adams, "A Voyage to the Mobile and Tomeh in 1700, with Notes on the Interior of Alabama," *Ethnohistory* 28 (1981): 182. Though they continued to use male prisoners for ritual torture, Native American slave raiders preferred to seize women and children; they proved less troublesome while being conveyed over long distances. Women did perform most of the agricultural labor in Indian society, but it was subsistence agriculture that differed greatly from the work involved in staple production. For this reason many planters regarded Indians of either gender as poor substitutes for indentured servants or for enslaved African workers. Gallay, *Indian Slave Trade*, 90, 200.

80. *Records in the British Public Record Office Relating to South Carolina, 1663–1717*, 5 vols. (1928–1947), 1: 259, in Gallay, *Indian Slave Trade*, 61.

81. Jean-Baptiste Bénard de La Harpe, *The Historical Journal of the Establishment of the French in Louisiana*, Virginia, Koenig and Joan Cain, trans.; Glenn R. Conrad, ed. (Lafayette: University of Southwestern Louisiana Press, 1971), 73.

imperial taxes). By 1715 Charles Town was the principal entrepôt for the slave trade in North America. It was not only the volume but also the bidrectional flow of slaves that made the port distinctive—vessels carried enslaved men, women, and children to and from its wharfs. The number of Indians exported by South Carolinians since 1674 probably exceeded the number of Africans they imported.[82] In 1715 as many as one-fourth of all lowcountry planters may have claimed ownership of one or more Native Americans.[83] The colony showed no signs of halting the Indian slave trade, so tribes in the southeast had to take matters into their own hands.

In early April 1715, rumors spread that the Yamasee Indians, who assisted whites in the recent Tuscarora war, "were discontented, and threatened to rise." Bearing messages from Governor Craven, several Indian traders returned to Pocotaligo Town and "offered them every kind of satisfaction for the wrong which had been done to them."[84] The Indians appeared satisfied but the next day Yamasee warriors "broke the Peace . . . & kill'd presently, after their Warr hoop, as many of our People as happen'd to be in their Towns upon the Account of Trade."[85] Traders who were not killed outright were put to death "in the most cruel manner in the world." Thomas Nairne, author of the 1710 promotional tract *A Letter from South Carolina*, "suffered horrible torture, during several days, before he was allowed to die." The Yamasee

82. Estimates of the number of southeastern Native Americans taken captive vary widely, but the total was certainly high enough to have a negative impact on social and religious structures and to put tribes on the defensive. Alan Gallay estimates that "30,000 to 50,000 is likely the range of [Southern] Amerindians captured directly by the British, or by Native Americans for sale to the British, and enslaved before 1715." [Gallay, *Indian Slave Trade*, 299–301.] According to an article in *Gentleman's Magazine* in 1755, the number of Native American slaves transported from the interior to Charles Town soared from 76 in 1712 to 419 in 1714. ["Record of Annual Slave Imports, 1706–1739 as It Appears in *Gentleman's Magazine* of 1755," (XXV), 344, reprinted in Wood, *Black Majority*, 151.] Between 1717 and 1755, many lowcountry residents would become involved in the Indian trade, exchanging manufactured goods for deerskins and other items. This activity was less provocative than the trade in captive Indians and involved a wide range of South Carolinians, including servants and slaves. Barker, "Indian Traders," in Greene et al, *Money, Trade, and Power*, 141.

83. Ramsey, *The Yamasee War: A Study of Culture, Economy, and Conflict in the Colonial South* (Lincoln: University of Nebraska Press, 2008), 165.

84. "George Rodd to his Employer in London (forwarded by him to the King)," May 8, 1715, in *Calendar of State Papers, Colonial Series, America and West Indies, 1574–1739*, vol. 28, (1714–1715), 166–69.

85. Le Jau to the Secretary, May 10, 1715, in *The Carolina Chronicle*, 152.

then proceeded eastward to Port Royal and "sacked and plundered" the town, killing any whites that were not fortunate enough to board a ship anchored nearby. As Yamasee warriors attacked plantations throughout the South Carolina lowcountry, the Lower Creek, Apalachee, Savannah, Euchee, Cherokee, and Catawba Indians joined in the effort "to seize the whole Continent and to kill us or chase us all out of it." One frightened colonist reported that, "it is some years, as we learn from prisoners, that the Indians have been preparing." He feared that the various tribes "will presently form a large body to cut us to pieces."[86] William Byrd of Virginia told the Board of Trade and Plantations that the Yamasee and Cherokee were the two most powerful nations in the southeast; if they and other Indians should jointly attack Carolina, "it would be impossible to prevent their destroying that province, Charles Town being the only place fortified."[87]

Alexander Spotswood, governor of Virginia, informed the Board of Trade in London that a subordinate who just returned from South Carolina found "the whole Country in ye greatest Consternation, the Indians having just then fallen unexpectedly upon ye People of the Frontier Plantations with unexampled Cruelty, and laid waste a great part of that Province." Many people had been "forced to desert their Habitations and leave their Houses and Effects a prey to the Heathen." Three months after the initial attacks at Pocotaligo, the English remained unsure which Indian nations were united against them, but "they very much fear the Chacktaws [*sic*], a numerous and warlike People, is in the Confederacy." To their dismay, the colonists soon learned that both the Choctaws and Chickasaws had killed South Carolina traders in their towns. In a separate communiqué, Spotswood wrote that if the French or Spanish "should now make such another Attempt upon Charles Town, as they did during the last War, they must infallibly Carry it, whilst all the force of the English is drawn to the Frontiers to withstand the Indians." The governor was reluctant to "wound his Maj't's [Majesty's] Ears with particular relation of the miserys his Subjects in Carolina labour under, and of ye Inhuman butchering and horrid Tortures many of them have been exposed to."[88]

86. "Rodd to his Employer...," May 8, 1715, *Calendar of State Papers*, vol. 28, 166–69. Stephen Oatis maintains that there was no preconceived conspiracy, but a series of Native American alliances set in motion by the Yamasee Indians' decision to wage war against the South Carolinians. Oatis, *A Colonial Complex*, 112–17.

87. "Journal, July 1715: Journal Book R," *Journals of the Board of Trade and Plantations*, vol. 3: March 1715–October 1718 (1924), 49–65.

88. "Alexander Spotswood to Josia Burchett, Esq'r, July 16, 1715," *The Official Letters of Alexander Spotswood, Lieutenant-Governor of the Colony of Virginia, 1710–1722*, R. A. Brock,

Colonists from outlying settlements flocked to Charles Town, seeking refuge. Governor Craven offered little reassurance, noting on May 6, 1715 that he and his fellow South Carolinians were "almost naked and defenseless, and know not how soon some of us may be in the hands of those monsters of mankind, the Indians."[89] Two weeks later, Minister Francis Le Jau, who fled his Goose Creek home and parish, wrote that, "the Indians that Surround us on Every Side but the Sea revolted from us by Unanimous Consent."[90] Residents and refugees were "block'd up" behind Charles Town's walls while the Yamasee and their allies exercised a "licentious cruelty in ravaging, burning, murdering and torturing all before them." Few took solace in the fact that the fortifications "may perhaps hold out some months," given the "miserable condition" of the people inside—"drove from their plantations, imprison'd between mud walls, stifled with excessive heats, oppress'd with famine, sickness, the desolation of their country, death of their friends, apprehension of their own fate, despairing of relief and destitute of any hopes to escape."[91]

Distressed by the unceasing "cries and groans of the women and children," George Rodd predicted that the colonists' misfortunes would "be increased every day by famine and disease."[92] His pessimism was not unfounded. Reverend Thomas Hassell offered up a disturbing passage from *Leviticus*: "When ye are gathered together within your cities, I will send the pestilence among you; and ye shall be delivered into the hand of the enemy."[93] Indians and microbes

---

ed., Collections of the Virginia Historical Society: New Series, vol. 2 (Richmond: Wm. Ellis Jones, 1885), 126; "Alexander Spotswood to the Lords Commissioners of Trade, July 15, 1715," in *Official Letters*, 119; "Alexander Spotswood to Mr. Secretary Stanhope, July 15, 1715," in *Official Letters*, 120–25.

89. Commons House Transcript, May 6, 1715, 4:389, quoted in Oatis, *Colonial Complex*, 142. Craven later proved his mettle, leading a 240-man military expedition into the "Yamasee lands" and winning some decisive engagements. Ibid., 144–45.

90. Le Jau to the Secretary, May 21, 1715, in *The Carolina Chronicle*, 159. One fallen Indian was alleged to have carried a letter addressed to the governor advising him "to quit the country, because they had determined to seize it." "Rodd to his Employer...," May 8, 1715, in *Calendar of State Papers*, vol. 28, 168.

91. Abel Kettleby and other planters and merchants trading to Carolina to the Council of Trade and Plantations, July 18, 1715, in *Calendar of State Papers, Colonial Series, America and West Indies, 1574–1739 CD-ROM*, Karen Ordahl Kupperman, John C. Appleby and Mandy Banton, eds. (London: Routledge, published in association with Public Record Office, 2000), Item 523, vol. 28 (1714–1715), 236–38.

92. "Rodd to his Employer...." May 8, 1715, in *Calendar of State Papers*, vol. 28, 166–69.

93. Oatis, *Colonial Complex*, 168. The biblical passage is from *Leviticus* 26:25.

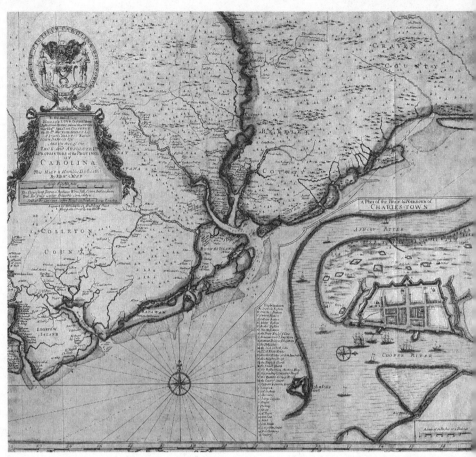

Detail from Edward Crisp, Thomas Nairne, John Harris, Maurice Mathews, John
Love, *A compleat description of the province of Carolina in 3 parts : 1st, the improved part
from the surveys of Maurice Mathews & Mr. John Love : 2ly, the west part by Capt. Tho.
Nairn: 3ly, a chart of the coast from Virginia to Cape Florida.* London, Edward Crisp,
[1711?]. Library of Congress, Geography and Map Division.

besieged Charles Town residents. Food, water, sanitation, and shelter were all
concerns; communicable illnesses only compounded refugees' problems.

One reason for the general sense of despair in Charles Town was the fact
that colonies to the north offered little assistance, and South Carolina, being a proprietary colony, was unlikely to be rescued by His Majesty's troops.
In October 1715 Governor Spotswood of Virginia reported that "None of ye
Provinces on ye Continent have yet sent any Assistance of Men to So Carolina, except this Colony alone and No. Carolina." Virginia authorities agreed

to send men to assist South Carolinians on the understanding that the latter would "send an equal number of Slaves to work on their plantation during their Absence"—but "not one [slave] hath been sent, nor any great prospect of their being sent at all." Spotswood considered the lack of remuneration "a bad return of the Friendship of this Governm't," one that was likely to "have as ill an Effect upon the like dispositions of other Governm'ts to assist one another on like occasions."[94]

The Lords Proprietors, vociferous opponents of the Indian slave trade and the colony's anti-proprietary faction, claimed to be unable to hire relief ships; they were unwilling to mortgage their Charter to raise money for the colony's defense. On July 8, 1715, however, the proprietors petitioned George I for assistance, pledging their Charter as "virtual security for what his Majesty shall please to advance them in arms, ammunition and other necessaries for the defence of the province." Members of the Board of Trade and Plantations responded that any transport ships dispatched from the colonies to fetch men and supplies "would have too long a voyage, and come too late for the intended service." When the Board suggested that the proprietors ought to surrender the government of the province, "they said they were willing to do it, for an equitable consideration and not otherwise."[95]

With the enemy just twelve miles outside Charles Town, counting coins was a luxury that the South Carolinians could not afford. On July 18, 1715, twenty-four Carolina planters and merchants sent a petition to the Board of Trade and Plantations, recounting the "deplorable condition" of the colony and begging for trained soldiers, firearms, ammunition, and a royal proclamation prohibiting British subjects from trading firearms or gunpowder to Indians. Hopeful that they would survive the present crisis, the petitioners also requested that a chain of frontier forts be constructed for the colony's future defense. But at present there were more urgent priorities; the colonists were "in imminent danger of being massacred by savages" who were most likely "incourag'd, directed and supply'd" by the Spaniards at St. Augustine and the French at Mobile. The petitioners insisted that this was not one colony's war . . . it was the first phase of an all-out attempt by Indians and Catholics to drive all Englishmen and their Church from North America. Should South

---

94. "Alexander Spotswood to Mr. Secretary Stanhope, October 24, 1715," in *Official Letters of Alexander Spotswood*, 133–35.

95. "Journal, July 1715: Journal Book R," *Journals of the Board of Trade and Plantations*, vol. 3, 49–65. Governor William Byrd of Virginia informed the Board that "these attempt of the Indians had never yet happened but against proprietary governments." Ibid.

Carolina miscarry, "all the other Colonys wou'd soon be involv'd in the same ruin."[96]

Governor Spotswood voiced the same concern, writing: "a Triumph over that very Province, w'ch has been ye most famous for keeping ye Indians under Subjection and the Booty taken from it might invite all the Heathen upon this Continent to Unite their Forces and try to over-run the rest of our Colonys."[97] For nearly half a century, competition for power and wealth had gone unchecked in South Carolina. Should the Spanish join the fight, or should the colony's black majority rise up, South Carolinians would indeed be at war against everyone, much as Thomas Hobbes had predicted.

On July 29, 1715, when the planters' and merchants' petition was still in transit, the Board of Trade and Plantations heard eyewitness testimony from Mr. Beresford, "lately arrived from Carolina." The colony was in "very bad circumstances," the Indians having destroyed most of the interior settlements and "so harrassed the province that all the women and children are retired into Charles Town." South Carolina's fourteen hundred male colonists were "in arms and defending their out-plantations, as well as they can and endeavouring to keep the Indians from Charles Town." Unless the king dispatched men, arms, and ammunition, the colonists "will be obliged to desert the province."[98]

At that moment, most of the colony's lands were in the hands of their original inhabitants. As refugees poured in to Charles Town and fighting raged in the "out-settlements," Minister Francis Le Jau expressed his hope that "all Persons who have suffer'd or are in Danger of suffering in this Miserable Juncture of Time would think of Repentance."[99] But despite the massacre of hundreds of colonists, the "deplorable" condition of exiles in Charles Town, and little hope of rescue, planter George Rodd's principal source of grief remained his financial loss: "When I consider ... that I had about 16 slaves, and the best estate in the Province, which would have produced several hundred pounds sterling in a year or two, and that I have lost everything in a moment etc. etc., it seems to me a hundred times worse than death."[100] Rodd's

96. "Abel Kettleby and other planters and merchants trading to Carolina to the Council of Trade and Plantations," July 18, 1715, in *Calendar of State Papers, Colonial Series, 1574–1739,* 236–38.

97. "Spotswood to Mr. Secretary Stanhope, July 15, 1715," in *Official Letters,* 122.

98. "Journal, July 29, 1715: Journal Book R," *Journals of the Board of Trade and Plantations,* vol. 3, 49–65.

99. Le Jau to the Secretary, August 23, 1715, in *The Carolina Chronicle,* 166.

100. "Rodd to his Employer ...," May 8, 1715, in *Calendar of State Papers,* vol. 28, 166–69.

extraordinary reaction to the loss of his property showed that "the Evil Spirit of Covetiousness & self Interest" that Le Jau considered "the true & Immediate Causes of our Desolation" would prove harder to kill than Englishmen.[101] Self-aggrandizement—the driving force behind for South Carolina's founding and development—was not likely to be "chased out" of the colony, though the war would deal a fatal blow to the very lucrative Indian slave trade. That pernicious industry and the abominable behavior of agents in the affiliated deerskin trade were, in the opinion of many, the chief causes of the conflict. One month into the war, Le Jau reflected that "the Indian Trade … brought Justly what we Suffer upon us." He estimated that "those Indians owe above 50,000 £ to our Traders wch they are not able to pay."[102] Three years earlier Le Jau had denounced traders for interfering with his efforts to bring the Gospel to Native Americans: "[The traders] do not care to have Clergymen so near them who doubtless would never approve those perpetual wars they promote amongst the Indians for the onely reason of making slaves to pay for their trading goods; and what slaves! Poor women and children, for the men taken prisoners are burnt most barbarously."[103]

As the war raged in South Carolina, William Byrd informed the Board of Trade and Plantations that "this misfortune was in a great measure owing to the Carolinians themselves, for their traders have so abused and so imposed upon the Indians in selling them goods at exorbitant prices, and receiving their peltry at very low rates, that they have been thereby very much disgusted." Another Virginian, Mr. Crawley, testified in London that the Yamasee had started the insurrection because "the Indian traders had very much misused them." Crawley claimed the traders failed to adequately compensate Native Americans for livestock and provisions they seized, that they would beat and abuse them, and that "they have frequently debauched the Indians wives and daughters, and that when they would not consent, they have proceeded so far as to force them."[104]

South Carolina's enslaved Africans were not involved in the coming of war, but they played a significant role in the fighting. In May 1715 Francis Le Jau wrote that Captain Thomas Barker's force consisted of "90 men on

---

101. Le Jau to the Secretary, August 23, 1715, in *The Carolina Chronicle*, 166.

102. Le Jau to the Secretary, May 21, 1715, in *The Carolina Chronicle*, 159. By 1711 the Yamasee Indians' collective trade debt was about one hundred thousand deerskins; other tribes were in similar straits. Ramsey, *Yamasee War*, 24.

103. Le Jau to the Secretary, May 27, 1712, in *The Carolina Chronicle*, 116.

104. "Journal, July 1715: Journal Book R," *Journals of the Board of Trade and Plantations*, vol. 3, 49–65.

Horseback and 12 Negroes," and Colonel Moore led "a Strong Body of White
Men & Negroes."[105] In August Le Jau reported that, following a successful
ambush, three hundred Indians "amused themselves in firing against a small
fort where we had 30 men, white and black." The same letter speaks of a
"blow given by 70 white men & about 40 negroes and Indians"—evidence
that whites were desperate enough to call on anyone, regardless of color, free
or enslaved, who might help subdue their enemies.[106] In an effort to recruit
whites, the Assembly offered a bounty of £25 for men ages sixteen to thirty,
and £22 for boys ages thirteen and sixteen, to join the colony's defensive
force. After much bloodshed and some startling defeats in the field, Governor
Craven cobbled together the province's first professional army—a multieth-
nic mix that included six hundred South Carolinians, four hundred enslaved
Africans, 170 "friendly" Indians, and three hundred troops from North Carolina and Virginia.[107] Whites were compensated with wages or bounties but
the promise of freedom for slaves who killed or captured an enemy seems to
have been ignored by South Carolinians after the war.[108]

As it turned out, Charles Town was never overrun, and South Carolinians
gradually regained much of the ground they lost in the summer of 1715. Authorities again displayed their penchant for strategic alliances; by forging a
treaty with the powerful Cherokee nation in early 1716, the colony neutralized
the threat posed by tribes that were still at war with the English. Rather than
being expelled from their American Eden, flawed as it was, South Carolinians
prevailed, and it was the Yamasee and some of their allies who were driven
out.[109] But the colony was hardly in a position to celebrate. The conflict left a
landscape dotted with burned plantations, ruined crops, and dead livestock.

105. Le Jau to the Secretary, May 21, 1715, in *The Carolina Chronicle*, 159.
106. Le Jau to the Secretary, August 22, 1715, in *The Carolina Chronicle*, 161.
107. Oatis, *Colonial Complex*, 146. The South Carolina Assembly ordered the militia
to arm more slaves than allowed in previous legislation; as many as half of the forces
raised by South Carolina during the Yamasee War may have been slaves. Jerry Cooper,
The Rise of the National Guard: The Evolution of the American Militia, 1865–1920 (Lincoln:
University of Nebraska Press, 2002), 3.
108. Gallay, *Indian Slave Trade*, 347. Conversely some slaves were liberated by Yamasee
warriors who raided plantations and led the Africans to freedom in Florida.
109. The war did not terrify or disarm the colony's major enemies; the Yamasee and
Apalachicola would conduct sporadic raids against South Carolinians for another decade. The war's greatest impact could be seen in it colonial defense, imperial politics,
and South Carolinian's identity in the face of outside threats. Oatis, *Colonial Complex*,
141.

Debts from just the first year of the war totaled £80,000.[110] The lucrative deerskin trade, which saw 121,355 skins shipped from Charles Town in 1707, plunged to only 4,702 hides exported in 1716.[111]

The colony also became burdened with the cost of maintaining six frontier garrisons; the Governor even paid £960 of his own money to purchase the indentures of thirty-two Scots—probably rebel officers taken at the battle of Preston—to man the new defensive outposts.[112] In terms of casualties, the colony lost approximately four hundred people, or 7 percent of the white population. The departure of settlers who fled for their safety, or because they faced financial ruin, only exacerbated those losses. The war also led to a decrease in the population of enslaved Africans, some of whom died in the fighting and some of whom fled during the chaos.[113]

The Yamasee War altered the structure of South Carolina's commerce. As settlers returned to lands and dwellings they abandoned in 1715, shipments of rice, livestock, lumber, and naval stores gradually resumed, but two other mainstays of the economy were harder hit. The crumbling of Indian alliances and the deaths of approximately ninety traders disrupted far-flung networks that delivered deerskins and captive Native Americans to Charles Town. With new oversight and tighter regulations, the deerskin trade eventually rebounded; not so the Indian slave trade.[114] New treaties, a dearth of experienced traders, and a shrinking market for Carolina Indians sounded the death knell for that heinous enterprise. The sale of prisoners from the recent

110. William Christie MacLeod, *The American Indian Frontier* (New York: Routledge, 2013), 287; Junius P. Rodriguez, *Encyclopedia of Slave Resistance and Rebellion*, vol. 2 (Westport, CT: Greenwood Publishing, 2007), 581. Rodriguez states that losses in the war totaled $400,000.

111. Crane, *Southern Frontier*, 112.

112. Wallace, *History of South Carolina*, vol. 1, 207–12.

113. Christina Snyder, *Slavery in Indian Country: The Changing Face of Captivity in Early America* (Cambridge: Harvard University Press, 2010), 77. Drawing on a variety of sources, historian Larry Ivers determined that in 1715 the colony housed approximately six thousand white Protestants; one-fifth of whom were French Huguenots. Ivers calculates that about two hundred were indentured servants, mainly "orphans, convicts, and financially poor of both sexes." Eight thousand were enslaved Africans or African Americans, and two thousand were Indian slaves, mainly women and children. Hundreds of "settlement Indians" also lived within colony bounds. The overall total, according to Ivers's estimates, was about seventeen thousand. Ivers, *This Torrent of Indians*, 6.

114. Between 1699 and 1715, approximately 54,000 skins were shipped annually from Charles Town; in 1750 the total was 150,000, and it represented one-fifth of the colony's exports. Edgar, *South Carolina, A History*, 136.

war brought slavers a quick profit, but then the supply of captive Native Americans dwindled.[115] As a result, the South Carolina economy depended more than ever on the labor of enslaved Africans, many of whom had risked life and limb defending the colony.

In 1717 Joshua Gee, author of the widely read *The Trade and Navigation of Great Britain Considered*, informed the Council of Trade and Plantations of "the dismall condition of the Proprietary Governmt. Of Carolina" and warned that the colony was "in danger of becoming a land of negroes."[116] Anxious to recoup their losses and confident in the quality and marketability of their rice, lowcountry planters redoubled their efforts. They were well on their way to replicating a Barbadian plantation system that produced immense profits for a fortunate few, and misery, hardship, and death for a great many others.

115. Ramsey, *Yamasee War*, 180. Due to captives taken during the war, the number of enslaved Native Americans in the colony actually peaked in 1724 when two thousand toiled on South Carolina farms and plantations. Snyder, *Slavery in Indian Country*, 78.

116. "Joshua Gee to the Council of Trade and Plantations," March 18, 1717, Colonial State Papers, Item 505, vol. 29 (1716–1717), 271–72.

Four

"Dreadfull Visitations"

One year into the Yamasee War, Dr. Francis Le Jau reported that "it appears that the Terrible Judgments we have felt make a good Impression." A number of colonists had withdrawn from the "Croud of Willful transgressors" whose actions invited God's wrath.[1] As it turned out, repentant South Carolinians comprised a distinct and capricious minority. Eight months later Le Jau wrote, "I ask Communicants & upon occasion dying men whether their conscience reproaches them with no Evil done by them & which ought to be remedied, they commonly answer [']No![']...and in Short will not part with any thing they may possess unjustly."[2] The war pushed the colony to the very brink of collapse, but in its wake, most South Carolinians focused on recouping their losses, not pondering religious interpretations of their recent ordeal. Mere competency was not the goal of immigrants (or the Lords Proprietors); it was the potential for outright prosperity that motivated men and women to assume the many risks that life in South Carolina entailed.[3]

The colony's postwar years were marked by political upheaval and economic instability. Still reeling from the recent conflict, Charles Town's inhabitants faced new challenges, including a growing underclass comprised of war refugees, widows, orphans, destitute and chronically ill individuals, victims of disasters and epidemics, vagrants, streetwalkers, and rogues. Poor relief and the maintenance of law and order were issues that would require the attention and cooperation of churchmen and legislators alike. Records kept by the Assembly and St. Philip's parish comprised a barometer of sorts—a

1. Le Jau to the Secretary, March 19, 1716, in *The Carolina Chronicle*, 173.

2. Le Jau to the Secretary, November 16, 1716, in *The Carolina Chronicle*, 189.

3. French Huguenots might be considered an exception, given their refugee status, but they eventually displayed a strong propensity for profitable enterprise and were among the colony's most successful planters. "Competency" implied modest prosperity or a comfortable standard of living; the term is especially common in histories of Puritan communities. Kupperman, *Providence Island*, 126; Virginia DeJohn Anderson, *New England's Generation: The Great Migration and the Formation of Society and Culture in the Seventeenth Century* (Cambridge: Cambridge University Press, 1991), 123.

misery index based on reactionary laws, burial records, and charitable disbursements.

☙

Once the Yamasee War ended, survivors had to get on with the business of living. For many, that was easier said than done. Four hundred white casualties, most of them males, caused a spike in the number of widows and fatherless children in the colony.[4] Many families who took refuge in Charles Town showed no inclination to head back to outlying settlements. South Carolina's frontier was precarious; the best that many widows could hope for was a quick marriage to a merchant or tradesman, or a chance to operate a tavern or boarding house in the city. Victims of the recent war also included men who had suffered traumatic injuries, losing limbs and economic self-sufficiency in one cruel stroke. In addition, epidemics left numerous orphans in their wake; aged, infirm, and deranged colonists were also unable to provide for themselves. Unfortunately what Charles Town and virtually every other colonial city lacked was a relief system capable of dealing with the victims of disaster.

Some of the most desperate refugees in Charles Town were recent immigrants. In early 1716, striving to "strengthen that Frontier and to encourage new comers," the Assembly had reserved certain tracts for "such of his Majesty's Protestant Subjects as should come and settle."[5] The prospect of free land attracted approximately five hundred Europeans; Mr. Boon reported the unhappy result to authorities in London: "[T]hen to the utter ruin of the new comers, and in breach of their publick Faith, the Proprietors, in April, 1719, ordered all those Lands to be surveyed for their own use.... Hereby the old Setlers in that Frontier, missing the reinforcement of the new comers, again deserted their Settlements and left them open to the Enemy, and the new comers are reduced to that want and poverty that most of them are daily

---

4. In a letter to the Board of Trade dated January 12, 1720, Governor Robert Johnson reported that South Carolina had "not above half of the number of Indians subject to this government as they had in the year 1715," when the twenty-three nations appear to have consisted of 28,041 men. "Papers in the State Paper Office, London," in *Collections of the South Carolina Historical Society*, vol. 2 (Charleston: South Carolina Historical Society, 1858), 239.

5. *An Act to grant several Privileges, Exemptions and Encouragements, to such of his Majesty's Protestant Subjects as are desirous to come into and settle in this Province*, ratified February 16, 1716–7; repealed by the Lords Proprietors, July 22, 1718, in *The Statutes at Large of South Carolina, Volume Third, Containing the Acts from 1716, Exclusive, to 1752, Inclusive*, ed. Thomas Cooper (Columbia: A. S. Johnston, 1838), 3.

perishing, having spent all their substance, and those that have anything left, removing off the Province."[6] To the chagrin of authorities, many of the displaced and indigent settlers retreated to Charles Town, exacerbating the growing relief crisis. Disgruntled residents composed a letter to the Board of Trade that blamed the Lords Proprietors for the debacle.

Poverty and privation haunted the colony since the first days of settlement. One of the earliest references to hardship in colony records was a 1685 act that alluded to "many poor tradesmen, laboring men, freemen, dwelling in the said town."[7] Their indigence was less attributable to war or calamities than to economic circumstances in the fledgling colony, but subsequent legislation demonstrated that other inhabitants were also in need. Beginning in 1690, numerous acts stipulated that one-half of the fines collected for various offenses would be used to aid "the poor people of Charles Towne."[8] In 1694 the Assembly passed *An Act for the Poor*; the language of the act is unknown but the law was in force for two years.[9] In 1696 new legislation steered all donations "given by any person whatsoever to the Poore of Carolina, or any other charitable use" to a five-man committee that would distribute the funds "equally, indifferently and according to the necessity of each person." Since voluntary donations might prove insufficient, committee members were empowered to take up to ten pounds annually from the "publick money of this Province" for the "necessary reliefe" of "the lame, the impotent, old, and blind men, and for the children thereof," and "such other persons being poore and not able to worke." The latter clause signified the Assembly's intention to provide relief only to "deserving poor" who were unable to provide for themselves. In the lawmakers' eyes, indigence was no excuse for indolence, so committee members and Justices of the Peace were empowered "to imploy any poore person in such worke as to them shall seeme most fitt, and also to bind any poore child or children to be apprentices."[10]

6. "Rede'd from Mr. Boon, June 16, 1720," Board of Trade, vol. 10, Q. 203, State Paper Office, cited in Rivers, *Early History of South Carolina*, 49–50. The letter was dated January 29, 1719.

7. *An Act for Clearing the Lotts and Streets of Charles Town, and for the settlement and regulation of a Night Watch in the said Town*, April 11, 1685, *The Statutes at Large of South Carolina*, vol. 7, 1–3.

8. *An Act for the settling and continuing a Watch in Charles Town*, Dec. 22, 1690, *The Statutes at Large of South Carolina*, vol. 2, 4–5.

9. "An Act for the Poor," June 20, 1694, *The Statutes at Large of South Carolina*, vol. 2, 78.

10. "An Act for the Poor," March 16, 1695/96, Ibid., 116–17.

New legislation passed in 1698 required the Commissioners of the poor and seven freeholders to levy a tax on residents of Charles Town "for the use of the Poor of the said Town." The "poor tax" would be collected by constables and "disposed of by the Commissioners to the Poor at their discretion." Because so many "sick and lame seamen" had been discharged in Charles Town and "left here upon the charge of the public," the act stipulated that masters of vessels needed to take their ailing seamen with them or provide "sufficient security" to pay for their care.[11] This was just the first inkling of what would become a major concern in coming years—that Charles Town was becoming a refuge for "Idle, vagrant, and viciously inclined People," including immigrants, seamen, and paupers from the countryside or other colonies.

One aspect of the colony's Barbadian heritage was the role of the Anglican parish as the basic unit of local government. In forging this link between church and state, Barbados authorities had drawn on the 1601 Elizabethan Poor Law and the 1662 Settlement Act. In 1704 the South Carolina Assembly passed *An Act for the Establishment of Religious Worship in the Province*, calling for the erection and staffing of six Anglican churches in the colony. The legislation created St. Philip's parish in Charles Town (the congregation having been established in 1681) and provided a residence, land, cattle, and slaves for the use of the Rector and his successors.[12] The fact that enslaved humans were part of the compensation package for the most prominent clergyman in the colony said much about South Carolinians' values at that time. The Assembly revised the 1704 "Church Act" on numerous occasions, creating ten parishes and merging all political and judicial districts with them. The likeness of administrative units and parish names in South Carolina and Barbados offered additional proof of Barbadian immigrants' hegemony in the new colony.

Each parish in South Carolina had both ecclesiastical and civil responsibilities; the latter included public health and poor relief, though parishes would draw on a colony-wide pool of funds generated by the poor tax.[13]

11. *An Act for the better Relief of the Poore*, Oct. 8, 1698, Ibid., 135–36.

12. *An Act for the Establishment of Religious Worship in the Province, According to the Church of England, and for the erecting of Churches for the Publick Worship of God, and also for the Maintenance of Ministers and the building convenient Houses for them*, Nov. 4, 1704, *The Statutes at Large of South Carolina*, vol. 2, 236–46. On March 1, 1710–11, the Assembly ratified *An Act for the Erecting of a New Brick Church at Charlestown, to be the Parish Church of St. Philip's, Charlestown*, Ibid., 352.

13. *An Additional Act for the Establishment of Religious Worship in the Province . . .*, *The Statutes at Large of South Carolina*, vol. 2, Nov. 30, 1706, 259–61; April 8, 1710, 338–42;

Under the law, individuals were required to seek aid from relatives before petitioning the churchwardens for relief, and alms were reserved for parishioners, at least in theory. Because the roster of parish officials included some of the wealthiest men in Charles Town, the almsgiving process ensured that the elite were keenly aware of the circumstances and needs of people at the bottom of society. This put significant power in the churchwardens' hands; the very survival of the petitioner might depend on their verdict. It was not a job that men relished; the churchwardens' role proved so onerous that fines had to be imposed on individuals who refused to serve.

When churchwardens concluded that a person or family was "deserving" of aid, they considered a number of options, including provision of food or clothing; cash disbursements; subsidized medical care; payments to third parties to house, nurse, or care for the sick and indigent; placement of orphans or infants of sick or impoverished mothers in foster homes; and arrangement of apprenticeships or schooling for older children.[14] The cost and duration of outdoor relief varied widely. One certainty is that the funds made available through charitable donations and the poor tax were insufficient to provide relief for the hundreds of people huddled in Charles Town during the war. Unfortunately that situation only worsened in the years to come.[15]

Many residents of rural parishes—including some of the colony's wealthiest planters—resented paying taxes to support Charles Town's growing underclass. In a sense, slaveholders were already supporting the colony's largest group of impoverished individuals—their slaves—and they had no desire to feed, clothe, house, or otherwise care for the urban poor. During one epidemic, Minister Francis Le Jau proposed that his wealthy Goose Creek congregation make charitable donations on communion days; the resulting torrent of protest caused him to abandon the plan.[16]

June 7, 1712, 366–76. The act passed on April 8, 1710, reserved funds from the fur trade for the maintenance of ministers.

14. Michael D. Byrd, "The First Charles Town Workhouse, 1738–1775: A Deterrent to White Pauperism?" *South Carolina Historical Magazine* 110, nos. 1–2 (January–April, 2009): 37; Barbara L. Bellows, *Benevolence Among Slaveholders: Assisting the Poor in Charleston 1670–1860* (Baton Rouge: Louisiana State University Press, 1993), 4; Waterhouse, *New World Gentry*, 102, 108.

15. The number of single women and women heading single-parent households who ended up in the Charleston workhouse climbed dramatically in the 1740s and 1750s. Walter J. Fraser, Jr., "The City Elite, 'Disorder,' and the Poor Children of Pre-Revolutionary Charleston," *South Carolina Historical Magazine* 84, no. 3 (July 1983): 169.

16. Society for the Propagation of the Gospel in Foreign Parts: MS. Letters, Ser. A, vol. 4, No. 58, Feb. 9, 1711, in Edgar Legare Pennington, "The Reverend Francis Le Jau's Work

In 1712 the Assembly passed *An Act for the better relief of the Poor of this Province*. It noted that "the necessity, number and continual increase of the poor, not only in Charlestown, but in other parts of this Province, is become very great and burthensome." Each parish was charged with nominating two "sober, discreet and substantial persons" to be overseers of the poor. Churchwardens would collect and redistribute the poor tax, while overall care of the poor belonged to the Vestry.[17] The act also contained measures "for preventing any poor persons coming from the parish where they are inhabitants or settled, to be chargeable to any other parish." Residency could only be established over a three-month period, and "not by reason of sickness, lameness or the like." If an individual traveled to Charles Town in search of medical treatment, his or her home parish was required to provide appropriate compensation to St. Philip's parish.[18]

When the Yamasee War compelled terrified colonists to seek safety in Charles Town, refugees with little more than the clothes on their backs overwhelmed St. Philip's limited resources. The town's residency requirement became moot at that point. In 1715 residents and evacuees had to deal with a food shortage; one later wrote, "We are ready to eat up one another for want of provisions, and what we can get is very bad."[19] During the conflict, outmigration became an increasingly attractive but illegal option. Some colonists preferred "to leave their Homes and Land ... [rather] than endure a lingering War and an Insupportable Tax." Between 1715 and 1718, approximately 150 of the 1,400 of the families in the colony departed for less traumatic settings.[20] The situation improved when treaties with the Creek and Cherokee reopened outlying settlements, but many evacuees remained in Charles Town, intensifying the competition for food, housing, jobs, and charitable relief.

As Minister Francis Le Jau, perhaps the most God-fearing man in the colony, huddled behind Charles Town's walls, he reflected on the "very frequent & Dreadfull Visitations upon this place" he had witnessed during his nine

---

Among Indians and Negro Slaves," *The Journal of Southern History* 1, no. 4 (Nov. 1935): 447. Six years later, Le Jau died after several months' illness; his body was interred at the foot of the altar of the Goose Creek church. [Ibid., 449.] He originally came to South Carolina to replace the only SPG missionary in the colony, Samuel Thomas, who died of yellow fever in 1706. McCandless, *Slavery, Disease, and Suffering*, 14.

17. Waterhouse, *New World Gentry*, 93.

18. *An Act for the better relief of the Poor of this Province*, December 12, 1712, *The Statutes at Large of South Carolina*, vol. 2, 593–98.

19. Aptheker, *American Negro Slave Revolts*, 174n.

20. Oatis, *Colonial Complex*, 167.

years in South Carolina.[21] Though Le Jau had witnessed numerous signs of God's displeasure, he may have underestimated the full compass and duration of divine wrath. South Carolinians had battled Spaniards, Frenchmen, Indians, pirates, and rebellious slaves, but armed conflict was only one cause of death and destruction in the fledgling colony. Fearful storms, fires, epidemics, and other disasters preceded his arrival in 1706 and such "visitations" seemed to gather force after his death in 1717.

Deadly hurricanes blasted Charles Town in 1686, 1700, 1713, and 1714, the last two occurring during Le Jau's time in the colony. The "dreadful hurry cane" of 1686 was "wonderfully horrid and destructive." An unsigned letter to the Lords Proprietors reported that "the greatest part of our houses are blown down ... long incessant rains have destroyed almost all our goods ... our corn is all beaten down ... our cattle are in great danger of running wild ... the food of our hogs is likewise destroyed." The colonists had "too great reason to fear the near approach of famine to complete all our miseries." The litany of "sad consequences" was meant to inform the proprietors "what we may reasonably expect for the future."[22] In 1700 a hurricane destroyed Charles Town's wharves and generated a storm surge so powerful that residents had to take refuge on their rooftops. Several vessels carrying Scots from the ill-fated Caledonia expedition were anchored off Charles Town when the tempest struck; they were "all shattered in pieces and all the people lost, and not a man saved."[23]

In 1713 another hurricane made landfall just north of Charles Town, causing "such an inundation from the sea ... that a great many lives were lost." Every vessel in the harbor, save one, was driven ashore and the city's front wall and parapet were "undermined and washed away." According to Le Jau, the Ashley and Cooper rivers "joined for some time" at the height of the storm; it was "miraculous how any of us came to escape from the great Hurricane." At least seventy people drowned, and countless houses, barns, and plantations were ruined.[24] The following year a storm destroyed thirty-four vessels

21. Le Jau to the Secretary, May 10, 1715, in *The Carolina Chronicle*, 153.

22. "Paper to the Lords Proprietors c. 1686," quoted in Rubillo, *Hurricane Destruction*, 34–35.

23. "Letter to the Lords of the Admiralty," October 1700, quoted in Rubillo, *Hurricane Destruction*, 36.

24. Thomas Lamboll, n.d., quoted in David Ramsay, *Ramsay's History of South Carolina, from its first settlement in 1670 to the year 1808* (Charleston: Walker, Evans & Co., 1858), 29–30fn. In 1719 Governor Robert Johnson noted that "Charles Towne was formerly ... enclosed with a regular fortification but in the year 1713 by a violent hurricane were

and compelled the Assembly to revise an earlier act "for preventing the Sea's further Encroachment" because the existing fortifications did not protect the city from the "violent storms and hurricanes, that for these two years last past hath been upon us."[25]

Fires also wreaked havoc in Charles Town, leaving residents homeless and impoverished. On February 1, 1698, several weeks after a sudden and unnerving earthquake, a major conflagration burned approximately one-third of the town. The loss of fifty or so buildings persuaded the Assembly to pass a number of ordinances to prevent future blazes, including a provision that the commissioners were empowered "to give all such directions for the pulling down or blowing up any such house or houses" to create firebreaks. The owner of every house in Charles Town was assessed "forty pounds current money" for the purchase of "six lathers [ladders] of severall sizes, fifty leather buckets, and six fire hooks."[26] Another destructive fire occurred in 1699, and the very next year an inferno burned "most of the town."[27] With no government relief or insurance, victims often found themselves at the mercy of the elements and creditors alike.[28]

all thrown down and ruined." Robert Johnson to the Proprietors, January 12, 1719, in Merrens, ed., *Colonial South Carolina Scene*, 58.

25. *An additional Act to an additional Act to an Act entitled An Act for preventing the Sea's further encroachment on the Wharfe of Charles Town, and for repairing the Bastions, Half-moon and Redoubts of the same*, Dec. 18, 1714, *Statutes at Large of South Carolina*, vol. 7, McCord, ed., 60–61.

26. *An ACT for settling a Watch in Charles Town, and for preventing of Fires*, Oct. 8, *1698, Statutes at Large of South Carolina*, vol. 7, 7–11. In 1701 the Assembly approved funds for "one engine for quenching of fire." In 1713 the town imported a fire engine from England; it came equipped with wheels and double-action handles that permitted several men to pump water. Robert M. Hazen and Margaret Hindle Hazen, *Keepers of the Flame: The Role of Fire in American Culture, 1775–1925* (Princeton: Princeton University Press, 1992), 121.

27. Daniel Crooks, Jr., *Charleston is Burning!, Two Centuries of Fire and Flames* (Charleston: The History Press, 2009), 14; Nicholas Butler, "Rediscovering Charleston's Colonial Fortifications," A Weblog for the Mayor's "Walled City" Task Force, http://walledcity taskforce.org/educational-resources/time-line/. The threat of fire actually curtailed the production of naval stores in the town; a 1704 statute was amended to ban the boiling of "any pitch, tarr, rosin, or turpentine within the bounds of Charlestown." *Statutes at Large of South Carolina*, vol. 7, 41–43.

28. Legislators responded by passing additional acts intended "to Prevent and suppress Fire in Charles Town. See *An Additional Act to an Act Entitled 'An Act to prevent and suppress Fire in Charles Town. December 18, 1713, Statutes at Large of South Carolina*, vol. 7, 58–60.

Epidemics were surely the most frequent and prolonged "Dreadfull Visitations" that punished inhabitants of South Carolina, regardless of race. Most people never lived to see their fortieth birthday; residents of Charles Town died at twice the rate of those in other cities and towns.[29] The colony's annual mortality rate probably exceeded that of any other British colony in North America. Between 1702 and 1717, thirty-four Anglican ministers died or resigned for health reasons; once they arrived in South Carolina, only four lived more than twenty years. Shortly before he died, Francis Le Jau informed his superiors in London of the hardships that he and his family had endured in South Carolina: "I have cruelly sufferd by Sickness & want, & my family has no cloathes these 2 years & I lost 2 young Slaves that dyed, and a third is adying I fear, and I am above 200£ in debt for bare Necessaryes & we live very hard upon Indian corn we buy at 10 sh a busell with little or no meat." Charles Woodmason later referred to the colony as "the grave of the clergy."[30]

Thousands of slaves also perished suddenly, and often terribly, in South Carolina. About one-third of the Africans transported to the colony died within twelve months. To the dismay of authorities who were anxious to encourage immigration, South Carolina developed a reputation as a charnel house best suited for individuals with a death wish. Shortly after he first set foot in the colony, Governor William Sayle informed the Proprietors that he "never was in a sweater [*sic*] climate then this is."[31] But reality quickly set in for Sayle and other immigrants, many of whom perished from dysentery, respiratory disorders, helminthic (worm) infestations, tetanus, malaria, smallpox, and more common distempers known as "dry bellyach" and "flux."[32] Colonists warned outsiders about the "sultry and suffocating" conditions that prevailed in the summer, though unflattering descriptions of South Carolina's

29. Byrd, "First Charles Town Workhouse," 44.

30. Le Jau to the Secretary, March 18, 1717, in *The Carolina Chronicle*, 202; "Charles Woodmason to Bishop Terrick," October 19, 1766, *The Carolina Backcountry of the Even of the Revolution: The Journal and Other Writings of Charles Woodmason, Anglican Itinerant*, Richard J. Hooker, ed. (Chapel Hill: University of North Carolina Press, 1953), 85;

31. H. Roy Merrens and George D. Terry, "Dying in Paradise: Malaria, Mortality, and the Perceptual Environment in Colonial South Carolina," *Journal of Southern History* 50, no. 4 (November 1984): 534, 549; Mr Johnston to Ld Bp of Sarum, Charles Town, Septr 20th 1708, in Klingberg, ed., *Carolina Chronicle: Papers of Commissary Gideon Johnston*, 19; Letter of William Sayle to the Proprietors, in Cheves, ed., *Shaftesbury Papers*, 175, quoted in Merrens and Terry, "Dying in Paradise," 539.

32. McCandless, *Slavery, Disease, and Suffering*, 6. McCandless argues that the lowcountry's virulent disease environment "helped shape its economic, political, racial, and cultural destiny." Ibid., 60.

climate were less widely circulated than promotional tracts that continued to attract gullible Europeans.[33]

A 1708 pamphlet "prepared by the Lords proprietors of Carolina" depicted the colony as "a most pleasant healthful and fruitful Country" where "artificers are of high esteem" and any maid or single woman" would "think themselves in the Golden Age . . . for if they be but Civil, and under 50 years of Age, some honest Man or other, will purchase them for their Wives." Rhetoric encountered reality once immigrants stepped off the boat. In 1711 one female settler remarked that spending a summer in the lowcountry was comparable to being baked in an oven; another colonist said that the winter months made South Carolina "the pisspot of the world." A German traveler later observed that the health of lowcountry residents, both white and black, was ruined by "the numerous fevers which every summer and autumn so generally prevail." He concluded, "Carolina is in the spring a paradise, in the summer a hell, and in the autumn a hospital."[34]

Recurring tropical diseases were a dire consequence of scorching summers and the arrival of vessels at Charles Town's busy wharves, especially the notorious slave ships that carried deadly pathogens from Africa and the West Indies. Malaria first appeared in South Carolina in 1684 and resurfaced sporadically, often with devastating results.[35] Colonists who recovered from a bout with the disease were more susceptible to other illnesses and infections, often described as "pestilential feavers" or "mortal distempers." The region's greatest natural killer was yellow fever, which likely followed the same route as malaria, tracing the contours of the early slave trade. The first yellow fever epidemic in the Americas was probably the deadly outbreak that wracked Barbados in 1647; the disease arrived in South Carolina in 1699, striking down

33. George Milligen-Johnston, "A Short Description of the Province of South Carolina," in *Colonial South Carolina: Two Contemporary Descriptions*, ed. Chapman J. Milling (Columbia: University of South Carolina Press, 1951), 126.

34. Robert Horne, "A Brief Description of the Province of Carolina on the coasts of Florida," (1708), quoted in Smith, *White Servitude in Colonial South Carolina*, 49; Mary Stafford to Mrs. Randall, August 23, 1711, *South Carolina Historical Magazine*: 4; Johann David Schoepf, trans. and ed., *Travels in the Confederation, 1783–1784*. By Alfred J. Morrison (1788; reprint Philadelphia: William J. Campbell, 1911), 172.

35. In 1716 the minister of St. Paul's Parish noted that because of an outbreak of malaria, few births had taken place that year and most of the newborns "are already deceased." Rev. William Tredwell Bull to the Secretary, May 16, 1716, series A, volume 11, 148, *Papers of the Society for the Propagation of the Gospel in Foreign Parts* (London), quoted in Merrens and Terry, "Dying in Paradise," 542.

one-sixth of the population.[36] Among the 170 or so victims were the chief justice, the receiver-general, the provost marshal, five ministers, and nearly half of the Assembly. Charles Town resident Hugh Adams described the crisis: "The Distemper raged, and the destroying Angel slaughtered so furiously with his revenging Sword of Pestilence . . . that the dead were carried in carts, being heaped up one upon another."[37] In 1706 news of another yellow fever outbreak prompted Spanish and French forces to launch a joint attack on the weakened colony. The invasion was repulsed, but the militia had to be stationed a quarter-mile outside Charles Town to avoid infection. People fortunate enough to survive bouts of malaria and yellow fever became recognizable by their unnatural ashen complexion.[38]

The much-dreaded smallpox battered South Carolina only twice in the seventeenth century, but more frequently thereafter. In late 1711 Reverend Gideon Johnston wrote: "Nver [*sic*] was there a more sickly or fatall season than this for the small Pox, Pestilential ffeavers, Pleurisies, and fflex's have destroyed numbers here of all Sorts, both Whites Blacks and Indians." He continued: "The Town looks miserably thin, and disconsolate . . . I verily think, it is a Sort of Plague, a kind of Judgemt upon the Place (ffor they are a sinfull People)." Johnston's church looked "thin and naked" and "there is scarce any thing to be heard but Sighs and Complaints, and sad accents of Sorrow at every corner."[39]

36. J. R. McNeill, "Yellow Jack and Geopolitics: Environment, Epidemics, and the Struggles for Empire in the American Tropics, 1650–1825." *OAH Magazine of History* (April 1, 2004) 18 (3): 11; Bellows, *Benevolence Among Slaveholders*, 2. In the colonial period, yellow fever was the most dreaded disease in the Lowcountry. Smallpox was "less mysterious" and common to other cities in North America. Viewed in combination with malaria, yellow fever "helped establish the lowcountry's reputation as a dangerous unhealthy place." McCandless, *Slavery, Disease, and Suffering*, 58–63.

37. Letter of Hugh Adams, Charleston, February 25, 1700, in *Diary of Samuel Sewall,* 1700–1714, Massachusetts Historical Society *Collections*, 5th series, vol. 4, 11–12, quoted in John Duffy, "Yellow Fever in Colonial Charleston," *The South Carolina Historical and Genealogical Magazine* 52, no. 4 (October 1951): 191. In Boston Reverend Cotton Mather referred to the illness in Charleston as "the horrible plague of Barbados."

38. Weir, *Colonial South Carolina*, 39–40. In 1750 following two years of yellow fever outbreaks, Anglican minister Robert Stone wrote, "Many are dead. Many are running away to new settlements. The country is very sickly . . . Forty two is looked upon to be the common age of man." Robert Stone to the Secretary, March 6, 1750, quoted in David Duncan Wallace, *South Carolina: A Short History* (Columbia: University of South Carolina Press, 1961), 190.

39. John Duffy, *Epidemics in Colonial America* (Baton Rouge: Louisiana State University Press, 1953), 75; Commissary Johnston to the Secretary, S: Carolina, November 16,

The 1712 *Act for the more effectual preventing the spreading of Contagious Distempers* funded construction of a small brick lazaretto or "pest house" on nearby Sullivan's Island. Anyone in Charles Town exhibiting signs of a "malignant contagious disease" would be sent there and could not reenter the town without permission of the commissioner of health. In addition, every incoming ship was to be inspected and anyone showing signs of a "contagious distemper" would also be exiled to the island. Vessels bearing infected persons were to be quarantined in the harbor for a minimum of twenty days.[40] Despite these measures, smallpox reappeared in Charles Town in 1718, and then five more times by mid-century.[41]

Hurricanes, fires, and "distempers" were deadly, but usually short-lived. Some hazards actually lived in the lowcountry, laying low and biting someone every now and then. Mary Stafford remarked that in the woods she encountered "swarms of Insects and some very troublesome." She noted, "There is great quantitys of Snakes allsoe." In 1705 Hannah Williams of Charles Town sent someone in England "some of Our Vipers & several sorts of Snakes Scorpions & Lizards in a Bottle & of the Other Insex [sic]." Williams also sent off a "Westo Kings Tobacco pipe & a Queens Petticoatt made off [sic] Moss"; in return, she requested newspapers and "medicions." Thomas Ashe described the South Carolina alligator as a "voracious greedy Creature, devouring whatever it seizes on." These predators, some being "from 16 to 20 foot," had "sharp keen Teeth." The reptile did not attack men on land, "except when asleep or by surprise," but in the water "it's more dangerous." Colonists who settled in coastal Georgia seemed even less enthusiastic about their surroundings. Thomas Causton said, "We have some grumbletonians here," referring

---

1711, in Klingberg, ed., *Carolina Chronicle: Papers of Commissary Gideon Johnston*, 99–100.

40. "An Act for the more effectual preventing the spreading of Contagious Distempers," June 7, 1712, *Statutes at Large of South Carolina*, vol. 2, 382; Marion Stange, *Vital Negotiations: Protecting Settler's Health in Colonial Louisiana and South Carolina, 1720–1763* (Goettingen: V&R unipress, 2012), 193–94. In subsequent years Sullivan's Island was employed chiefly for the quarantine of Africans arriving on slave ships. Suzannah Smith Miles, *Writings on the Islands: Sullivan's Island and the Isle of Palms* (Charleston: The History Press, 2004), 33–34.

41. Duffy, "Yellow Fever," 191–92. The end of Carolina's first half-century by no means marked an end to the colony's calamities. Reverend Alexander Garden arrived at Charles Town in 1620; during his thirty-six years in the colony he experienced: "Monstrous hurricanes; the 'Great Fire' of 1740; five outbreaks of yellow fever and periodic swells of malaria, smallpox, and typhus." Fred E. Witzig, *Sanctifying Slavery & Politics in South Carolina: The Life of the Reverend Alexander Garden, 1685–1756* (Columbia: University of South Carolina Press, 2018), preface.

to complaints about the region's torrential rains, sand flies, and ants, which "bite desperately." Alligators and venomous snakes also put off Georgians; James Oglethorpe went so far as to bring a wounded alligator into Savannah where children "pelted and beat him to Death."[42]

During the Yamasee War, South Carolinians had to deal (once again) with human predators—pirates who cruised the coast in search of booty. Brigands sailing under the black flag attacked merchant vessels coming out of Charles Town, taking prisoners, demanding tribute from authorities, and nearly wrecking the colony's faltering economy. After the war Britain's heightened naval presence in the Caribbean exacerbated the problem by driving pirates toward the Carolinas.[43] In the spring of 1718, Edward Teach ("Blackbeard") and his fleet blockaded the port of Charles Town, virtually shutting down trade for nearly a week. After seizing nine or so vessels and taking several prominent citizens hostage, Teach and his men received the medicines they demanded.[44]

Stede Bonnet, the "Gentleman Pirate" from Barbados, also raided merchant vessels along the coast of both Carolinas. When he and thirty-three henchmen, several of whom hailed from Charles Town, were captured at Cape Fear and brought to trial, many members of the town's underclass—sailors, servants, pardoned pirates, former smugglers, and others—insisted that the prisoners be released. According to assistant attorney general Thomas Hepworth, an armed mob "threatened to set the town on fire about our ears" in their effort to free the pirates. Bonnet escaped, but twenty-two of his men were speedily tried and hanged.[45] When Bonnet was recaptured, a sympathetic Governor Johnson responded to public pressure (especially from Bonnet's female admirers) and delayed his execution. Not everyone in Charles

42. Mary Stafford to Mrs. Randall, August 23, 1711, *South Carolina Historical Magazine*: 4; Hannah Williams to _____, Feb. 6, 1704/5, Charles Town, in "Early Letters from South Carolina Upon Natural History," *The South Carolina Historical and Genealogical Magazine* 21, no. 1 (January 1920): 5; Ashe, *Carolina, or a Description*, in Salley, *Narratives*, 155; Thomas Causton to his Wife, March 12, 1733, quoted in Walter J. Fraser, *Savannah in the Old South* (Athens: University of Georgia Press, 2005), 10.

43. Nelson, *Common Law in Colonial America: Volume II*, 74.

44. Prominent among those medicines would have been mercurial preparations for the treatment of syphilis. Robert E. Lee, *Blackbeard the Pirate: A Reappraisal of His Life and Times* (Winston-Salem, NC: John F. Blair, Publisher, 2002), 39–49.

45. Three of Bonnet's men—John William Smith, Samuel Booth, and Jonathan Clarke—were originally from Charles Town. Daniel Defoe, *A General History of the Pyrates* (London, 1724; reprinted, Mineola, NY: Dover Publications, 1999), 104.

Town was enamored of the pirate; angry merchants confronted the governor "in a mass" and demanded that Bonnet be strung up immediately.[46] After seven delays at the governor's behest, Bonnet was hanged at White Point Garden on December 10, 1718. The following year a British man-of-war was stationed at Charles Town to help suppress pirate activity in Carolina waters.[47] Despite the stigma and dangers involved, some townsmen remained eager to join the pirate ranks.[48] But most South Carolinians remained on dry land; when it came to exploitation they preferred to prey on Africans, Native Americans, and each other.

During the Yamasee War, the Lords Proprietors suffered a crushing blow to their credibility and their influence, which had long been on the wane.[49] The colonists' umbrage at the lack of support from England, when virtually every settlement in South Carolina was overrun or under siege, led to a final rejection of the proprietors' authority. "The end of Obedience is Protection," wrote Thomas Hobbes in *Leviathan*. Security was an essential part of the social contract: "The Obligation of Subjects to the Soveraign, [sic] is understood to last as long, and no longer, than the power lasteth, by which he is able to protect them." No covenant—or *Fundamental Constitutions*—could supersede men's natural right to protect themselves "when none else can protect them." In December 1719 Arthur Middleton and other leading planters and merchants conducted a virtual coup d'état in which they repudiated Governor Robert Johnson and propriety rule and named James Moore Jr. as provisional governor.[50] In a letter to the Board of Trade, the revolutionaries claimed that

46. Defoe, *General History of the Pyrates*, 101–11; Colin Woodard, *The Republic of Pirates* (Boston: Harcourt, 2007), 299–301.

47. Hughson, *The Carolina Pirates*, 48–60, 298, 364.

48. Public Records, vol. 8, 24, cited in Wallace, *History of South Carolina*, 372.

49. The proprietors had disallowed a series of laws that would have placed duties on imports, further regulated the Indian trade, retired outstanding bills of credit, and allowed paper money to be printed and circulated in the colony. They lost the support of the Dissenters in the 1704 religious/political fracas and caused further ill will when they insisted on keeping the lands of the defeated Yamasee for themselves. [Roper, *Conceiving Carolina*, 5.] The proprietors were led astray by the lobbying efforts of South Carolina merchants who were much better represented in London than the colony's planters. The proprietors' opposition to duties, money policies, and the abolition of the Indian trade infuriated the planters, as did the decision to grant the Yamasee lands to themselves except for that given to a Scottish baronet. Hewitt, "State in the Planters' Service," in Greene et al., *Money, Trade, and Power*, 66–67.

50. Johnson was on good terms with many of the rebellious colonists; he may even have colluded in the "Revolution of 1719." In 1729, when the British Crown gained title

the "confused, negligent and helpless Government of the Lords Proprietors
... forced us, as the only means for our preservation, to renounce all obedience to the Lords, and to throw ourselves at the foot of the throne of his most
sacred Majesty, King George; humbly imploring him ... to take us into his
immediate protection and Government."[51] The king appointed a royal governor in 1720; nine years later the Lord Proprietors sold their rights in both
North and South Carolina to the Crown.[52] Their "Grand Model" had col-
lapsed under the weight of the ambition and enterprise meant to sustain it.
Only belatedly did the proprietors come to recognize the Faustian aspects of
their deal with the Barbadians and the shortcomings of a social contract that
engendered opposition, inequity, and exploitation.

---

to the lands of South Carolina for £22,500, Johnson was appointed the colony's second
royal governor. [Alexander Moore, "Marooned: Politics and Revolution in the Bahamas
Islands and Carolina," in LeMaster and Wood, eds., *Creating and Contesting Carolina*,
257–58.] In 1720 the king appointed Francis Nicholson as governor of Carolina; the
Goose Creek men soon thwarted Nicholson's play to incorporate the town and appoint
a self-perpetuating council of nineteen men. Hart, *Building Charleston*, 28.

51. "Lrs from the new pretended Council and Assembly of Carolina, dated at Charles
Town, the 24 Decr, 1719, relating to their having deposed their Govr, &c.," Board of
Trade, vol. 10, Q. 199, State Paper Office, cited in William James Rivers, *A Chapter in the
Early History of South Carolina* (Charleston: Walker, Evans & Cogswell, 1874), 39.

52. Rising merchants and planters hoped that the rejection of proprietary rule and
conversion to a royal colony would better integrate South Carolina into the British
Empire's expanding trade networks, thereby providing even greater financial opportunities. However, the rapid decline of the colony's currency exacerbated the political divi-
sions between planters and merchants well into the 1720s. Planters used their legislative
muscle to solidify their control over the colony; when the acting governor opposed their
schemes regarding the money supply, the planter-dominated Assembly "brought the
colony's government to a standstill" in 1728. [Hewitt, "State in the Planters' Service,"
in Greene et al, *Money, Trade, and Power*, 65–67.] The proprietors' vision of "an ordered
social landscape" was "in tatters" by the 1730s. Ambitious planters refused to be constrained by the land grant system laid out in the Grand Model. Instead, they relied on
inheritance and available lines of credit to acquire vast landholdings that far exceeded
their ability to plant and cultivate such acreage. Edelson, *Plantation Enterprise*, 94–95.

Five

Reapers

⚜⚜⚜⚜⚜⚜⚜⚜⚜⚜⚜⚜⚜⚜⚜⚜⚜⚜⚜⚜⚜⚜⚜⚜

South Carolina's grueling first half-century laid the groundwork for extraordinary economic growth, but only in narrow commercial sectors. Years before the destructive Yamasee War, Thomas Nairne described South Carolina planters as men who "live by their own and their Servants Industry, improve their Estates . . . and make those Commodities which are transported from hence to Great Britain, and other Places."[1] During the 1720s a shift in the colony's commercial orientation was evident at Charles Town's wharves: shipments were increasingly bound for Europe rather than the West Indies. More and more of those cargoes were rice; the crop was in the process of turning a farm colony into a plantation colony.[2]

Between 1720 and 1740, burgeoning rice exports brought unprecedented riches.[3] The Earl of Shaftesbury's vision for Carolina was coming to fruition, at least for some colonists. In just a matter of decades, lowcountry rice barons would be counted among the wealthiest men in the world. There were important changes in politics as well. Bolstered by economic success and unencumbered by meddlesome proprietors, the colony's government enjoyed broader public support. The relentless pursuit of profits by merchants and

1. Nairne, *Letter from South Carolina*, 39–40.

2. McCusker and Menard, *Economy of British America*, 179–83. A plantation colony uses many low-skilled workers to produce a "labor-intensive crop subject to substantial scale economies." The colonies are characterized by a highly uneven distribution of income. The crops typically produced in farm colonies require fewer laborers. The distribution of income in farm colonies is more equitable and workers produce an array of goods and services for local consumption. [Ibid., 24.] Regarding these contrasting growth processes, McCusker and Menard cite Robert Baldwin, "Patterns of Development in Newly Settled Regions," *Manchester School of Economic and Social Studies*, vol. 24 (1956), 161–79.

3. The colony shipped 6.5 million pounds of rice in 1720, approximately 19 million pounds in 1730, 43 million pounds in 1740, and 72 million pounds in 1770. The market saw a number of temporary but severe downturns during that span. Stephen G. Hardy, "Colonial South Carolina's Rice Industry and the Atlantic Economy; Patterns of Trade, Shipping, and Growth," table 5.1, in Greene et al., *Money, Trade, and Power*, 125–26.

Carolina. By H. Moll Geographer. London, 1717. Map Collection, South Carolina Department of Archives and History.

planters created the illusion of common purpose. Ironically the stability that the "Grand Model" was supposed to foster occurred only after South Carolinians overthrew proprietary rule in 1719.[4]

&

In the 1720s, despite indications that South Carolina might soon become a "flourishing colony," petitions by Grand Juries and parish leaders responsible for poor relief revealed that the number of paupers in Charles Town was on the rise. The recruitment of "Poor Protestants" to counter the rapid growth of the slave population (particularly in the lowcountry) only exacerbated the relief crisis.[5] In the 1730s the Assembly increased the poor tax and approved construction of a workhouse that would keep some of the city's beggars and derelicts out of sight.[6] Meanwhile slave traders continued to import Africans, and colonists rushed to purchase them despite the paranoia, violence, disease, and human suffering that the flesh trade engendered. Even though the brutal subjection of thousands of African men, women, and children put virtually everyone in South Carolina at risk, most colonists did not share in the windfall that rice plantations generated in the 1730s and 1740s.

The Yamasee War sounded the death knell for the Indian slave trade in South Carolina but not for African slavery. In 1714, one year before hostilities with the Yamasee and their allies commenced, Charles Town slave traders conducted a brisk trade, importing 419 slaves from Africa and Barbados.[7] During the next two years, as South Carolinians battled for the colony's very

4. Emma Hart concluded that in the 1740s, "circumstances were finally colluding to make Charles Towne as attractive a destination for new arrivals as its founder, Lord Ashley, had hoped it might be." She maintains the proprietors "believed that their new society would be successful only with towns at its heart." Hart, *Building Charleston*, 36–37.

5. "The Present[ment] of the Grand-Jury," March 20, 1733, *South Carolina Gazette*, April 6, 1734; "The Petition of The Vestry, Church Wardens and other Inhabitants of The Parish of St. Philip's Charles Town," January 6, 1734/5, St. Philip's Parish Vestry Minutes 1732–1755, Book 1, April 10, 1732–April 7, 1755; "Bill to provide a full supply for subsisting poor Protestants coming from Europe and Settling in his Majesty's new Townships in this Province," April 29, 1735, *The Journal of the Commons House of Assembly of South Carolina, Nov. 8, 1734—June 7, 1735*, A. S. Salley, ed., 212.

6. In 1740 legislation sent runaway servants and slaves to the workhouse until owners claimed them. "An Act for the better ordering and governing Negroes and other Slaves in this Province," May 10, 1740, *The Statutes at Large of South Carolina*, vol. 7, 397–417.

7. Richard Waterhouse points out that "virtually all slaves imported into Carolina were the property of English merchants; in this important area of trade the Charles Town merchants usually acted only as factors." Waterhouse, *New World Gentry*, 5.

existence, 148 additional enslaved Africans arrived. Once peace was restored, rice planters and others clamored for additional slaves. Traders responded enthusiastically, delivering more than five hundred Africans to Charles Town each year until 1720, when slave imports topped six hundred for the first time.[8] At that point, South Carolina's black population neared twelve thousand; two out of every three people in the colony (excluding Native Americans) had been forcibly transported from Africa or were of African descent.[9] In the decade that followed, slave imports for some years would nearly triple the 1720 total. South Carolinians had no intention of deviating from the perilous course on which the colony embarked half a century earlier.

Between 1715 and 1717, concerns about the colony's black majority were overshadowed by the immediate threat of annihilation by Native Americans. However, once the conflict ended, whites returned to their pre-war anxieties about the Africans they simultaneously loathed and considered indispensable. That paranoia reached new heights when a "very wicked and barbarous plot" by Lowcountry slaves to "destroy all the white people in the country and then to take the town" was exposed in May 1720. Twenty-three blacks were arrested; six were convicted and sentenced to be burned, hanged, or deported. Primus, the lead conspirator, was hanged alive in chains.[10] The Lords Commissioners for Trade and Plantations informed King George I that the slave uprising in South Carolina had the potential to become "a new revolution,

8. Coclanis, *Shadow of a Dream*, 64; "Record of Annual Slave Imports, 1706–1739," as it appears in *Gentleman's Magazine* of 1755 (25), 344, reprinted in Wood, *Black Majority*, 151. Estimates of slave imports vary; R. C. Nash writes that "until 1720 slave imports were modest, rarely numbering more than 200 per year. However, with the expansion of rice, naval stores, and later, indigo production using slave labor, imports increased to 2,000 to 3,000 per year." R. C. Nash, "The Organization of Trade and Finance in the Atlantic Economy: Britain and South Carolina, 1670–1775," in Greene et al., *Money, Trade, and Power*, 83.

9. "An Exact Account of the Number of Inhabitants who pay Tax in the Settlement of South Carolina for the year 1720 with the Number of Slaves in each parish." Records in the British Public Record Office Relating to South Carolina, 9:22–23, in Colanis, *Shadow of a Dream*, 64n. According to the report, the colony had 1,305 taxpayers in 1720; by extrapolation, South Carolina must have housed approximately 6,525 whites that year.

10. "Anonymous Letter to Mr. Boone in London, June 24, 1720," MS. Public Records of South Carolina, vol. 8, 24–27; Joshua Coffin, *Account of some of the Principal Slave Insurrections* (New York: American Anti-Slavery Society, 1860), 11; Junius P. Rodriguez, *Encyclopedia of Slave Resistance and Rebellion*, vol. 1 (Westport, CT: Greenwood Publishing, 2007), 107. News of the conspiracy came on the heels of unrest on the frontier and reports that the colony was under threat of attack by Spanish privateers. The Assembly rewarded the slave who exposed the plot.

which would probably have been attended by the utter extirpation of all your Majesty's subjects in this province."[11]

The colony's brush with disaster prompted a revision of the *Act for the Better Ordering and Governing of Negroes and other Slaves*. While acknowledging the value of the "labor and service of negroes and other Slaves," the new law posed harsher penalties for black offenders, especially recidivists.[12] The 1720 conspiracy made it clear that Africans held in outlying areas needed closer supervision. According to an anonymous letter sent to London, the "principal rogues" in the plot to seize Charles Town lived on a plantation where slaves had not been properly managed.[13] Previous legislation stipulated that any farm or plantation with six or more "Negroes or slaves" must have at least one white person in residence, but there was no limit on how many slaves one white could supervise.[14]

An act passed in 1726 required owners of twenty or more blacks to employ one white man for every ten male slaves. The Assembly anticipated the new law would provide "great encouragement to such persons to transport themselves from Great Britain and other parts, when they are sure of employment upon their arrival."[15] The act tightened controls on Africans in the countryside, but had little effect in Charles Town where whites had long been

---

11. "Representation of the Board of Trade to the King upon the State of His Maj: Plantations in America," [September 8, 1721], in *The State Records of North Carolina, Vol. II, 1713 to 1728*, ed. William L. Saunders (Raleigh: P. M. Hale, 1886), 421. In 1722 the Assembly passed an act that basically incorporated Charles Town along the lines of New York City but the measure died in London when the Crown disallowed it. Bruce Mc-Cully maintains that George I rejected Charles Town's bid for civic autonomy (or "municipal oligarchy") not on constitutional principle, but due to Whitehall's sensitivity to "the pressure of interested parties on both sides of the Atlantic." Bruce T. McCully, ed., "The Charleston Government Act of 1722: A Neglected Document," *The South Carolina Historical Magazine* 83, no. 4 (October 1982): 303–19.

12. "An Act for the Better Ordering and Governing of Negroes and other Slaves," Feb. 23, 1722, *The Statutes at Large of South Carolina*, vol. 7, 371–84.

13. The plantation belonged to Andrew Percivall. Regarding his slaves, it was reported that "work does not agree with them." "Anonymous Letter to Mr. Boone in London, June 24, 1720," MS.

14. "An Act for the Better Ordering and Governing of Negroes and Slaves," June 7, 1712, *The Statutes at Large of South Carolina*, vol. 7, 352, 365. The penalty for noncompliance was forty shillings.

15. "An Act for the better securing this Province from Negro Insurrections, and for encouraging of poor people by employing them in Plantations," March 11, 1726, in Cooper, ed., *The Statutes at Large*, vol. 3, 272.

concerned about the "insolent" behavior of blacks.[16] Legislation drafted four-teen years earlier mentioned groups of armed slaves in Charles Town capable of "wicked designs."[17] Since that time, slave traders had done a brisk busi-ness and the number of Africans in and about Charles Town had increased substantially.[18] Though the majority of slaves lived on plantations, residents of St. Philip's parish owned nearly fourteen hundred slaves in 1720.[19] During the day those "city slaves" mingled with unsupervised country slaves who were sent to Charles Town on errands. Blacks' proclivity for gathering in large numbers was especially troubling. During the 1720s South Carolina's white population saw very stagnant growth. Even so the prospect of a two-to-one black-to-white ratio did not deter colonists from importing an average of nine hundred Africans each year during the 1720s.[20]

16. In 1720 Charles Town housed approximately the same number of black and white residents but visitors from outlying parishes and sailors, newly imported slaves, foreign-ers, and so on, arriving and departing daily from city wharves could skew the black-white ratio on any given day. In parishes such as St. James Goose Creek, St. John's (Berkeley), St. Andrews and St. James Santee, blacks accounted for more than 70 percent of the population. Wood, *Black Majority*, 146–47.

17. "An Act for the Better Ordering and Governing of Negroes and Slaves," June 7, 1712, *The Statutes at Large of South Carolina*, vol. 7, 354.

18. "Record of Annual Slave Imports, 1706–1739 as it appears in *Gentleman's Maga-zine* of 1755" in Wood, *Black Majority*, 151. *The Gentleman's Magazine* article data (9,758 imports in 1720–29 or an average of 976 per year) contradicts information given by Ju-nius Rodriguez who maintains that between the war's end and 1728, the number of en-slaved Africans imported into South Carolina each year rarely dropped below 1,700. The *Gentleman's Magazine* lists only two years (1726–1727) that the total number of slaves arriving in Charles Town exceeded 1,700. [Rodriguez, *Encyclopedia of Slave Resistance and Rebellion*, Volume 2, 581.] Only those who survived the Middle Passage are included in these totals; losses in the range of 12 to 17 percent of the Africans aboard were common during this period, as opposed to the 24 percent mortality aboard Royal African Com-pany ships in the 1680s. David W. Galenson, *Traders, Planters and Slaves: Market Behavior in Early English America* (Cambridge: Cambridge University Press, 2002), 38–39.

19. Wood, *Black Majority*, 147. Between 1732 and 1775, sixty-four plantations averag-ing 267 acres operated within a five-mile radius of Charleston. According to the *South Carolina Gazette*, forty-two plantations averaging 438 acres were six to ten miles away, seventy-three plantations averaging 619 acres were eleven to twenty miles away, and fifty-seven plantations averaging 844 acres were twenty-one to fifty miles from Charles-ton. Edelson, *Plantation Enterprise*, 283.

20. Menard, "Transitions to African Slavery," in Morgan, *Slavery in America A Reader*, 40. South Carolina's white population increased by 3,475 between 1720 and 1730 while the black population showed a net increase of 8,132. Coclanis, *Shadow of a Dream*, 64.

Anxieties stemming from the colony's racial imbalance reached all the way to London. In 1720 Governor Johnson reported that "since the Indian Warr, which broke out in April, 1715, we are increased about 100 Inhabitants, we having lost about 400 in the Warr, and have had the accession of about 500 from England, Ireland and other places."[21] That same year, the Assembly estimated that there were nine thousand whites and twelve thousand blacks in the colony. In their view, prodigious increases in the pitch and tar trade had "occasioned ye Inhabitants to buy Blacks to the great Indangering [of] this Province." In 1721 the Lords Commissioners for Trade and Plantations proposed that more white servants be encouraged to move to the province. In a report on the "State of His Majesty's Plantations on the Continent of America," the Commissioners predicted that South Carolina, which had just shucked off proprietary rule, "will no doubt, under the happy influence of your Majesty's immediate protection, become a flourishing colony."[22]

Although trade was "not hitherto very considerable," the colony's lack of ships meant its imports and exports were "carried on by the Merchants of Great Britain, who reap a considerable advantage thereby." South Carolinians purchased £23,000 of British goods per annum and their "southernly

21. "Letter from Col. Johnson, Govr of Carolina, to the Board, dated 12 January, 1719–20," Board of Trade, vol. 10, Q. 201, State Paper Office, in Rivers, *Early History of South Carolina*, 92. A report dated March 14, 1720/1 estimated that the "exact account of the number of Inhabitants who pay Tax" in St. Philip's Parish was 283; according to the same source the number of slaves in Charles Town at that time was 1,390. [Ibid., 55–56.] Peter Coclanis estimates that St. Philip's parish had a permanent white male population of 283 in 1722; seventeen other white male parishioners lived outside of Charleston. By 1732 that number had increased nearly 25 percent to 350. The city's transient population varied; in February and March—the peak of the shipping season—there were four hundred to five hundred sailors in Charleston, but that total fell drastically in the summer months. As a result, the average number of white transients at any given time between 1722 and 1732 was 350; these would be added to the city's residential population. These totals do not include British naval squadrons that occasionally visited the city. The crude death rate for this period was "very high"—between fifty-two and sixty per thousand, indicating that Charleston deserved its reputation as a "great charnel-house." Coclanis, *Shadow of a Dream*, 166–74.

22. "Copy of a Representation of the Lords Commissioners for Trade and Plantations to the King upon the State of His Majesties Colonies & Plantations on the Continent of North America, dated September the 8th 1721," in John Romeyn Brodhead, ed., *Documents relative to the colonial history of the State of New-York: procured in Holland, England and France* (Albany: Weed, Parsons and Company, 1855), 610. In 1721 the colony exported twenty-five thousand barrels of rice, fourteen thousand pounds of pitch, and seven thousands pounds of tar. Sirmans, *Colonial South Carolina*, 132–33.

situation" would make them "always dependent on Great Britain" for com-modities. Being the "southern frontier" of the British plantations in America and "lying much exposed to the incursions both of the French [French] & Spaniards, as well as to the insults of the Indians," South Carolina needed his Majesty's "immediate assistance and protection." Toward that end, the Lords Commissioners recommended the dispatch of at least four regiments to the colony.[23]

In the early 1720s, pitch and tar generated considerable income for South Carolinians, but the elimination of the bounty on naval stores from 1725 to 1729 caused a downturn from which the industry never fully recovered. Another flagging sector of the economy was beef and pork production; the Yamasee War dealt that business a crippling blow and exports never again reached prewar levels. Smaller farmers who depended on the sale of livestock and naval stores found themselves on the margins of society, both economi-cally and politically.[24] The deerskin trade continued to generate profits but even those shipments dropped in volume and, as in the past, they enriched only a small number of influential men.[25] After 1724 rice coming out of low-country plantations clearly constituted the colony's most significant com-mercial offering.[26] Ideally the burgeoning rice trade would improve the status of everyone in the colony, but that was not the case. Ordinary planters lacked the capital and the workers necessary to create and operate a rice plantation.

23. "Copy of a Representation," in Brodhead, ed., *Documents*, 610. As South Carolin-ians established plantations further into the interior, conflicts with Native Americans became more likely. Prior to the Yamasee War, most whites did not view the Indian slave trade as a threat to the growing rice and indigo trades. According to Gary Hewitt, col-onists assumed that conquest and enslavement of Native Americans would facilitate expansion—"conquest, trade, and plantation agriculture were complementary . . . all three could be promoted by the state with the same policies." Hewitt, "State in the Planters' Service," in Greene et al, *Money, Trade, and Power*, 50.

24. Waterhouse, *New World Gentry*, 50.

25. Between 1699 and 1715, an average of fifty-four thousand deerskins were exported from South Carolina each year. In 1715 South Carolina exported 55,806 deerskins; that total dropped to 4,702 in 1716 but by 1722 deerskin exports rebounded to 59,827. The trade remained active but never again approached the 1707 volume when 121,355 hides were shipped from Charleston. ["Deerskin Exports from Virginia and South Carolina, 1699–1724," in Thomas L. Purvis, *Colonial America to 1763* (New York: Infobase Publish-ing, 1999), 96.] An act passed in 1723 required the office of trade commissioner to be filled by a process of compromise—the lower house nominated the commissioner, but the governor appointed him. Nelson, *Common Law in Colonial America: Vol. II*, 78.

26. The colony exported about 1.5 million pounds of rice in 1710, 6 million in 1720, and nearly 20 million by 1730. The surging exports of the 1720s made rice South Carolina's

Many were literally pushed aside, physically and politically, by the emerging planter gentry. The substantial revenues generated by rice exports went into rice planters' coffers, as well as those of agents, shipowners, and the king. The rigorous labor of Africans in lowcountry rice fields affected virtually everyone in the region, but not necessarily in a positive way.

The profits garnered from slave labor in South Carolina spawned controversy in neighboring Georgia in the 1730s and 1740s. When planters there waged a campaign to eliminate that colony's ban on slavery, the Trustees argued that slavery produced indolence and inequality among free whites; colonists would become indebted in order to purchase slaves; the importation of Africans would lead to insurrections; slave labor would reduce opportunities for poor whites to find work; non-slaveholders would be inclined to leave the colony; and the Spanish would likely entice enslaved Africans to rebel or to flee. South Carolina had set an example that the Trustees did not want Georgia to follow.[27] Some colonists supported the Trustees' ban on slavery: "We are laborious, and know that a White Man may be by the Year more usefully employed than a Negro. We are not rich, and becoming Debtors for slaves, in case of their running away or dying, would inevitably ruin the poor Master, and he become a greater Slave to the Negro Merchant, than the Slave he bought could be to him.... How miserable would it be to us, and to our Wives and Families, to have an Enemy without, and more dangerous ones in our Bosom!" Though few South Carolinians voiced objections to slavery on moral grounds, a number of Georgians did so in earnest: "It's shocking to human Nature, that any Race of Mankind, and their Posterity, should be sentenced to perpetual Slavery." They concluded that "they [Africans] are thrown amongst

---

unquestioned staple; by the late 1740s the crop would account for nearly 60 percent of South Carolina's total exports by value. McCusker and Menard, *Economy of British America*, 176; Edelson, *Plantation Enterprise*, 77. Edelson notes that the emergence of rice after 1720 "changed South Carolina's external relationship to the Atlantic economy, opening lines of credit, generating private fortunes, and drawing hundreds and then thousands of new slaves to the colony every year to grow more rice for export." [Ibid., 54.] Rice prices received by lowcountry planters nearly doubled between 1720 and their peak in 1738. During the same period, rice output rose from 6.5 million pounds to 43 million pounds in 1740. Peter C. Mancall, Joshua L. Rosenbloom, and Thomas Weiss, "Slave Prices and the South Carolina Economy, 1722–1809," *The Journal of Economic History* 61, no. 3 (September 2001): 629.

27. Anon., *An Account Shewing the Progress of the Colony of Georgia in America from its First Establishment* [1741], reprinted in *The Clamorous Malcontents: Criticisms & Defenses of the Colony of Georgia, 1741–1743*, ed. Trevor R. Reese (Savannah: The Beehive Press, 1973), 190–92.

us to be our Scourge one Day or another for our Sins; and as Freedom to them must be as dear as to us, what a Scene of Horror must it bring about!"[28]

Advocates of slavery in Georgia countered that: Europeans were unfit for labor in a tropical climate; slaves were cheaper to maintain than indentured servants; the latter tended to be lazy and degenerate; it was more difficult for blacks to escape and remain undetected; and South Carolina slave holders had an insurmountable economic advantage.[29] Based on the general tide of opinion, ongoing violations of the ban on slavery, and dire economic predictions regarding the competitive advantage enjoyed by South Carolinians—"they having their Labour so much cheaper, will always ruin our Market"—Georgia's Trustees repealed the prohibition in 1750. They reluctantly concluded, "In its Infancy the Introduction of Black Slaves or Negroes would have been of dangerous Consequence but at present it may be a Benefit to the said Colony and a Convenience and Encouragement to the Inhabitants thereof."[30]

Paupers in Charles Town derived no "convenience and encouragement" from slave labor. A widow or disabled soldier might profit from charitable donations or distributions from the poor tax, but Charles Town's relief crisis seemed to grow in tandem with the economy. Many colonists who were solvent before the Yamasee War found themselves in financial straits in its wake. A 1719 report prepared for the Board of Trade pointed out that, besides the cost of fortifications in Charles Town and on the frontier, "the debts contracted by the late bloody Indian Warr and the several expeditions against the Pirates and the alarms caused by Incursions from St. Augustine, has brought a heavy debt upon the Inhabitants who have now lost all publick credit."[31]

28. Number IX, "To his Excellency General Oglethorpe," January 3, 1739, *Colonial Records of the State of Georgia*, 427.

29. Number VIII. "To the Honorable the Trustees for Establishing the Colony of Georgia in America," December 9, 1738, *The Colonial Records of the State of Georgia*, vol. 3 (Atlanta: Franklin Printing and Publishing Company, 1905), 422–25.

30. Ibid., 423; August 8, 1750, *Journal of the Trustees for Establishing the Colony of Georgia in America, July 20, 1732-June 23, 1752* (Atlanta: Franklin Printing and Publishing Company, 1904), 57–62.

31. "Copy of the General Assembly's Answer to the [eight] Queries sent by the Honble the Lords Commissioners of trade and plantations relating to the State of South Carolina, January 29, 1719," Papers Relating to the American Plantations, Etc., *Report of the Royal Commission on Historical Manuscripts*, issue 11, part 4 (London: H. M. Stationery Office, 1887), 254. The process of dismantling Charles Town's walls beginning in 1718 marked the town's architectural passage from medieval to modern. Peter A. Coclanis, "The Sociology of Architecture in Colonial Charleston: Pattern and process in an Eighteenth-Century Southern City," *Journal of Social History* 18, no. 4 (1985): 609.

The 1721 *Act for establishing County and Precinct Courts* included provisions that addressed the legion of South Carolinians who could not pay their debts, or worse. It stated that "divers careless persons" spent their time in "punch-houses, &c., instead of betaking themselves to labor." Some scalawags ran up debts in country stores and then made their escape "to North Carolina, and other parts of America, for fear of arrests and lying in prison."[32] The new law allowed any man who owned nothing but the clothes on his back to be "set at liberty, and stand forever discharged of all his debts." It gave bankrupt individuals a second chance; but anyone who lied under oath regarding their worth was to lose both ears and serve four years as a soldier in a remote garrison.[33] The problem was not so easily solved: one year later the Assembly passed *An Act for the relief of Poor Debtors*, because "many of the white men in this Province are daily deserting this Settlement upon account of their debts." Because the departure of indigent whites rendered the colony "less capable of withstanding of our foreign and domestick enemies," any person in prison for debt above forty shillings would be discharged of the debt and released if he was "not worth forty shillings."[34]

Some planters and merchants profited handsomely during the 1720s, but the economic recovery was erratic. In 1722 a "most violent rain" fell for three days and nights without intermission, causing "great destruction of grain and other necessaries of life."[35] One survivor described the storm as "the greatest flood attended with a hurricane that has been known since the country was settled." He reported that "great numbers of cattle, horses, hogs and some people were drowned ... deer were found frequently lodged on high trees."[36] The next year floods destroyed a third of the rice crop; profits plummeted

32. In 1621 the Lords Commissioners noted that North Carolina had become "a place of refuge for all the vagabonds, whom either debt, or breach of the Laws have driven from other Colonies on the Continent; and pirates have too frequently found entertainment amongst them." "Copy of a Representation of the Lords Commissioners for Trade and Plantations to the King," 609.

33. "An Act for establishing County and Precinct Courts," September 20, 1721, *The Statutes at Large of South Carolina*, vol. 7, 174–75. William Nelson points out that the proprietary government of South Carolina had "used common law to establish effective governance in the Charles Town area ... but proved largely unable to impose legal order on outlying regions." Nelson, *Common Law in Colonial America: Vol. II*, 5.

34. "An Act for the relief of Poor Debtors," June 23, 1722, in Cooper, ed., *The Statutes at Large*, vol. 3, 173.

35. Le Jau to the Secretary, January 22, 1713, in *The Carolina Chronicle*, 136.

36. George F. Frick and Raymond P. Stearns, *Mark Catesby: The Colonial Audubon* (Urbana: University of Illinois Press, 1961), 24, quoted in Rubillo, *Hurricane Destruction*,

further when Parliament eliminated the bounty on naval stores. In 1728 a drought savaged the rice harvest; that calamity was followed by an outbreak of yellow fever and two major hurricanes. In the second tempest, twenty-three ships were driven ashore and residents once again sought refuge on rooftops. That same year raids by Yamasee Indians provoked fears of another war and led to a preemptive raid on the Yamasee village near St. Augustine. Then yellow fever killed "multitudes of the inhabitants of Charles Town, both white and black." In 1731 a major fire burned many of the city's six hundred homes and businesses. That was followed by a 1732 smallpox outbreak that killed so many whites—133 according to one report—that the tolling of funeral bells was prohibited. Many inhabitants of Charles Town fled to the countryside in search of healthier surroundings; not so Governor Johnson, who remained at his post and lost his wife, son, and three servants as a result. "City slaves" also perished in large numbers, though no bells tolled to mark their passing.[37]

During the 1720s paper money remained a disruptive issue, pitting merchants against planters who were keen on promoting agricultural expansion. Colonists further down the food chain could only pray that legislation crafted by the gentry might in some way prove helpful, or at least not hurt them too badly.[38] Political infighting continued to foster difficulties for rich and poor alike. Battles over special interests pushed the colony toward a political meltdown: inhabitants of northern parishes refused to pay taxes in 1727, the legislature failed to meet between mid-1728 and 1731, taxes went uncollected, and the judicial system operated on an intermittent basis. In England, a committee appointed by the Commons reported that South Carolina was "in a very distressed and calamitous condition."[39] By 1730 some residents had been in that condition for fifteen or more years and the number of people who appealed to the churchwardens for aid was on the rise. Poverty was not limited to Charles Town; the spread of rice cultivation created greater economic inequality, enriching the lowcountry elite but pushing small planters out to

---

40. Mark Catesby reported conditions after the flood: "Panthers, Bears, and Deer, were drowned, and found lodg'd on the Limbs of Trees. The smaller Animals suffered also in this Calamity; even Reptiles and Insects were dislodged from their Holes, and violently hurried away[.] . . ." Mark Catesby, *Natural History of Carolina, Florida, and the Bahama Islands* (London, 1731–47), quoted in Amy R. W. Myers, *Empire's Nature: Mark Catesby's New World Vision* (Chapel Hill: University of North Carolina Press, 1998), 74.

37. Hewatt, *Historical Account*, 317; Duffy, *Epidemics*, 193. Additional outbreaks occurred in 1738, 1745, and 1748.

38. Hewitt, "The State in the Planters' Service," in Greene et al., *Money, Trade, and Power*, 51–55.

39. Weir, *Colonial South Carolina*, 108–10.

the periphery where war, disease, and natural disasters had also taken their toll.

In 1729 the Lords Proprietors arrived at a financial settlement with the Crown, making Carolina a royal colony. Shortly thereafter, the king appointed Robert Johnson as the colony's first Royal Governor, and Parliament passed favorable legislation regarding naval stores and rice.[40] Those developments helped restore stability and revitalized South Carolina's economy. One of Governor Johnson's priorities was the creation of twenty-thousand-acre townships that would stretch in a protective arc around Charles Town from the Savannah River to the North Carolina border. These remote settlements were to be manned by European immigrants who would strengthen the colony's defenses, provide commodities that would find ready markets in Charles Town, and counteract the growth of the colony's African population.[41]

The people recruited for the new townships were destitute Protestants from Britain or Continental Europe. This effort to populate the frontier with

---

40. In 1721 the Board of Trade noted that English merchants involved in Carolina's rice trade "often complained that the advantage they formerly reaped by supplying Portugal with Rice hath been almost entirely lost since the act . . . whereby Rice is made one of the Enumerated Commodityes and the Importation thereof restrained to Great Britain." ["Representation of the Board of Trade," September 8, 1721, in Saunders, ed., *The State Records of North Carolina*, 423.] Northern Europeans consumed the majority of South Carolina's rice exports, though all shipments had to pass through a British port en route to their final destination. Until 1720, London was the major port for transshipment of Carolina rice. [Nash, "The Organization of Trade and Finance in the Atlantic Economy," in Greene et al., *Money, Trade, and Power*, 87; Peter A. Coclanis, "Rice Prices in the 1720s and the Evolution of the South Carolina Economy," *The Journal of Southern History* 48, no. 4 (November 1982): 532.] English laws passed in 1704 required Carolinians to ship their rice to London for reexport to Europe; in 1730 Parliament eased these restrictions, allowing Carolina planters to export their crop to Iberia as well as Britain. [John Solomon Otto, *The Southern Frontiers, 1607–1860: The Agricultural Evolution of the Colonial and Antebellum South* (New York: ABC-CLIO, 1989), 39.] By 1720 South Carolina planters had passed through the first of "three principal stages in the sociocultural development of most colonies: simplification, elaboration, and replication" [Roper, *Conceiving Carolina*, 6.] Three decades of political maneuvering to use state power "to help Indian trade, conquest, and plantation development coexist" and to "subordinate trade and conquest to the needs of the plantation economy" paid off in the 1730s when rice production and the importation of Africans both soared. Hewitt, "The State in the Planters' Service," in Greene et al., *Money, Trade, and Power*, 68.

41. In 1732 the king granted a charter for the colony of Georgia; it was expected to protect South Carolina from Spanish invasion but provisions that included limited land tenure and a ban on slavery that stifled settlement.

thousands of "poor Protestants" repeated mistakes that the colony had made in the past; the result was a significant increase in the number of paupers. Some immigrants never ventured to the frontier; others went there and failed, or were dismayed by the hardscrabble conditions and quickly retreated to Charles Town. There they merged into the city's burgeoning population of poor families and destitute individuals, many of whom had borne the brunt of natural and human-caused disasters and were in need of food, shelter, and medical care. Churchwardens were hard-pressed to refuse charity to the homeless, even though many petitioners did not qualify for relief by law. When Governor Johnson died in 1735, his successor described him as the "common Father" of the "Poor and Unfortunate who sought a Retreat here," and pledged to "make Provision for the poor Protestants already arrived, and daily expected to arrive." South Carolina may have offered "Shelter from Cruelty and Oppression," but it hardly relieved newcomers from the "Pressure of Poverty," as Johnson intended.[42] At midcentury, Governor James Glen noted that one-fifth of South Carolinians could only afford a "bare subsistence." Had he included the colony's forty thousand enslaved Africans in his estimate, the governor could have reported that nearly 70 percent of the people in his colony endured a bare subsistence.[43]

In the 1720s and the 1730s, the intensification of the plantation system in the lowcountry fostered even more oppressive conditions for enslaved Africans.[44] Slaves constituted a major part of planters' estates, but individual

42. "The Speech of the Honourable Thomas Broughton ... in General Assembly met May 27, 1735," *The American Weekly Mercury*, June 26-July 3, 1735. On July 26, 1735, the *South Carolina Gazette* announced the arrival of "two hundred Palatines; most of them being poor, they were obliged to sell themselves and their children for their passage ... within a fortnight of the time of their arrival, or else to pay one pistole more to be carried to Philadelphia." They became the first settlers in Orangeburg Township.

43. "James Glen to the Board of Trade," March, 1751; "An attempt towards an estimate of the value of South Carolina." Records in the British National Archives relating to South Carolina (microfilm, SCDAH), v. 24, 303–30, cited in Tim Lockley, "Rural Poor Relief in Colonial South Carolina," *The Historical Journal* 48, no. 4 (2005): 963. As of 1720 South Carolinians claimed ownership of approximately twelve thousand black men, women, and children. In the next two decades, thirty-two thousand more Africans were imported, yet there were only 39,155 blacks in the province in 1740. In sum, enslaved Africans in South Carolina were dying faster than they could be replaced. Edward Countryman, *How Did American Slavery Begin?*, 5.

44. Peter McCandless states that the suffering produced by the rice plantation economy "was obscured by elites who did not want to expose it and the illiteracy of most of those who suffered." Lowcountry rice plantations "provided an especially welcoming environment for diseases transmitted by mosquitoes and water-borne parasites.... The

blacks were expendable. Despite greater mortality and a lower birth rate among plantation slaves, the constant arrival of "choice parcels" of Angolans and other Africans ensured that the black population continued to grow.[45] In 1737 an immigrant wrote that "Carolina looks more like a negro country than like a country settled by white people."[46] Two years later, on September 9, 1739, a revolt that originated in Stono, fifteen miles west of Charles Town, led to the deaths of twenty-one whites. The resulting *Act for the better ordering and governing Negroes and other Slaves in this Province*—legislation that mirrored Barbados's notorious slave code—provided a legal framework for the intimidation and subjugation of Africans and African Americans in South Carolina for the next 125 years.[47]

adoption of African slavery was not a response to an unhealthy environment. It was a major cause of it, along with human alterations of the landscape required for rice cultivation." [McCandless, *Slavery, Disease, and Suffering*, 8–14, 58.] Philip D. Morgan and others have argued that the coming of the task system improved slaves' lives in terms of the domestic economy, patterns of resource use, consumption, accumulation, and independence of spirit. [Stephen Innes, ed., *Work and Labor in Early America* (Chapel Hill: University of North Carolina Press, 1988), 28.] The development of plantations made South Carolina even deadlier for whites as well. Planter Henry Ravenel and his wife had sixteen children between 1750 and 1779. Eight died before the age of five, only six lived beyond their twenty-first birthday, and none of the couple's seven daughters lived to be twenty.

45. The *American Weekly Mercury* reported that between November 1, 1734, and November 1, 1735, the port of Charles Town imported 2,671 "Negroes from Africa" and another 236 from the West Indies. [*The American Weekly Mercury*, December 11–December 18, 1735]. As plantations expanded and the labor regime became more intense, infant mortality rose and the birth rate and average life expectancy declined. [Nagle and Sanders, eds., *English in the Southern United States*, 72.] Between 1735 and 1775 the Charles Town slave trade involved hundreds of merchants, but a clique of ten merchants in overlapping firms imported 57 percent of the enslaved Africans in these years. Nearly all these slave traders also bought and sold rice and dry goods on commission. Most small country factors were not involved in the African slave trade. Nash, "The Organization of Trade and Finance in the Atlantic Economy," in Greene et al., *Money, Trade, and Power*, 83.

46. "Letter from Samuel Dyssli, December 3, 1737," *South Carolina Historical and Genealogical Magazine* 23 (July 1922): 90. Dyssli noted, "In Charleston and that neighborhood there are calculated to be always 20 blacks, who are called negroes, to one white man, but they are all slaves."

47. "An Act for the better ordering and governing Negroes and other Slaves in this Province," May 10, 1740, *The Statutes at Large of South Carolina*, vol. 7, 397–417. Twelve days after the Stono rebellion the Upper House had drafted a "Bill for the Better Ordering and Governing of Negroes and Other Slaves." The May 10 act was a revised and expanded final version of the September 21 legislation.

Treaties signed in the wake of the Yamasee War introduced a period of relative calm on the frontier, but Native Americans continued to be at risk in other ways.[48] In the summer of 1739, eleven "chief men among the Catawbas and Cheraw Indians" came to Charles Town to speak with the governor. They carried news that they had executed five renegade members of their tribe accused of killing a white family. It was a much-appreciated gesture, but a most inopportune time for the Indians to be in the city. An outbreak of smallpox had recently killed as many as four hundred colonists, and a subsequent yellow fever epidemic struck down "nineteen and twenty on a Day."[49] One of the two diseases soon exterminated as many as half of the people in the Catawba nation. Other southeastern tribes were also devastated by the epidemic; approximately one-third of the Cherokee died as well. Noting the avarice, brutality, and death all around him, Minister Stephen Roe of Charles Town declared that he was "almost wearied out with the perverseness of the people added to the unhealthfulness of the country."[50]

On November 18, 1740, a fire broke out in the "most valuable part" of Charles Town, leaping from one structure to the next "with astonishing violence and fierceness." In less than six hours, the blaze consumed more than three hundred buildings as well as huge quantities of rice, naval stores, lumber, and "7 or 8,000" deerskins awaiting export. Total damages amounted to £250,000; merchant Robert Pringle described the city's smoldering ruins as "a dismal scene which much surpassed anything I ever saw." The next day, Governor Bull appealed to "all Christian and well-disposed people" to contribute to the support of those in need; he personally contributed £100 currency for "Releif [sic] of such poor People who have been Ruined by the late

---

48. The Assembly asserted its power over the colony's economic affairs with legislation passed shortly after the Yamasee War. The members asserted that the Indian trade served the interests of traders and their merchant partners, not those of the colony. No longer would traders receive preferential treatment when it came to legislation. Hewitt, "The State in the Planters' Service," in Greene et al., *Money, Trade, and Power*, 58.

49. Entry dated September 25–29, 1739, in William Stephens, "A Journal of the Proceedings in Georgia, Beginning October 20, 1737," in *The Colonial Records of the State of Georgia, Vol. 4: Stephens' Journal 1737–1740* (Atlanta: Franklin Printing and Publishing Company, 1906), 423. The loss of so many people to smallpox and yellow fever in the summers of 1738 and 1739 spelled disaster for many families. The outbreaks also dealt a punishing blow to the economy as productivity dropped and colonists living in the country refused to bring goods into the city or to patronize its merchants.

50. *South Carolina Gazette*, July 7, 1739; McCandless, *Slavery, Disease, and Suffering*, 191; "Stephen Roe to the Secretary," July 13, 1739, SPG Letter Books, B7: 227, in Ibid., 59.

dreadful fire."[51] It would take years for some merchants to recover their losses, but they were fortunate compared to Charles Town's poorest inhabitants, many of whom lost everything they had, including any real hope of recovery.

Seven months after the Charles Town conflagration, preacher Jonathan Edwards of Northampton, Massachusetts, warned his congregation that they were "already under a Sentence of Condemnation to Hell," and that justice called for "an infinite Punishment of their sins." Sinners should anticipate "*sudden* unexpected Destruction . . . the Fire is made ready." Directly overhead were "black Clouds of God's Wrath." The "Floods of God's Vengeance" awaited; "the Bow of God's Wrath is bent."[52] The sermon, "Sinners in the Hands of an Angry God," was printed in Boston and widely distributed throughout the colonies.[53] The images that Edwards used must have resonated with South Carolinians who had endured catastrophic fires, hurricanes, floods, and Indian attacks. New England Puritans took Edwards's message to heart and flocked to churches and their Bibles, but in Charles Town, where many people had just been burned out of their homes and businesses by an angry God (if Reverend George Whitefield was correct), residents redoubled their efforts in their quest for mammon. Catastrophes were not divine mandates; they were obstacles to be overcome on the road to prosperity.[54]

51. *South Carolina Gazette*, November 27, 1740; *Journal of the Commons House of Assembly*, September 12, 1739–March 26, 1741, 408; "Robert Pringle to Andrew Pringle," November 22, 1740, in *Letterbook of Robert Pringle, Vol. 1*, 273; "Letter from Charleston," *Gentleman's Magazine* (January 1741), 55, quoted in Kenneth Scott, "Sufferers in the Charleston Fire of 1740," *The South Carolina Historical Magazine* 64, no. 4 (October 1963): 203–11.

52. Jonathan Edwards, *Sinners in the Hands of an Angry God, A Sermon Preached at Enfield, July 8th 1741* (Boston: Printed and Sold by S. Kneeland and T. Green, 1741), 4–14. Edward's sermon was printed separately nine times in Great Britain and North America, and appended to an extensive number of other works. Jonathan M. Yeager, *Jonathan Edwards and Transatlantic Print Culture* (New York: Oxford University Press, 2016), 10.

53. Edwards's sermon made "remarkable Impressions on many of the Hearers" according to the frontispiece of the printed version. Edwards was one of the leading voices of the First Great Awakening; the evangelical revival he led in Northampton, Massachusetts, between 1733 and 1735, sparked similar revivals from New England to Georgia. In 1740 Edwards helped arrange a visit to America by George Whitefield, the most prolific and controversial revivalist of the era.

54. Charles Town had some dissenting ministers with strong ties to New England revivalists but the Anglican commissary, Alexander Garden, was one of the revival's severest critics. The revival "did not spread very deeply in South Carolina culture." [Frank Lambert, *Inventing the "Great Awakening"* (Princeton: Princeton University Press, 1999),

From the colony's earliest days, greed was a driving force, shaping growth, fostering competition, and inviting self-destructive behavior. John Locke's *Two Treatises of Government*, published when rice was just an experimental crop in the lowcountry, advanced the notion of natural rights. If Locke hoped to alter the colony's course, his efforts came too late; by the time his writings reached Charles Town, South Carolina's Barbadian heritage was indisputable and irreversible.[55] With rice as an economic engine, a planter oligarchy would soon emerge and hasten the colony ever deeper into the dark abyss of slavery. Consequences be damned, South Carolina had become a slave society— one where profits trumped prophecies, even those of renowned clergymen.

Long after its first half-century had drawn to a close, South Carolina remained a land of opportunity for well-connected white men who arrived with money in their pockets and a penchant for exploiting every opportunity and available resource, including fertile lands and enslaved Africans. But blind ambition was no guarantee of success; both merchants and planters had to make prudent decisions and demonstrate resilience in the face of adversity. Disasters would weed out the weak, the unlucky, and the unprepared. Some calamities took the form of wind, fire, or disease; others came about through human agency. In South Carolina's second fifty years, as rice and indigo planters accumulated vast fortunes, countless men, women, and children fell by the wayside. The chaff of lowcountry society, they were victims of bad decisions, bad luck, and bad policies. As in the past, many of the colony's most terrible wounds continued to be self-inflicted. Failure was often personal, but on occasion, calamity hunched down on the South Carolina landscape and spread misery near and far.

143.] Evangelicals "learned that the dominant elites in southern slave society were too strong to challenge." Alan Gallay, "Planters and Slaves in the Great Awakening," in John B. Boles, ed., *Masters and Slaves in the House of the Lord: Race and Religion in the American South, 1740–1870* (Lexington: University Press of Kentucky, 2015), 20.

55. Locke advanced two notions of slavery. He defined and defended "the perfect condition of slavery" as "the state of war continued, between a lawful Conqueror, and a Captive," but he opposed arbitrary rule and argued that "[t]he natural liberty of man is to be free from any superior power on earth." Locke, *Second Treatise of Civil Government* (1690), Ch. 4, Secs. 22, 24. Locke owned shares in English slave trading companies.

Epilogue

AN HONEST RECKONING

In *Leviathan* Thomas Hobbes emphasized the importance of law and the need for a sovereign with absolute authority.[1] Between 1670 and 1720, Carolinians did have a sovereign—in fact, six sovereigns, albeit at a distance. During that span Charles II, James II, William III, Mary II, Anne, and George I, respectively, ruled England. These monarchs, however, were hardly exemplars of absolute rule. Charles I was executed by his subjects, James II was chased off of the throne, and the rest were often distracted by internal rebellions or wars with rival nations. Of course no Englishman expected the Crown to pay much attention to a hardscrabble colony planted south of Virginia; that was the responsibility of the Lords Proprietors of Carolina. As it turned out, the Proprietors were poor substitutes for the monarchical oversight that Hobbes preferred.[2] The colony's first fifty years are often called "the era of Proprietary rule," but those years actually marked the *disintegration* of proprietary rule.

Given the remoteness of colonies in general, Hobbes thought their governance should be committed to "an Assembly of men," but few such Assemblies resided "in the Province it selfe." The Virginia and Bermuda governments, established decades before *Leviathan* was published, had been "committed to Assemblies in London" that appointed governors for each colony, rather than "commit the Government" to any body politic in the Americas.[3] Between 1670 and 1720, South Carolina had a plethora of governors—the Proprietors and Grand Council appointed nineteen different men to the position (three

---

1. Hobbes, *Leviathan*, 62–64.

2. The influence of Carolina's proprietors waxed and waned not only abroad but also at home. In July 1681, Shaftesbury was charged with high treason and placed in the Tower of London. He was released and died in exile in Holland in January 1683. Seven months later John Locke took refuge in Holland following discovery of the Rye House Plot; he remained there until 1689, returning to England after the "Glorious Revolution."

3. Hobbes, *Leviathan*, 162–63.

served dual nonconsecutive terms).[4] Not only did these governors fail to bring stability, the actions of some—James Moore being a prime example—created new problems for the colony. Crises stemming from ineffective leadership were compounded by infighting between the "Dissenters" and the "Goose Creek Men," and by disagreements between the colonists and the Lords Proprietors.[5] During South Carolina's first half-century, the most stable source of authority was the Commons House of Assembly, but that body was dominated by colonists who were deeply engaged in the freewheeling competition for power and wealth that Hobbes envisioned. Rather than curtail the insidious and inflammatory Indian slave trade, they attempted to restrict it to licensed traders.[6] Rather than halt the importation of enslaved Africans, they discussed ways to recruit white settlers. Not only did members of the Assembly pass much questionable legislation, but as private citizens they conducted themselves and their business enterprises in ways that deprived others of their liberty, their property, their happiness, their health, their security, and sometimes their lives.[7] While some South Carolinians strove for the common

4. In 1691 Carolina had a governor in Charles Town and a deputy governor in the Albemarle region. In 1710 the Lords Proprietors appointed separate governors for North Carolina and South Carolina, essentially dividing the two colonies. Alan Gallay, ed., *Colonial Wars of North America, 1512–1763: An Encyclopedia* (New York: Routledge, 1996), 508. According to Louis Roper, "the men who were expected to govern Carolina maintained presences in various parts of England's Atlantic empire . . . [they] held political and commercial interests in and had familiarity with places on both sides of the ocean, physically and mentally." Roper, *Conceiving Carolina*, 7.

5. In 1704 the Goose Creek men allied themselves with the proprietors against the Dissenters; this alienated the one group in Carolina that had supported the Lords Proprietors because of their promise of religious toleration. [Roper, *Conceiving Carolina*, 5.] In 1709 Francis Le Jau wrote, "I wish some things here were carryed on more for the glory of God than for private ends . . . We are infected with Railers, Scoffers, & Atheistical persons, and those pretened [*sic*] to be the mighty Statesmen; God keep us from seeing the World govern'd by their principles." Dr. Francis Le Jau to the Secretary, August 5, 1709, in *The Carolina Chronicle*, 58.

6. South Carolina authorities proved ineffective in enforcing laws relating to the Indian Trade and by 1714 most traders ignored the requirement to obtain licenses. In April 1715 Yamasee leaders complained about traders who threatened to seize their families and sell them into slavery as payment for large debts they had accumulated. Ivers, *This Torrent of Indians*, 1–4, 38–50.

7. Northern colonies whose climate and topography were not suited to the production and export of cash crops had less obvious pathways to prosperity, but they also "experienced a less powerful drive toward coerced labor and commercial competition." LeMaster and Wood, eds., *Creating and Contesting Carolina*, 6.

good, too many others—including many of their elected representatives—did not.

The subtitle of Bernard Mandeville's expanded version of *Fable of the Bees*, published in 1723, was *Private Vices, Publick Benefits*. In his metaphorical hive, the "worst of all the Multitude did something for the Common Good." Had Mandeville visited Charles Town and the surrounding lowcountry at that time, he might have concluded that in the colony of South Carolina, *vices* were public and *benefits* were private. His ideas about the potential for envy, competition, and exploitation to generate "publick benefits" may not have changed, but the boldness with which the colony's planter and merchant elites engaged in those behaviors—their blatant scheming and avarice—suggested that in a true Hobbesian environment, the "worst of the multitude" would inevitably come to wield power over the rest.

Cupidity, conflict, and poor leadership were not Carolina's only problems in its first half-century. For nearly twenty-five years, planters were unable to identify a cash crop that would sustain their individual ambitions and the colony at large. In the absence of such a commodity, the deerskin trade provided valuable income. The Indian slave trade that followed on the deerskin trade's heels depopulated southeastern tribes and posed a great danger to the colony. The shipment of Native Americans to Barbados and other English colonies enabled a small number of Carolinians to become wealthy at the expense of the entire Province—whites and Indians alike. In a similar vein, ambitious merchants and planters imported thousands of Africans, regardless of the great harm they wreaked on those captives and on their own colony.

By 1708 more than half of the people in South Carolina were enslaved; it was a recipe for disaster. This demographic anomaly was not an accident of fate; it stemmed from the proprietors' flawed assumptions and from the colony's Barbadian heritage. The planting of a colony in North America did not *require* the labor of enslaved Native Americans and Africans. South Carolina's commitment to slave labor was fostered by individuals intimately familiar with techniques that generated immense fortunes in the West Indies. The Lords Proprietors wanted to stock their Province with men who knew how to generate profits in a colonial setting ... men who could identify, plant, harvest, and sell a staple crop. They needed planters who had responded to market opportunities in the past and would do so in the future. They found such men in Barbados—former sugar planters had no reason to deviate from a formula that had already proven successful. Whether to place responsibility for the creation of a slave society in South Carolina on the proprietors, or on the Barbadians they recruited, or on other colonists who quickly adopted the latter's mind-set and methods, is a moot point. What is certain is that it was a poisoned wellspring from which the colony drank. In no other colony in North America did slaveholders establish and maintain hegemony from the outset. South Carolina was not doomed to slavery by necessity; it adopted that vile institution by choice . . . and paid the price for centuries to come.[8]

It is difficult to analyze the past uncritically, to describe behavior that we consider shameful without injecting a note or tone of censure. For historians, objectivity is as essential as it is difficult; as Lynn Hunt pointed out, moral judgments blur our understanding of the past. It could be argued, however, that humanity transcends historical periods—that in every age, people recognize inhumanity when they see it. Along those lines historians who describe brutality and injustice in former times are not obliged to rationalize them or downplay their effects just because they were commonplace. Peter Wood, author of *Black Majority: Negroes in Colonial South Carolina from 1670 through the Stono Rebellion*, recently pointed out that in the past several decades, historians who have spoken of inequality in early America have been criticized for "exaggeration, presentism, or alarmist hyperbole." Wood says, "We live in a nation in denial" and suggests that in discussions of the South, we substitute the term "slave labor camp" for the word "plantation." Gary Nash believes the concept of historical inevitability tends to free past generations from responsibility for their actions, "no matter how deplorable," because it holds that larger forces—environmental and geographic, moral and political, or economic and social—dictated the way individuals acted. Only in recent years, he writes, has the refusal to "acknowledge and explore human culpability" been overturned.[9]

---

8. A century after the first arrival of enslaved Africans at Charles Town, Thomas Jefferson penned this reflection on the institution of slavery: "Indeed I tremble for my country when I reflect that God is just: that his justice cannot sleep forever." When Jefferson wrote these words in 1781, South Carolina was the only state with a black majority and probably the state most determined to perpetuate the use of slave labor. Subsequent events proved that Jefferson's fears were not unwarranted. Jefferson, *Notes on the State of Virginia*, Query XVIII, in Ford, ed., *The Writings of Thomas Jefferson*, 4: 232.

9. Sabine Cherenfant, *Presentism: Reexamining Historical Figures Through Today's Lens* (New York: Greenhaven Publishing, LLC, 2019), 7; Lynn Hunt, "The Problem with Presentism is That It Blurs Our Understanding of the Past," in Ibid., 12; Peter Wood, "Slave Labor Camps in Early America," in Cherenfant, *Presentism*, 223; Gary Nash, "The Concept of Inevitability in the History of European-Indian Relations," in Carla Gardina Pestana and Sharon V. Salinger, ed., *Inequality in Early America* (Hanover: University Press of New England, 1999), 16–17. A recent work of note by Fred Witzig examines the life of Reverend Alexander Garden of Charles Town—a "minister . . . husband, father,

Collectively, leading scholars have painted a grim picture of colonial South Carolina. Max Edelson dryly reminds us that planters "wrenched slaves into this new world of work with violence." Every master was free to brutalize his slaves, "backed by the coercive power of the state and sanctioned by a version of the Barbados slave code." Describing the "rising refinement of material life" of rice planters, Edelson plainly states, "This contrast between white urban pleasures and black rural suffering indicts planters for their luxury, as well as their brutality. It also explains how they were able to shield themselves from an ever-present awareness of their moral accountability." Alan Gallay considers it unfair to expect past people "to consider an institution wrong that their generation viewed as legitimate and moral," but he goes on to say that Carolina's slave trade—the most large-scale enslavement of Indians in the English Empire—was "undertaken illegally by Carolina laws and moral standards." Gallay notes that the colony's "great" men ruled "in order to line their pockets, not serve the common good," and over three centuries ago, the proprietors castigated South Carolina officials for "wrongheaded and immoral behavior."[10]

In the opening pages of *Slavery, Disease, and Suffering in the Southern Lowcountry*, Peter McCandless describes the sanitization of lowcountry history. After a thorough examination of the historical record, he arrived at an explanation for much of the "immense suffering" in South Carolina: "One can call it greed or, more prosaically, economic forces, local and global, that produced the plantation system and ultimately a perverse denial of its epidemiological consequences."[11] Peter Coclanis cautions that no one "should moralize excessively" about the "flawed" behavior of South Carolinians, yet he seems taken

---

friend, religious administrator, and spiritual pastor" who also became "a slave master, a land speculator, a doyen of high society, and a pioneer in slave education." Witzig acknowledges that Garden was "blinded to a debilitating moral defect—slavery" and offers two contrasting interpretations: "Perhaps . . . [Garden's] failings were too much shared by everyone . . . or perhaps the reader will reckon their [Garden's and Charles Town's] story nothing but a tragedy, a horrific tale of exploitation and abuse." Witzig, *Life of the Reverend Alexander Garden, 1685–1756*, preface.

10. Edelson, *Plantation Enterprise*, 83, 164–65; Gallay, *Indian Slave Trade*, 63–65. Charles Joyner observed that "Slavery can be made to appear either benign or barbaric . . . depending on what evidence is emphasized and what evidence is suppressed." Joyner, *Down by the Riverside*, xvi.

11. McCandless, *Slavery, Disease, and Suffering*, 16. McCandless wonders whether carriage drivers in Charleston talk about "how much people suffered to produce this unique slice of Old South ambiance," whether they describe the diseases that "constantly assailed and thinned the population," and whether tourists understand that the

aback by the colony's "shocking mortality" and "mass misery," and ultimately describes the Carolina lowcountry as an "inconsolable landscape, evoking loneliness, gloom, melancholy...a dismal little corner of the world in a brutish period long past." [12]

The darkness of *this* particular historical narrative is not the product of the author's imagination. Rather, the bleak interpretation presented in these pages is based on the experiences of *all* inhabitants of South Carolina, not just the "great men" celebrated in outdated historical accounts. Without question, certain colonists should be singled out for their role in raising Charles Town up from a rude settlement to a bustling seaport—the most important one in the Southeast. The cast of notables includes merchants whose international connections were crucial to the colony's growth, planters whose operations produced vast quantities of rice, advancing South Carolina's interests in commercial networks that crisscrossed the Atlantic, and officials, clergymen, and families, such as the Pinckneys and Rutledges, who made significant contributions in their time. But an honest reckoning of the colony's first half-century must give due consideration to the *other* people in South Carolina—men, women, and children of different races and ethnicities who endured not only the calamities that tested the mettle of the colony's elite, but also a host of other crises and hardships. This work examines the challenges that humble colonists faced, the setbacks they experienced, and the impact of policies and practices they did not initiate. In the first fifty years, success was hard earned and often slow in coming, unlike the storms, fires, epidemics, and violence that destroyed property, lives, and dreams in a heartbeat.

In every historical study, certain things are left out or given scant mention. One shortcoming of most accounts of colonial America is the lack of information about individual women and children.[13] Extant records from South

---

stink of dung and urine in Charleston would have been exacerbated by "the smells of cesspits, hog and cattle pens, slaughterhouses, dead dogs, cats, and humans." Ibid., 3–4.

12. Coclanis, *Shadow of a Dream*, 28–30, 143. In another recent work, L. H. Roper addresses Proprietary South Carolina's "often shabby and occasionally sordid story" (Roper, *Conceiving Carolina*, 2). Matthew Jennings's essay, "Cutting one anothers Throats": British, Native, and African Violence in Early Carolina," and other entries in LeMaster and Wood, ed., *Creating and Contesting Carolina: Proprietary Era Histories*, are fine examples of much-needed revisionist histories that advance our understanding of South Carolina in the colonial period.

13. Some of the best recent scholarship on specific women in colonial South Carolina appears in volume 1 of *South Carolina Women: Their Lives and Times*. Essays cover "The Lady of Cofitachequi"; Huguenot Judith Giton; Mary Fisher, Sophia Hume, and the

Carolina's first fifty years offer tantalizing snippets, but not much else. In November 1718 a sea battle took place between pirates and four ships armed to defend Charles Town. When one of the pirate ships was defeated and the hatches opened, South Carolinians found thirty-six women from London. They were among the 106 convicts and servants being transported to Virginia and Maryland when their vessel, the *Eagle*, was taken on the high seas.[14] The names and individual fates of those women are lost to history. In a similar vein, the only thing we know about Mary Newman, buried in Charles Town in July 1720, was that parish records described her as "a poor-woman." Three months later, another "poor woman" was interred, but the parish secretary did not even have a name to enter in his ledger. In Charles Town the interment of women who died in poverty and relative anonymity only accelerated in the next few decades. According to St. Philips's parish register, thirty people "from the workhouse" were buried in the 1740s; many of them were widows or impoverished single mothers. In the same decade, at least one hundred other Charles Town inhabitants were buried at parish expense.[15] The peril that children in early Carolina faced is also evident in St. Philip's parish records.[16] The first entry in the list of recorded burials for 1720–21 was that of "Mortimer, a Child" on May 10, 1720; another child was buried on May 24, and six more children were buried in June. Only two children were buried in July, but in July of the following year, seven of the eight parishioners buried in Charles Town were children.[17]

Quakers of Colonial Charleston; Mary-Anne Schad and Mrs. Brown (overseers' wives); and Eliza Lucas Pinckney and Harriott Pinckney Horry. *South Carolina Women*, Spruill, Littlefield, and Johnson, eds., 1–109.

14. Shirley Carter Hughson, "The Carolina Pirates and Colonial Commerce, 1670–1740," *The Johns Hopkins University Studies in Historical and Political Science*, Herbert B. Adams, ed., 12th series, vols. 5–7 (Baltimore: Johns Hopkins University Press, May–July 1894): 115–19.

15. Alexander S. Salley, Jr., ed., *Register of St. Philip's Parish, Charles Town, South Carolina, 1720–1758* (Charleston: Walker, Evans & Cogswell Co., 1904), 269–71. Outbreaks of yellow fever in 1745 and 1748 may have been responsible for some of the thirty deaths but the highest morbidity in the workhouse was in 1740, 1742, and 1747.

16. In 1682 Thomas Ashe wrote that the air in Carolina was "so serene and excellent a temper, that the Indian Natives prolong their days to the Extremity of Old Age." Ashe admitted that the summer months sometimes brought on "Touches of Agues and Fevers ... [but] never Fatal." English children born in the colony were "strong and lusty, of sound Constitutions, and fresh ruddy Complexions." Ashe, *Carolina, or a Description*, in Salley, *Narratives*, 141.

17. Salley, ed., *Register of St. Philip's Parish*, 223–25.

Thanks to the work of various scholars we know about some of the women who inhabited South Carolina in its first half-century. Several historians have written about Judith Giton, the Huguenot who came to Carolina in 1686. She bore five children before dying in 1711 at age forty-six. Giton predeceased her husband, Pierre Manigault, and when he died he bequeathed two enslaved women and a child to Judith's daughter and namesake. Pierre gave Gabriel, Judith's youngest son, a sizeable estate, including an enslaved woman, girl, and child; he also gave each of his granddaughters a young female slave.[18] Colony and family records offer this information about Judith and her five children. But how much do we know about the three enslaved women, three enslaved girls, and two enslaved children that Judith's offspring inherited? Unfortunately these gaps in our historical knowledge encompass the majority of the women and children who lived in South Carolina between 1670 and 1720, especially Native Americans and enslaved Africans.

This work has called attention to the intimidation, physical abuse, and unabashed exploitation of slaves in Barbados and South Carolina. During the proprietary period, virtually everyone in the lowcountry had reason to fear what the morrow might bring. The difference was that the elite were able to control their destinies to some degree; they had money and power and options that others lacked. The colony's demographic profile sprang from the actions of planters and merchants atop the socioeconomic pyramid—men who bought and sold Africans and Native Americans, established quotas and tariffs, drafted repressive slave codes, and monopolized the Indian trade. Between 1670 and 1720, southeastern tribes remained a formidable presence, but their interactions with English officeholders, colonists, and traders gnawed at their own autonomy and cultures like some internal parasite. European diseases were merely the coup de grâce.

It would not be difficult to paint a significantly different picture of South Carolina's early years—one that accentuates the positive(s). Doctor Henry Woodward is credited with being the first English settler in South Carolina. In 1666 Woodward chose to remain with Native Americans at Port Royal when his fellow explorers departed for England. He spent "some considerable time amongst the natives," learning their language and customs. Once Charles Town was established, Woodward acted as interpreter, ambassador, and quartermaster, procuring corn and other provisions from the Westos, Yamasee, and Lower Creek Indians. Hailed by the Lords Proprietors for his

18. Caroline T. Moore and Agatha Aimar Simmons, ed., *Abstract of the Wills of the State of South Carolina: 1670–1740* (Columbia, 1960), 18–19, in Van Ruymbeke, "Judith Giton," 37.

"industry and hazard," Woodward was given two thousand acres and appointed Indian agent.[19] Scholars hail Woodward's "crucial role in the success of the Carolina colony," noting his diplomatic skills in extending the colony's trade network and opening a "new arena of competition between the Spanish and British empires in North America."[20] However, if one considers the impact of that rivalry on colonists in Florida, South Carolina, and Georgia, as well as the effects of the Indian trade on southeastern tribes, Woodward's legacy suffers quite a blow. Intermittent warfare with the Spanish hardly improved the lives of South Carolinians, and the exchange networks that Woodward initiated fairly devastated the tribes he befriended. Charles Town's appetite for deerskins fostered sweeping changes in Native American culture, corrupting Indians' relationship to their natural environment. It also lured them into a pernicious dependence on European goods and weapons, advancing their economic and political subordination.[21] The Indian slave trade poisoned relations between the tribes in the southeast and culminated in a war that pushed the colony to the brink of extinction.[22] In many ways Henry Woodward paved the way for the destruction of Native Americans and their culture.

19. Joseph W. Barnwell, "Dr. Henry Woodward, the First English Settler in South Carolina, and Some of His Descendants," *South Carolina Historical and Genealogical Magazine* 8, no. 1 (January 1907): 30–32.

20. Eric E. Bowne, "Dr. Henry Woodward's Role in Early Carolina Indian Relations," in LeMaster and Wood, eds., *Creating and Contesting Carolina*, 89; Daniel S. Dupre, *Alabama's Frontiers and the Rise of the Old South* (Bloomington: Indiana University Press, 2018), 68–70.

21. The destructive influence of the "Indian trade" is described in many works; see Kathryn E. Braund, *Deerskins and Duffels: Creek Indian Trade with Anglo-America, 1685–1815* (Lincoln: University of Nebraska Press, 1993), passim; Joseph M. Hall, Jr., *Zamumo's Gifts: Indian-European Exchange in the Colonial Southeast* (Philadelphia: University of Pennsylvania Press, 2009), passim. Trade with Europeans also exposed Native Americans to diseases for which they had no immunity, exacerbating the process of depopulation that accompanied the Indian slave trade. Paul Kelton, "The Great Southeastern Smallpox Epidemic, 1690–1700: The Region's First Major Epidemic?," in Ethridge and Hudson, eds., *Transformation of the Southeastern Indians*, 21–37; Paul Kelton, *Epidemics & Enslavement: Biological Catastrophe in the Native Southeast, 1492–1715* (Lincoln: University of Nebraska Press, 2007), passim.

22. It would be difficult to overstate the impact of diseases that the Indian trade spread. In 1707 John Archdale wrote that it "pleased Almighty God to send unusual Sicknesses amongst them, as the Smallpox, etc., to lessen their Numbers." [Archdale, *A New Description*, in Salley, Jr., *Narratives*, 285.] For every seven Native Americans

An author intent on writing a positive account of South Carolina's first half-century could quote Thomas Nairne, who wrote: "There is no Place in the Continent of *America*, where People can transport themselves to greater Advantage." Nairne's testimony that "the Indians with whom we are in Friendship . . . [are] reckon'd a very considerable Part of our Strength" speaks well of the colonists' relations with their Native American neighbors.[23] In 1707 Charles Town traders dealt "near 1,000 miles into the Continent," expanding British influence and South Carolina's commercial prospects.[24] On the other hand, deeper investigation reveals that between 1670 and 1715, between thirty and fifty thousand Southern Indians were captured, exported, and sold in the slave trade initiated by Nairne's contemporaries.[25] In 1708 Nairne contacted the Earl of Sunderland, the British secretary of state, to outline a plan whereby Englishmen could conquer the southeast, enslave any Native Americans who resisted, and then "build a plantation economy worked by African and Indian slaves on the ruins of Indian villages."[26] Seven years later, Nairne's Yamasee allies—those with whom the colony was "in friendship"—tied him to a stake and pierced his flesh with "slivers of resinous fat pine wood" which were then set afire. He was tortured for three days before he expired.[27]

For a glowing account of early Carolina, writers can turn to Dr. Francis Le Jau, the SPG missionary so often quoted in this and other works. Le Jau thought South Carolina had "the finest climate I ever saw." He reported to his superiors in London that he was healthy and "well contented" in his new home. He was impressed by the gentility, politeness, and "handsome way of living" that he observed. In his view, poor families could "live very well" in the province—"they shall have plenty of things necessary for life if they be

---

dwelling in the lowcountry in 1576, there was only one there in 1776. Coclanis, *Shadow of a Dream*, 47.

23. Nairne, *Letter from South Carolina*, 8–32; Rowland et al., *History of Beaufort County*, 91.

24. Archdale, *A New Description*, in Salley, ed., *Narratives*, 363. In 1707 the Goose Creek men pushed through legislation that concentrated the deerskin trade in Charleston; this gave a significant advantage to merchants who acted as intermediaries between the town and traders operating in their interior. Hart, *Building Charleston*, 25.

25. Gallay, *Indian Slave Trade*, 299. Francis Le Jau blamed intertribal violence on white traders who encouraged "that Bloody Inclination in order to get Slaves." S.P.G., series A., vol. 4, No. 64, April 22, 1708, cited in Pennington, "Reverend Francis Le Jau's Work . . .," 446.

26. Hewitt, "The State in the Planters' Service," in Greene et al., *Money, Trade, and Power*, 55.

27. Nairne, *Letter from South Carolina*, 31–32; Crane, *Southern Frontier*, 169.

industrious." Le Jau's early letters make a fine promotional tract; the missionary left a flattering description of the colony, if one ignores his later correspondence. In 1715 Le Jau calculated that he had been ill for six of his ten years in South Carolina. His Goose Creek parishioners, a notoriously unprincipled lot, "would do any thing for money." Le Jau grieved to see his fellow Christians abuse slaves and instigate tribal wars. After the members of Le Jau's church ignored his pleas for financial assistance, the distraught missionary warned any who were inclined to follow in his footsteps that they "must prepare to suffer great hardships and crosses" in South Carolina.[28]

Scholars who prefer to portray prominent individuals need look no further than Arthur Middleton, one of the colony's foremost planters and politicians. Born in South Carolina, Middleton was trained as a merchant in London and returned to the lowcountry in 1703. He served in both houses of the Assembly and became a member of the Council. Middleton later led the opposition against the proprietors, sat on the royal council, and became acting governor in 1725. Active in the militia as well as the Anglican Church and free schools, Middleton bequeathed more than eighteen thousand acres of land to his heirs. His grandson was second president of the First Continental Congress and a signer of the Declaration of Independence. Middleton's accomplishments were certainly notable, but historians really ought to mention that his fortune derived in part from his father's sugar plantations in Barbados (virtual killing fields for enslaved Africans), and Middleton's involvement in both the African and Indian slave trades. In South Carolina, his family profited handsomely from the labor of enslaved 3,500 African men, women, and children.[29] Middleton used his political influence to amass large land grants; he and his descendants eventually owned twenty-eight plantations. As acting governor, Middleton dissolved the general assembly five times in two years—a period of "near anarchy"—and the Commons House of Assembly censured him.[30] He had eight children, but five died in infancy. In 1737 Middleton succumbed to malaria or one of the other lowcountry diseases that

28. Le Jau to the Secretary, in *The Carolina Chronicle*, 16–62, 88–89, 108–11, in McCandless, *Slavery, Disease, and Suffering*, 14–16, 59.

29. Barbara Doyle, Mary Edna Sullivan, Tracey Todd, *Beyond the Fields: Slavery at Middleton Place* (Columbia: University of South Carolina Press, 2008), 11–13. In 1684 Arthur Middleton, Sr., was displaced from the council for trespassing on the privileges of the Lords Proprietors by shipping Indian slaves to Barbados. Edward McCrady, "Slavery in the Province of South Carolina, 1670–1770," *Annual Report of the American Historical Association for the Year 1895* (Washington: Government Printing Office, 1896), 642.

30. Sirmans, *Colonial South Carolina*, 158.

killed countless Africans who worked in his fields.[31] Arthur Middleton's career demonstrated that a man just needed capital and the will to act as if he had "a Right to every thing…even to one another's body" in order to succeed in colonial South Carolina.[32]

To portray the entrepreneurial spirit of early South Carolinians, one might lionize Charles Lowndes, who emigrated from St. Kitts with his family and his slaves. When the South Carolina Assembly passed *An Act to encourage Charles Lowndes, Esqr. to make a New Machine to pound and Beat Rice*, it distinguished the Goose Creek resident as a man whose energy and vision might benefit the entire colony.[33] But the historical record, when fully disclosed, tells otherwise. Two years later Lowndes announced his intention to go to the West Indies. Shortly after his estate was sold at auction in 1736, Lowndes narrated "a full Account of the Misfortunes he met with since his Arrival in this Province."[34] He later described "unjust Proceedings against him" and said he would clear his name or die "by cutting an Arterie or shooting himself through the Head." Lowndes confessed that he was "very much tempted to kill all his Children." Jailed for not supporting his family, Lowndes composed a "Memorial" that blamed several contemporaries for his downfall. He wrote a letter inviting an associate to his funeral, and then shaved, dressed, lay down with a "loaden Pistol" in each hand, and "blew out his Brains."[35]

31. Alexander Moore, "Middleton, Arthur (1681–7 September 1737)," *American National Biography*, online (February, 2000), accessed Jan. 30, 2019.

32. Hobbes, *Leviathan*, 62. Hobbesian notions persisted in South Carolina far into the future. In 1861, slaveholder Leonidas Spratt worried that the competition for enslaved African-Americans coming from the Gulf States might result in an increase in "pauper labor" in South Carolina and "democracy may gain a foothold." South Carolina planters attempted to reopen the slave trade and, when that failed, 'to advocate for slavery in the abstract—essentially, slavery regardless of race." Slaveholders would "no longer have to fear masterless whites that they long struggled to control." Keri Leigh Merritt, *Masterless Men, Poor Whites and Slavery in the Antebellum South* (Cambridge: Cambridge University Press, 2017), 91.

33. "An Act to encourage Charles Lowndes, Esqr. to make a New Machine to pound and Beat Rice, and appropriate the benefit thereof to himself," June 9, 1733, *The Statutes at Large of South Carolina, Volume Sixth, containing the Acts from 1814 to 1838*, David McCord, ed. (Columbia: A. S. Johnston, 1839), appendix, 620–21.

34. *South Carolina Gazette*, January 25, 1734. Lowndes's letter, dated November 5, 1735, was paraphrased in the *South Carolina Gazette*, June 5, 1736.

35. George Bigelow Chase, *Lowndes of South Carolina: An Historical and Genealogical Memoir* (Boston: A. Williams and Co., 1876), 12–17. The *South Carolina Gazette* reported Lowndes's suicide and carried an announcement that his remaining slaves would be

Scholars have written remarkable books, many of them cited in this work, that describe the emergence of South Carolina's lucrative rice and indigo trades and the rise of a "New World Gentry." But the disappointments, failures, personal tragedies, and transgressions that occurred in earlier decades also comprise worthwhile historical narratives.[36] Thomas Hobbes postulated that wherever the sole restraint on men's conduct was their own moral code, there would be "continual fear, and danger of violent death" ... civility would be replaced by "a condition of War of every one against every one."[37] Between 1670 and 1720, colonists in South Carolina may not have considered themselves an "enemy to every man," but they had enemies enough. Threatened by their Spanish rivals, by the Native Americans they exploited, and by the Africans they enslaved and abused, most whites did live in continual fear. For some, it was the price they paid for the riches they accumulated. For many, there were no riches, and the possibility of a sudden, violent death was overshadowed by the misery of their day-to-day existence—a grim slog marked by sickness, grief, and want.

---

sold to the highest bidder. Lowndes's wife returned to St. Kitts with his eldest son, but his two younger sons remained in Carolina. [*South Carolina Gazette*, June 5, 1736.] Rawlins Lowndes later became Provost Marshal, Speaker of the House, and President of South Carolina (1778).

36. Waterhouse, *New World Gentry*, passim.

37. Hobbes, *Leviathan*, 62. In 1711, Francis Le Jau observed that in South Carolina, "[m]any believe nothing at all of Religion; the Contagion I perceive is passed into mean Persons & illiterate Men who argue most blasphemously & live scandalously." Le Jau to the Secretary, July 10, 1711, in *The Carolina Chronicle*, 93.

BIBLIOGRAPHY

Primary Sources

Assorted Historical Documents

"A Briefe Relation of the Voyage Unto Maryland by Father Andrew White." In C. C. Hall, ed., *Narratives of Early Maryland, 1633–1684*. New York: Charles Scribner's Sons, 1910.

"Copy of a Representation of the Lords Commissioners for Trade and Plantations to the King upon the State of His Majesties Colonies & Plantations on the Continent of North America, dated September the 8th 1721." In John Romeyn Brodhead, ed., *Documents relative to the colonial history of the State of New-York: procured in Holland, England and France*. Albany: Weed, Parsons and Company, 1855.

"Deposition of John Cole of Stepney, Middlesex, mariner, age 39, and late Commander of the 'John' of London." In Peter Wilson Coldham, *Lord Mayor's Court of London, Depositions Relating to Americans, 1641–1736*. Arlington: National Genealogical Society, 1980.

"Governor Gibbes' Speech to the Assembly, May 15, 1711." Reprinted in David Duncan Wallace, *The History of South Carolina*, vol. 1. New York: American Historical Society, 1934.

"Grievances of the Inhabitants of Barbados." Cited in Hilary Beckles, *White Servitude and Black Slavery in Barbados, 1627–1715*. Knoxville: University of Tennessee Press, 1989.

"Instructions for Collonell Phillipp Ludwell, [*sic*] Governor of Carolina, May 20, 1692." In Alexander S. Salley, Jr., ed., *Commissions and Instructions from the Lords Proprietors of Carolina to Public Officials of South Carolina, 1685–1715*. Columbia: The State Co., 1916.

"Journal, July 715: Journal Book R." In *Journals of the Board of Trade and Plantations*, vol. 3, March 1715–October 1718, edited by K. H. Ledward. London: His Majesty's Stationery Office 1924. British History Online, accessed January 9, 2019, http://www.british-history.ac.uk/jrnl-trade-plantations/vol3.

"Minutes of Council of Barbados: Order for sundry payments to officers, and for payment of ten guineas to Alice Mills for castrating forty-two negroes according to sentence of the Commissioners for trial of rebellious negroes." Great Britain Public Office. *Calendar of State Papers*. Col. Entry Bk., vol. 12. London: Longman, 1908.

"Number VIII. To the Honorable the Trustees for Establishing the Colony of Georgia in America" (1738). In *The Colonial Records of the State of Georgia*, vol. 3, edited by Allen D. Candler. Atlanta: Franklin Printing and Publishing Company, 1905.

"Number X." In *The Colonial Records of the State of Georgia*, vol. 3, edited by Allen D. Candler. Atlanta: Franklin Printing and Publishing Company, 1905.

"Official Report on the State of the Province, 1708." In Yates Snowden and Harry Gardner Cutler, *History of South Carolina*, vol. 1. Chicago and New York: Lewis Publishing Company, 1928.

"Paper to the Lords Proprietors c. 1686." Quoted in J. G. Dunlop, "Spanish Depredations, 1686." *South Carolina Historical & Genealogical Magazine* 30, no. 2 (1929): 81–89.

"Petition of William Miles" (1725). *The Journal of the Commons House of Assembly of South Carolina, November 1, 1725–April 30, 1726*, edited by Alexander S. Salley, Jr. Columbia: Printed for the Historical Commission of South Carolina by the State Co., 1945.

"Report of Governor N. Johnson" (1708). In William J. Rivers, *A Sketch of the History of South Carolina to the Close of the Proprietary Government by the Revolution of 1719; With an Appendix Containing Many Valuable Records Hitherto Unpublished*. Charleston: McCarter & Co., 1856.

"Report of the War Board of the Indies to the Queen" (1674). Reprinted in José Miguel Gallardo, "The Spaniards and the English Settlement in Charles Town." *The South Carolina Historical and Genealogical Magazine* 37, no. 2 (April 1936): 49–64.

"The Representation and Address of several of the Members of this present Assembly return'd for Colleton County, and other the Inhabitants of this Province . . ." (1703). In William J. Rivers, *A Sketch of the History of South Carolina*. Charleston: McCarter & Co., 1856.

"Trade Revived." Pamphlet. Quoted in *Leigh Hunt's London Journal* 1, no. 29. London: Charles Knight, 1834.

A Brief, but Most True Relation of the Late Barbarous and Bloody Plot of the Negro's in the Island of Barbados on Friday the 21 of October, 1692. London: 1693. Quoted in Jerome Handler, "Slave Revolts and Conspiracies in Seventeenth-Century Barbados." *New West Indian Guide* 56, no. 1/2 (1982): 5–42.

Ash, John. "The Present State of Affairs in Carolina, by John Ash, 1706." In Alexander S. Salley, Jr., ed., *Narratives of Early Carolina 1650–1708*. New York: Barnes & Noble, 1911.

Colt, Sir Henry. "The Voyage of Sir Henrye Colt Knight to the Ilands of the Antilles." In Vincent T. Harlow, ed., *Colonising Expeditions to the West Indies and Guiana, 1623*. Publications of the Hakluyt Society, 2nd series, vol. 56. London, 1925.

Evelyn, John. *Diary and Correspondence of John Evelyn, F.R.S.*, 4 vols. Edited by William Bray. London: George Bell & Sons, 1906.

Fortescue, J. W., ed. "Petition of several persons interested in Barbados to the King." *Calendar of State Papers: Colonial Series, America and West Indies*. vol. 14. London: Mackie and Co., 1903.

Great Newes From the Barbados. Or, a True and Faithful Account of the Grand Conspiracy of the Negroes Against the English. London, 1676. Quoted in Jerome Handler, "Slave Revolts and Conspiracies in Seventeenth-Century Barbados." *New West Indian Guide* 56, no. 1/2 (1982): 5–42.

Hilton, William. "A Relation of a Discovery by William Hilton, 1664." In *Narratives of Early Carolina 1650–1708*, edited by Alexander S. Salley, Jr. New York: Barnes & Noble, 1911.

Horne, Robert. "A Brief Description of the Province of Carolina." In *Narratives of Early Carolina 1650–1708*, edited by Alexander S. Salley, Jr. New York: Barnes & Noble, 1911.

Horne, Robert. "A Brief Description of the Province of Carolina on the coasts of Florida." 1708. Quoted in Abbot Emerson Smith, *Colonists in Bondage: White Servitude and Convict Labor in America, 1607–1776*. Gloucester: Peter Smith, 1965.

Hunt, Leigh. *Leigh Hunt's London Journal*. London: Sparrow & Co. (1834): 227.

Laudonnière, René Goulaine de. *A notable historie containing foure voyages made by certaine French Captaines into Florida*. In Richard Hakluyt, *Principal Navigations, Voyages, Traffiques and Discoveries of the English Nation*, ed. Edmund Goldsmid, vol. 13, part 2. 1599.

Littleton, Edward. *The groans of the plantations, or, A true account of their grievous and extreme sufferings by the heavy impositions upon sugar and other hardships relating more particularly to the island of Barbados*. London: Printed by M. Clark, 1689. Quoted in Richard S. Dunn, *Sugar and Slaves: The Rise of the Planter Class in the English West Indies, 1624–1713*. New York: Norton, 1973.

Milligen-Johnston, George. "A Short Description of the Province of South Carolina." In *Colonial South Carolina: Two Contemporary Descriptions*, edited by Chapman J. Milling. Columbia: 1951.

Plantagenet, Beauchamp. *A Description of the Province of New Albion*. London: 1648. Quoted in Jerome Handler, "Slave Revolts and Conspiracies in Seventeenth-Century Barbados." *New West Indian Guide* 56, no. 1/2 (1982): 5–42.

Quexos, Pedro de. "June 2, 1526. Replies by Pedro de Quijos [Quexos] to interrogatories administered on behalf of Matienzo." In Shea Papers, Georgetown University Library. Cited in Margaret F. Pickett and Dwayne W. Pickett, *The European Struggle to Settle North America: Colonizing Attempts by England, France and Spain, 1521–1608*. Jefferson, NC: McFarland & Co., 2010.

Ribault, Jean. "The Whole and True Discovery of Terra Florida." In *Reading the Roots: American Nature Writing Before Walden*, edited by Michael P. Branch. Athens: University of Georgia Press, 2004.

Sandford, Robert. "A Relation of a Voyage on the Coast of the Province of Carolina." In *Narratives of Early Carolina 1650–1708*, edited by Alexander S. Salley, Jr. New York: Barnes & Noble, 1911.

Stephens, William. "A Journal of the Proceedings in Georgia, Beginning October 20, 1737." In *The Colonial Records of the State of Georgia, Vol. IV, Stephens' Journal 1737–1740*, edited by Lucian Lamar Knight, Milton Ready, and Kenneth Coleman. Atlanta: Franklin Printing and Publishing Company, 1906.

United States Commission on Boundary Between Venezuela and British Guiana. *Report and Accompanying Papers of the Commission Appointed by the President of the united States "to Investigate and Report Upon the True Divisional Line Between the Republic of*

Venezuela and British Guiana," vol. 1. Washington: Government Printing Office, 1897.

Wilson, Samuel. "An Account of the Province of Carolina." London, 1682. In Salley, ed., *Narratives of Early Carolina 1650–1708*. New York: Barnes & Noble, 1911.

Books (Primary)

Anonymous. *An Account Shewing the Progress of the Colony of Georgia in America from its First Establishment*. 1741. Reprinted in Trevor R. Reese, ed., *The Clamorous Malcontents: Criticisms & Defenses of the Colony of Georgia, 1741–1743*. Savannah: The Beehive Press, 1973.

Archdale, John. *A New Description of that Fertile and Pleasant Province of Carolina*. London, 1707. Reprinted in A. S. Salley, ed., *Narratives of Early Carolina 1650–1708*. New York: Barnes & Noble, 1911.

Archdale, John. *Records of the General Assembly: Acts, Bills and Joint Resolutions—Act of the General Assembly, March 2–16, 1696*. Columbia: South Carolina Department of Archives and History.

Ashe, Thomas. *Carolina, or a Description of the Present State of that Country*. London, 1682. In Alexander S. Salley, ed. *Narratives of Early Carolina 1650–1708*. New York: Barnes & Noble, 1911.

Benezet, Anthony. *Some Historical Account of Guinea: With an inquiry into the rise and progress of the slave trade*. London: J. Phillips, 1788.

Catesby, Mark. *Natural History of Carolina, Florida, and the Bahama Islands*. London, 1731–47. Quoted in Amy R. W. Myers, *Empire's Nature: Mark Catesby's New World Vision*. Chapel Hill: University of North Carolina Press, 1998.

Cheyes, Langdon, ed. *The Shaftesbury Papers and Other Records Relating to Carolina and the First Settlement on Ashley River Prior to the year 1676*. In *Collections of the South Carolina Historical Society*, vol. 5. Charleston: Published by the South Carolina Historical Society, 1897.

Cooper, Anthony Ashley. *Letters of the Earl of Shaftesbury, author of the Characteristicks, collected into one volume*. Glasgow: 1746. Eighteenth Century Collections Online; Gale.

Cooper, Thomas, ed. *The Statutes at Large of South Carolina, Volume Third, Containing the Acts from 1716 to 1752*. Columbia: A.S. Johnston, 1838.

Defoe, Daniel. *A General History of the Pyrates*. London, 1724. Reprinted Mineola: Dover Publications, 1999.

Defoe, Daniel. *Party-Tyranny*. 1701. Reprinted in *Narratives of Early Carolina 1650–1708*, edited by Alexander S. Salley, Jr. New York: Barnes & Noble, 1911.

Edwards, Jonathan. *Sinners in the Hands of an Angry God, A Sermon Preached at Enfield, July 8th 1741*. Boston: S. Kneeland and T. Green, 1741.

Forbes, Allyn B., ed. *Winthrop Papers, 1498–1649*, 5 vols. Boston: Massachusetts Historical Society Collections, 4th ser., vol. 5, 1929–47.

Ford, Paul L., ed. *The Writings of Thomas Jefferson*. New York: G.P. Putnam's Sons, 1892–99.

Grose, Francis. *A Classical Dictionary of the Vulgar Tongue*. London: Printed for S. Hooper, 1788.

Guild, June Purcell. *Black Laws of Virginia: A Summary of the Legislative Acts of Virginia Concerning Negroes from Earliest Times to the Present.* Richmond: Whittet & Shepperson, 1936.

Hall, Richard, comp. *Acts, Passed in the Island of Barbados: From 1643, to 1762 Inclusive.* London, 1764.

Hening, William Waller, ed. *The Statutes at Large; Being A Collection Of All The Laws Of Virginia, From The First Session Of the Legislature, In The Year 1619.* Richmond: Franklin Press, 1819.

Hewatt, Alexander. *An Historical Account of the Rise and Progress of the Colonies of South Carolina and Georgia*, vol. 1. London: Printed for Alexander Donaldson, 1779.

Hobbes, Thomas. *Leviathan: Or, The Matter, Form, and Power of a Common-Wealth Ecclesiastical and Civil.* London: Printed for Andrew Crooke, 1651.

Holland, Edwin C. *A refutation of the calumnies circulated against the southern & western states, respecting the institution and existence of slavery among them . . . by a South-Carolinian.* Charleston: A.K. Miller, 1822.

Jefferson, Thomas. *Notes on the State of Virginia*, Query XVIII. In *The Writings of Thomas Jefferson*, edited by Paul L. Ford, 232. New York: G.P. Putnam's Sons, 1892–99.

La Harpe, Jean-Baptiste Benard de. *The Historical Journal of the Establishment of the French in Louisiana.* [c.1730] Translated by Virginia Koenig and Joan Cain, edited by Glenn R. Conrad. Lafayette: University of Southwestern Louisiana Press, 1971.

Lawson, John. *A New Voyage to Carolina; Containing the Exact Description and Natural History Of That Country.* Chapel Hill: University of North Carolina Press, 1984.

Ledward, K. H., ed. *Journals of the Board of Trade and Plantations*, vol. 3, March 1715–October 1718. London: His Majesty's Stationery Office 1924. British History Online, accessed January 9, 2019, http://www.british-history.ac.uk/jrnl-trade-plantations/vol 3.

Le Jau, Francis. *The Carolina Chronicle of Dr. Francis Le Jau, 1706–1717.* Edited by Frank J. Klingberg. Berkeley: University of California Press, 1956.

Ligon, Richard. *A True History and Exact History of the Island of Barbados.* London, 1657. Karen Ordahl Kupperman, ed. Reprint, Indianapolis: Hackett Publishing, 2011.

Locke, John. *Two Treatises of Government.* Edited by Peter Laslett, rev. Cambridge: Cambridge University Press, 1988.

Mandeville, Bernard. *The Fable of the Bees and Other Writings.* Edited by E.J. Hundert. Indianapolis: Hackett Publishing, 1997.

Martyn, Benjamin. *An Impartial Enquiry into the State and Utility of the Province of Georgia*, 2nd edition. London: Printed for W. Meadows at the Angel in Cornhill, 1741.

McCord, David J., ed. *The Statutes of South Carolina, Volume Second, Containing the Acts from 1682 to 1716.* Columbia: A.S. Johnston, 1837.

McCord, David J, ed. *The Statutes at Large of South Carolina, Volume Seventh, Containing the Acts Relating to Charleston, Courts, Slaves, and Rivers.* Columbia: A.S. Johnston, 1840.

McCord, David J., ed. *The Statutes at Large of South Carolina, Volume Sixth, Containing the Acts from 1814 to 1838.* Columbia: A.S. Johnston, 1839.

Nairne, Thomas. *A letter from South Carolina: giving an account of the soil, air, product, trade, government, laws, religion, people, military strength, &c. of that province; together with the manner and necessary charges of settling a plantation there, and the annual profit it will produce.* London: A. Baldwin, 1710.

Norris, John. *Profitable Advice for Rich and Poor in a Dialogue, or Discourse between James Freeman, a Carolina Planter, AND Simon Question, a West-Country Farmer.* London, 1712. Reprinted in Jack P. Greene, ed., *Selling in a New World: Two Colonial South Carolina Promotional Pamphlets.* Columbia: University of South Carolina Press, 1989.

Pinckney, Elise, ed. *The Letterbook of Eliza Lucas Pinckney, 1739–1792.* Chapel Hill: University of North Carolina Press, 1972.

Reese, Trevor R., ed. *The Clamorous Malcontents: Criticisms & Defenses of the Colony of Georgia, 1741–1743.* Savannah: The Beehive Press, 1973.

Schoepf, Johann David. *Travels in the Confederation, 1783–1784.* Translated and Edited by Alfred J. Morrison. 1788. Reprint, Philadelphia: William J. Campbell, 1911.

Tertre, Pere Du. *Histoire Genrale des Antilles Habitees par Les Francais.* Paris: 1667–71. Cited in Thomas Southey, *Chronological History of the West Indies,* vol. 1. London: Longman, Rees, Orme, Brown, & Green, 1827.

Whitefield, George. *A Continuation of the Reverend Mr. Whitefield's Journal, from a few Days after his Return to Georgia to his Arrival at Falmouth on the 11th of March 1741 . . . The Seventh Journal.* London: W. Strahan for R. Hett, 1741.

Letters

"George Rodd to his Employer, May 8, 1715." In Karen Ordahl Kupperman, John C. Appleby, and Mandy Banton, eds., *Calendar of State Papers, Colonial Series, America and West Indies, 1574–1739,* vol. 28. London: Routledge, published in association with the Public Record Office, 2000.

"Hannah Williams to _____, Feb. 6, 1704/5, Charles Town." In Anonymous, "Early Letters from South Carolina Upon Natural History." *The South Carolina Historical and Genealogical Magazine* 21, no. 1 (January 1920): 3–9.

"Letter from Charleston." Quoted in Kenneth Scott, "Sufferers in the Charleston Fire of 1740." *The South Carolina Historical Magazine* 64, no. 4 (October 1963): 203–11.

"Letter from Samuel Dyssli, December 3, 1737." In R. W. Kelsey, "Swiss Settlers in South Carolina." *South Carolina Historical and Genealogical Magazine* 23, no. 3 (July 1922): 85–91.

"Letter of Henry Cromwell." 4th *Thurloes' State Papers.* Quoted in John Prendergast, *The Cromwellian Settlement of Ireland.* Baltimore: Genealogical Publishing Company, 2009.

"Letter of Hugh Adams." February 25, 1700. In *Diary of Samuel Sewall, 1700–1714.* Boston: Massachusetts Historical Society Collections, 5th series, volumes 11–12.

"Letter of Joseph West, June 26, 1670." In Alexander S. Salley, ed., *Narratives of Early Carolina 1650–1708.* New York: Barnes & Noble, 1911.

"Letter of rev. Jonas Michaelius (1628)." In *Narratives of New Netherland, 1609–1664,* vol. 8, edited by John Franklin Jameson, 126. New York: Charles Scribner's Sons, 1909.

"Letter of Thomas Newe, August the 23, 1682." Reprinted in Alexander S. Salley, Jr., ed., *Narratives of Early Carolina 1650–1708.* New York: Barnes & Noble, 1911.

"Lrs from the new pretended Council and Assembly of Carolina, dated at Charles Town, the 24 Decr, 1719, relating to their having deposed their Govr, &c." Board of Trade, Vol. 10, Q. 199, State Paper Office. Cited in William James Rivers, *A Chapter in the Early History of South Carolina*. Charleston: Walker, Evans & Cogswell, 1874.

"Pinckney to Mrs. Cheesman, [c. March 1742], to [Miss Mary Bartlett], [March 1742], and entry dated March 11, 1741/2." In Elise Pinckney, ed., *The Letterbook of Eliza Lucas Pinckney, 1739–1792*. Chapel Hill: University of North Carolina Press, 1972.

"Representation of the Board of Trade to the King upon the State of His Maj: Plantations in America." September 8, 1721. In William L. Saunders, ed., *The State Records of North Carolina, Vol. II, 1713 to 1728*. Raleigh: P.M. Hale, 1886.

"Rev. William Tredwell Bull to the Secretary." May 16, 1716. *Papers of the Society for the Propagation of the Gospel in Foreign Parts*, Series A, vol. 11. London: Society for the Propagation of the Gospel in Foreign Parts, n.d.

Acton, Lord. "Letter to Bishop Mandell Creighton, April 5, 1887." In John Emerich Edward Dalberg-Acton, *Historical Essays and Studies*. London: Macmillan, 1907. Database online. Appendix. Available from http://oll.libertyfund.org.

Glen, James. "An attempt towards an estimate of the value of South Carolina." Microfilm. Columbia: South Carolina Department of Archives and History. In Tim Lockley, "Rural Poor Relief in Colonial South Carolina." *The Historic Journal* 48, no. 4 (December 2005): 955–76.

Spotswood, Alexander. "Alexander Spotswood to Josia Burchett, Esq'r, July 16, 1715." In *The Official Letters of Alexander Spotswood, Lieutenant-Governor of the Colony of Virginia, 1710–1722* edited by R. A. Brock. Collections of the Virginia Historical Society: New Series, vol. 2. Richmond: Wm. Ellis Jones, 1885.

Vines, Richard. "Richard Vines to John Winthrop, July 19, 1647." In *Winthrop Papers, 1498–1649*, edited by Allyn B. Forbes, 5 vols. Boston: Massachusetts Historical Society Collections, 4th ser., vol. 5, 1929–47.

White, Edmund and J. G. Dunlop. "Letter from Edmund White to Joseph Morton." *The South Carolina Historical and Genealogical Magazine* 30, no. 1 (January 1929): 1–5.

Secondary Sources

Articles and Essays

Anonymous. "Early Letters from South Carolina Upon Natural History." *The South Carolina Historical and Genealogical Magazine* 21, no. 1 (January 1920): 3–9.

Anonymous. "Granting of Land in Colonial South Carolina." *The South Carolina Historical Magazine* 77, no. 3 (July 1976): 208–212.

Baldwin, Robert. "Patterns of Development in Newly Settled Regions." *Manchester School of Economic and Social Studies*, vol. 24 (1956): 161–79.

Barker, Eirlys M. "Indian Traders, Charles Town and London's Vital Link to the Interior of North America, 1717–1755." In Jack P. Greene, Rosemary Brana-Shute, and Randy J. Sparks, eds., *Money, Trade, and Power: The Evolution of Colonial South Carolina's Plantation Society*. Columbia: University of South Carolina Press, 2001.

Barnwell, Joseph W. "Dr. Henry Woodward, the First English Settler in South Carolina, and Some of His Descendants." *The South Carolina Historical and Genealogical Magazine* 8, no. 1 (January 1907): 29–41.

Beckles, Hilary. "A 'Riotous and Unruly Lot': Irish Indentured Servants and Freemen in the English West Indies, 1644–1713." *William and Mary Quarterly*, 3rd ser., 47, no. 4 (October 1990): 503–522.

Byrd, Michael D. "The First Charles Town Workhouse, 1738–1775: A Deterrent to White Pauperism?" *The South Carolina Historical Magazine* 110, no. 1/2 (January/April 2009): 35–52.

Carney, Judith. "Out of Africa: Colonial Rice History in the Black Atlantic." In Londa Schiebinger and Claudia Swan, eds., *Colonial Botany: Science, Commerce and Politics in the Early Modern World.* Philadelphia: University of Pennsylvania Press, 2005.

Childs, St. Julien R., ed. "A Letter Written in 1711 by Mary Stafford to her Kinswoman in England." *South Carolina Historical Magazine* 81, no. 1 (January 1980): 1–7.

Childs, St. Julien R. "The First South Carolinians." *The South Carolina Historical Magazine* 71, no. 2 (April 1970): 101–8.

Coby, Patrick. "The Law of Nature in Locke's Second Treatise: Is Locke a Hobbesian?" *The Review of Politics* 49, no. 1 (1987): 3–28.

Coclanis, Peter A. "Rice Prices in the 1720s and the Evolution of the South Carolina Economy." *The Journal of Southern History* 48, no. 4 (November 1982): 531–44.

Craton, Michael. "Property and propriety: Land tenure and slave property in the creation of a British West Indian plantocracy, 1612–1740." In *Early Modern Conceptions of Property*, edited by John Brewer and Susan Staves, 523–4. London: Routledge, 1996.

Duffy, John. "Yellow Fever in Colonial Charleston." *The South Carolina Historical and Genealogical Magazine* 52, no. 4 (October 1951): 189–97.

Dunlop, J.G. "Spanish Depredations, 1686." *The South Carolina Historical & Genealogical Magazine* 30, no. 2 (1929): 81–89.

Dunlop, J. G. and Mabel L. Webber, eds. "Paul Grimball's Losses by the Spanish Invasion." *South Carolina Historical and Genealogical Magazine* 29, no. 3 (July 1928): 231–37.

Dunn, Richard S. "The Barbados Census of 1680: Profile of the Richest Colony in English America." *The William and Mary Quarterly* 26, no. 1 (January 1969): 3–30.

Edelson, S. Max. "Defining Carolina: Cartography and Colonization in the North American Southeast, 1657–1733." In *Creating and Contesting Carolina: Proprietary Era Histories*, edited by Michelle LeMaster and Bradford J. Wood. Columbia: University of South Carolina Press, 2013.

Edmunson, George. "The Dutch in Western Guiana." *The English Historical Review*. S. R. Gardiner and Reginal L. Poole, eds. Vol. 14. London: Longmans, Green, and Co., 1901. 640–75.

Fraser, Walter J., Jr. "The City Elite, 'Disorder,' and the Poor Children of Pre-Revolutionary Charleston." *The South Carolina Historical Magazine* 84, no. 3 (July 1983): 167–79.

Gallardo, José Miguel. "The Spaniards and the English Settlement in Charles Town." *The South Carolina Historical and Genealogical Magazine* 37, no. 2 (April 1936): 49–64.

Gallay, Alan. "Planters and Slaves in the Great Awakening." In *Masters and Slaves in the House of the Lord: Race and Religion in the American South, 1740–1870*, edited by John B. Boles. Lexington: University Press of Kentucky, 2015.

Gaspar, David Barry. "With a Rod of Iron: Barbados Slave Laws as a Model for Jamaica, South Carolina and Antigua, 1661–1697." In *Crossing Boundaries: Comparative History of Black People in Diaspora*, edited by Darlene Clark Hine and Jacqueline McLeod. Bloomington: Indiana University Press, 1999.

Gouldner, Alvin W. "The Norm of Reciprocity: A Preliminary Statement." *American Sociological Review* 25, no. 2 (April 1960): 161–78.

Greene, Jack S. "Colonial South Carolina and the Caribbean Connection." *The South Carolina Historical Magazine* 88, no. 4 (October 1987): 192–10.

Hahn, Steven C. "The Mother of Necessity: Carolina, the Creek Indians, and the Making of a New Order in the American Southeast, 1670–1763." In Robie Ethridge and Charles M. Hudson, eds., *The Transformation of the Southeastern Indians, 1540–1760*. Jackson: University of Mississippi Press, 2002.

Handler, Jerome S. "Amerindians and their Contributions to Barbadian Life in the Seventeenth Century." *JBHMS* 35 (1977): 189–210.

Handler, Jerome S., ed. "Father Antoine Biet's Visit to Barbados in 1654." *JBHMS* 32 (May 1967): 56–76.

Handler, Jerome, S. "Slave Revolts and Conspiracies in Seventeenth-Century Barbados." *New West Indian Guide* 56, no. 1/2 (1982): 5–42.

Hughson, Shirley Carter. "The Carolina Pirates and Colonial Commerce, 1670–1740." *The Johns Hopkins University Studies in Historical and Political Science*, 12th series, vols. 5–7, Herbert B. Adams, ed. Baltimore: Johns Hopkins University Press, May–July 1894.

Jackson, Harvey H. "Hugh Bryan and the Evangelical Movement in Colonial South Carolina." *The William and Mary Quarterly*, 3rd series, 43 (October 1986): 594–614.

Kelsey, R. W. "Swiss Settlers in South Carolina." *South Carolina Historical and Genealogical Magazine* 23, no. 3 (July 1922): 85–91.

Kelton, Paul. "The Great Southeastern Smallpox Epidemic, 1690–1700: The Region's First Major Epidemic?" In Robbie Ethridge and Charles Hudson, eds., *The Transformation of the Southeastern Indians, 1540–1760*. Jackson: University Press of Mississippi, 2002.

Knight, Vernon J. and Sheree L. Adams. "A Voyage to the Mobile and Tomeh in 1700, with Notes on the Interior of Alabama." *Ethnohistory* 28, no. 2 (Spring 1981): 179–94.

Lockley, Tim. "Rural Poor Relief in Colonial South Carolina." *The Historical Journal* 48, no. 4 (December 2005): 955–76.

Mancall, Peter C., Joshua L. Rosenbloom, and Thomas Weiss. "Slave Prices and the South Carolina Economy, 1722–1809." *The Journal of Economic History* 61, no. 3 (September 2001): 616–39.

Matthews, Maurice. "A Contemporary View of Carolina in 1680." *The South Carolina Historical Magazine* 55, no. 3 (July 1954): 153–59.

McClain, Molly and Alessa Ellefson, "A Letter from Carolina, 1688: French Huguenots in the New World." *The William and Mary Quarterly*, 3rd Series, 64, no. 2 (April 2007): 377–94.

McCrady, Edward. "Slavery in the Province of South Carolina, 1670–1770." *Annual Report of the American Historical Association for the Year 1895* (1895): 631–73.

McCully, Bruce T., ed. "The Charleston Government Act of 1722: A Neglected Document." *The South Carolina Historical Magazine* 83, no. 4 (October 1982): 303–19.

McNeill, J.R. "Yellow Jack and Geopolitics: Environment, Epidemics, and the Struggles for Empire in the American Tropics, 1650–1825." *OAH Magazine of History* 18, no. 3 (April 2004): 9–13.

Melvin, Patrick. "Captain Florence O'Sullivan and the Origins of Carolina." *The South Carolina Historical Magazine* 76, no. 4 (October 1975): 235–49.

Menard, Russell. "Financing the Lowcountry Export Boom: Capital and Growth in Early South Carolina." *The William and Mary Quarterly* 51, no. 4 (October 1994): 659–76.

Menard, Russell. "Transitions to African Slavery in British America, 1630–1730: Barbados, Virginia and South Carolina." *Indian Historical Review* 15 (1988–89). Reprinted in Kenneth Morgan, ed., *Slavery in America: A Reader and Guide*. Athens: University of Georgia Press, 2005.

Merrens, H. Roy and George D. Terry. "Dying in Paradise: Malaria, Mortality, and the Perceptual Environment in Colonial South Carolina." *Journal of Southern History* 50, no. 4 (November 1984): 533–50.

Montiano, Manuel de. "Letters of Manuel de Montiano: Siege of St. Agustine [*sic*]." No. 248, Florida, Jan. 2, 1741. *Collections of the Georgia Historical Society* 7, no. 1. Savannah: Georgia Historical Society, 1909: 1–70.

Moore, Alexander. "Daniel Axtell's Account Book and the Economy of Early South Carolina." *The South Carolina Historical Magazine* 95, no. 4 (October 1994): 280–301.

Moore, Alexander. "Marooned: Politics and Revolution in the Bahamas Islands and Carolina." In *Creating and Contesting Carolina: Proprietary Era Histories*, edited by Michelle LeMaster and Bradford J. Wood. Columbia: University of South Carolina Press, 2013.

Nash, R.C. "Trade and Business in Eighteenth-Century South Carolina: The Career of John Guerard, Merchant and Planter." *South Carolina Historical Magazine* 96, no. 1 (January 1995): 6–29.

Navin, John J. "Servant or Slave? South Carolina's Inherited Labor Dilemma." *Proceedings of the South Carolina Historical Association* (2013): 77–90.

Otto, John Solomon. "Livestock-Raising in Early South Carolina, 1670–1700: Prelude to the Rice Plantation Economy." *Agricultural History* 61, no. 4 (Autumn 1987): 13–24.

Pennington, Edgar Legare. "The Reverend Francis Le Jau's Work Among Indians and Negro Slaves." *The Journal of Southern History* 1, no. 4 (November 1935): 442–58.

Proper, Emberson Edward. "Colonial Immigration Laws: A Study of the Regulation of Immigration by the English Colonies in America." *Studies in History, Economics and Public Law* 12, no. 2 (1900): 69.

Roberts, Justin and Ian Beamish. "Venturing Out: The Barbadian Diaspora and the Carolina Colony, 1650–1685." In *Creating and Contesting Carolina: Proprietary Era Histories*, edited by Michelle LeMaster and Bradford J. Wood. Columbia: University of South Carolina Press, 2013.

Roper, L. H. "The 1701 'Act for the better ordering of Slaves': Reconsidering the History of Slavery in Proprietary South Carolina." *The William and Mary Quarterly*, 3rd series, 64, no. 2 (April 2007): 395–418.

Ruymbeke, Bertrand van. "Judith Giton: From Southern France to the Carolina Low-country." In *South Carolina Women: Their Lives and Times*, vol. 1, edited by Marjorie Julian Spruill, Joan Marie Johnson, and Valinda W. Littlefield. Athens: University of Georgia Press, 2009.

Ruymbeke, Betrand van. "The Huguenots of Proprietary South Carolina: Patterns of Migration and Integration." In Jack P. Greene, Rosemary Brana-Shute, and Randy J. Sparks, eds., *Money, Trade, and Power: The Evolution of Colonial South Carolina's Plantation Society*. Columbia: University of South Carolina Press, 2001.

Scott, Kenneth. "Sufferers in the Charleston Fire of 1740." *The South Carolina Historical Magazine* 64, no. 4 (October 1963): 203–11.

Simmons, Slann Legare Clement, ed. "Early Manigault Records." *Transactions of the Huguenot Society of South Carolina* 59 (1954): 24.

Smith, Henry A. M. "The Baronies of South Carolina." II. *South Carolina Historical and Genealogical Magazine* 11, no. 4. (October 1910). 193–202.

Stanwood, Owen. "Between Eden and Empire: Huguenot Refugees and the Promise of New Worlds." *The American Historical Review* 118, no. 5 (December 2013): 1319–44.

Stanwood, Owen. "Imperial Vineyards: Wine and Politics in the Early American South." In Patrick Griffin, *Experiencing Empire: Power, People, and Revolution in Early America*. Charlottesville: University of Virginia Press, 2017.

Stewart, John, and J. G. Dunlop. "Letters from John Stewart to William Dunlop." *South Carolina Historical and Genealogical Magazine* 32, no. 1 (January 1931): 1–33.

Thompson, Peter, ed. "Henry Drax's Instructions on the Management of a Seventeenth-Century Barbadian Sugar Plantation." *The William and Mary Quarterly*, 3rd series, 66, no. 3 (July 2009): 565–604.

Wood, Peter H. "Black Labor, White Rice." In Gad J. Heuman, *The Slavery Reader*. New York: Routledge, 2003.

United States Commission on Boundary Between Venezuela and British Guiana. *Report and Accompanying Papers of the Commission Appointed by the President of the United States "to Investigate and Report Upon the True Divisional Line Between the Republic of Venezuela and British Guiana,"* vol. 1. Washington: Government Printing Office, 1897.

Dissertations

Lane, George W. "The Middletons of Eighteenth-Century South Carolina: A Colonial Dynasty, 1678–1787." Ph.D. diss., Emory University, 1990.

Meriwether, Robert L. "The expansion of South Carolina, 1729–1765." Ph.D. diss., Columbia University, 1940.

Books (Secondary)

2004. "Heath, Sir Robert (1575–1649)." *Oxford Dictionary of National Biography.* 9 Jan. 2019. http://www.oxforddnb.com.login.library.coastal.edu:2048/view/10.1093/ref: odnb/9780198614128.001.0001/odnb-9780198614128-e-1012178.

2004. "Yeamans, Sir John, first baronet (1611–1674), colonial governor." *Oxford Dictionary of National Biography.* 9 Jan. 2019. http://www.oxforddnb.com.login.library .coastal.edu:2048/view/10.1093/ref:odnb/9780198614128.001.0001/odnb-9780 198614128-e-30202.

2005. "Colonial administrators and post-independence leaders in Barbados (1627–2000)." *Oxford Dictionary of National Biography.* 9 Jan. 2019. http://www.oxforddnb .com.login.library.coastal.edu:2048/view/10.1093/ref:odnb/9780198614128.001 .0001/odnb-9780198614128-e-93228.

2008. "Courten, Sir William (c. 1568–1636), merchant and financier." *Oxford Dictionary of National Biography.* 9 Jan. 2019. http://www.oxforddnb.com/view/10.1093/ ref:odnb/9780198614128.001.0001/odnb-9780198614128-e-6445.

2008. "Modyford, Sir Thomas, first baronet (c. 1620–1679), planter and colonial governor." *Oxford Dictionary of National Biography.* 9 Jan. 2019. http://www.oxford dnb.com.login.library.coastal.edu:2048/view/10.1093/ref:odnb/97801986 14128.001.0001/odnb-9780198614128-e-18871.

Amussen, Susan Dwyer. *Caribbean Exchanges: Slavery and the Transformation of English Society, 1640–1700.* Chapel Hill: University of North Carolina Press, 2007.

Amy R. W. Myers, *Empire's Nature: Mark Catesby's New World Vision.* Chapel Hill: University of North Carolina Press, 1998.

Anderson, Virginia DeJohn. *New England's Generation: The Great Migration and the Formation of Society and Culture in the Seventeenth Century.* Cambridge: Cambridge University Press, 1991.

Applebaum, Herbert A. *Colonial Americans at Work.* Lanham: University Press of America, 1996.

Aptheker, Herbert. *American Negro Slave Revolts.* New York: Columbia University Press, 1943; reprint, International Publishers, 1993.

Baird, Charles W. *History of the Huguenot Emigration in America,* 2 vols. 1885. Reprint, Baltimore, 1973.

Baseler, Marilyn C. *"Asylum for Mankind": America, 1607–1800.* Ithaca, NY: Cornell University Press, 1998.

Beckles, Hilary. *White Servitude and Black Slavery in Barbados 1627–1715.* Knoxville: University of Tennessee Press, 1989.

Beckles, Hillary. *Natural Rebels: A Social History of Enslaved Women in Barbados.* New Brunswick: Rutgers University Press, 1989.

Bellows, Barbara L. *Benevolence Among Slaveholders: Assisting the Poor in Charleston 1670–1860.* Baton Rouge: Louisiana State University Press, 1993.

Blackburn, Robin. *The Making of New World Slavery: From the Baroque to the Modern, 1492–1800.* London: Verso, 1997; reprint, Verso, 1998.

Boles, John B., ed., *Masters and Slaves in the House of the Lord: Race and Religion in the American South, 1740–1870*. Lexington: University Press of Kentucky, 2015.

Branch, Michael P., ed. *Reading the Roots: American Nature Writing Before Walden*. Athens: University of Georgia Press, 2004.

Braund, Kathryn E. *Deerskins and Duffels: Creek Indian Trade with Anglo-America, 1685–1815*. Lincoln: University of Nebraska Press, 1993.

Brewer, John and Susan Staves, eds. *Early Modern Conceptions of Property*. London: Routledge, 1996.

Brock, R. A., ed. *The Official Letters of Alexander Spotswood, Lieutenant-Governor of the Colony of Virginia, 1710–1722*. Collections of the Virginia Historical Society: New Series, vol. 2. Richmond: Wm. Ellis Jones, 1885.

Brodhead, John Romeyn, ed. *Documents relative to the colonial history of the State of New-York: procured in Holland, England and France*. Albany: Weed, Parsons and Company, 1855.

Carney, Judith Ann. *Black Rice: The African Origins of Rice Cultivation in the Americas*. Cambridge: Harvard University Press, 2001.

Candler, Allen D., ed. *The Colonial Records of the State of Georgia*, vol. 3. Atlanta: Franklin Printing and Publishing Company, 1905.

Carter, Luther F., and Richard D. Young. *The Governor: Powers, Practices, Roles and the South Carolina Experience*. Center for Governmental Services, Institute for Public Service and Policy Research, the University of South Carolina, 2000.

Chapin, Joyce E. *An Anxious Pursuit: Agricultural Innovation and Modernity in the Lower South*. Charlottesville: University of North Carolina Press, 2012.

Chase, George Bigelow. *Lowndes of South Carolina: An Historical and Genealogical Memoir*. Boston: A. Williams and Co., 1876.

Clowse, Converse D. *Economic Beginnings in Colonial South Carolina 1670–1730*. Columbia: University of South Carolina Press, 1971.

Coclanis, Peter A. *The Shadow of a Dream: Economic Life and Death in the South Carolina Low Country 1670–1920*. New York: Oxford University Press, 1989.

Coffin, Joshua. *Account of Some of the Principal Slave Insurrections*. New York: American Anti-Slavery Society, 1860.

Coldham, Peter Wilson. *Lord Mayor's Court of London, Depositions Relating to Americans, 1641–1736*. Arlington: National Genealogical Society, 1980.

Conforti, Joseph A. *Saints and Strangers: New England in British North America*. Baltimore: Johns Hopkins University Press, 2006.

Cooper, Jerry. *The Rise of the National Guard: The Evolution of the American Militia, 1865–1920*. Lincoln: University of Nebraska Press, 2002.

Countryman, Edward. *How Did American Slavery Begin?* Boston: Bedford/St. Martin's Press, 1999.

Craig, Pamela Barnes. *American Women: A Library of Congress Guide for the Study of Women's History and Culture in the United States*. Library of Congress: 2001.

Crane, Verner. *The Southern Frontier, 1670–1732*. Tuscaloosa: University of Alabama Press, 2004.

Creighton, Charles. *A History of Epidemics in Britain*. London: The University Press, 1894.

Crooks, Jr., Daniel. *Charleston is Burning!, Two Centuries of Fire and Flames*. Charleston, SC: The History Press, 2009.

Dalberg-Action, John Emerich Edward. *Historical Essays and Studies*. London: Macmillan, 1907. Database online, Appendix. Available from http://oll.libertyfund.org.

David Ramsay. *Ramsay's History of South Carolina, from its first settlement in 1670 to the year 1808*. Charleston: Walker, Evans & Co., 1858.

Davis, David Brion. *Slavery and Human Progress*. New York: Oxford University Press, 1984.

Davis, Nicholas Darnell. *The Cavaliers & Roundheads of Barbados, 1650–1652: with some account of the early history of Barbados*. London: Argosy Press, 1887.

Doyle, Barbara, Mary Edna Sullivan, and Tracey Todd. *Beyond the Fields: Slavery at Middleton Place*. Columbia: University of South Carolina Press, 2008.

Duffy, John. *Epidemics in Colonial America*. Baton Rouge: Louisiana University State Press, 1953.

Dunn, Richard S. *Sugar and Slaves: The Rise of the Planter Class in the English West Indies, 1624–1713*. New York: Norton, 1973.

Dupre, Daniel S. *Alabama's Frontiers and the Rise of the Old South*. Bloomington: Indiana University Press, 2018.

Easterby, Harold J., ed. *The Colonial Records of South Carolina: The Journal of the Commons House of Assembly*. Columbia: South Carolina Archives Department, 1914.

Edelson, S. Max. *Plantation Enterprise in Colonial South Carolina*. Cambridge: Harvard University Press, 2006.

Edgar, Walter. *South Carolina, A History*. Columbia: University of South Carolina Press, 1998.

Ethridge, Robie, and Charles M. Hudson, eds. *The Transformation of the Southeastern Indians, 1540–1760*. Jackson: University of Mississippi Press, 2002.

Fischer, David Hackett. *Albion's Seed: Four British Folkways in America*. New York: Oxford University Press, 1989.

Fischer, Kirsten. *Suspect Relations: Sex, Race, and Resistance in Colonial North Carolina*. Ithaca: Cornell University Press, 2002.

Fiske, John. *Old Virginia and her Neighbors* Vol. 2. Boston: Houghton, Mifflin, and Co., 1897.

Frick, George F., and Raymond P. Stearns. *Mark Catesby, The Colonial Audubon*. Urbana: University of Illinois Press, 1961.

Galenson, David W. *Traders, Planters and Slaves: Market Behavior in Early English America*. Cambridge: Cambridge University Press, 2002.

Galenson, David W. *White Servitude in Colonial America: An Economic Analysis*. Cambridge: Cambridge University Press, 1981.

Gallay, Alan, ed. *Colonial Wars of North America, 1512–1763: An Encyclopedia*. New York: Routledge, 1996.

Gallay, Alan, ed. *Indian Slavery in Colonial America*. Lincoln: University of Nebraska Press, 2009.

Gallay, Alan. *The Indian Slave Trade: The Rise of the English Empire in the American South.* New Haven: Yale University Press, 2002.

Gately, Lain. *Tobacco: A Cultural History of How an Exotic Plant Seduced Civilization.* New York: Grove Atlantic Press, 2007.

Greene, Jack P. *Pursuits of Happiness: The Social Development of Early Modern British Colonies and the Formation of American Culture.* Chapel Hill: University of North Carolina Press, 1988.

Greene, Jack P., ed., *Selling in a New World: Two Colonial South Carolina Promotional Pamphlets.* Columbia: University of South Carolina Press, 1989.

Greene, Jack P., Rosemary Brana-Shute, and Randy J. Sparks, eds. *Money, Trade, and Power: The Evolution of Colonial South Carolina's Plantation Society.* Columbia: University of South Carolina Press, 2001.

Greer, Allan. *Property and Dispossession: Natives, Empires and Land in Early Modern North America.* Cambridge: Cambridge University Press, 2018.

Griffin, Patrick. *Experiencing Empire: Power, People, and Revolution in Early America.* Charlottesville: University of Virginia Press, 2017.

Guild, June Purcell, ed. *Black Laws of Virginia: A Summary of the Legislative Acts of Virginia Concerning Negroes from Earliest Times to the Present.* Richmond: Whittet & Shepperson, 1936.

Hall, Clayton C., ed. *Narratives of Early Maryland, 1633–1684.* New York: Charles Scribner's Sons, 1910.

Hall, Jr., Joseph M. *Zamumo's Gifts: Indian-European Exchange in the Colonial Southeast.* Philadelphia: University of Pennsylvania Press, 2009.

Hammond, David Scott. *Tropical forests of the Guiana Shield: Ancient Forests in a Modern World.* Cambridge: Cabi Publishing, 2005.

Hann, John H. *The Land Between the Rivers.* Gainesville: University Presses of Florida, 1988.

Harlow, Vincent T. *A History of Barbados: 1625–1685.* New York: Negro Universities Press, 1969.

Harlow, Vincent T., ed. *Colonising Expeditions to the West Indies and Guiana, 1623–1667.* Publications of the Hakluyt Society, 2nd series, vol. 56. London, 1925.

Harris, Tim. *Restoration: Charles II and His Kingdoms, 1660–1685.* London: Penguin Books, 2006.

Hart, Emma. *Building Charleston: Town and Society in the Eighteenth-Century British Atlantic World.* Charlottesville: University of Virginia Press, 2010.

Hatfield, April Lee. *Atlantic Virginia: Intercolonial Relations in the Seventeenth Century.* Philadelphia: University of Pennsylvania Press, 2004.

Hazen, Robert M., and Margaret Hindle Hazen. *Keepers of the Flame: The Role of Fire in American Culture, 1775–1925.* Princeton: Princeton University Press, 1992.

Hazlewood, Nick. *The Queen's Slave Trader: John Hawkyns, Elizabeth I, and the Trafficking in Human Souls.* New York: Harper Collins, 2004.

Heitzler, Michael James. *Goose Creek, South Carolina, A Definitive History 1670–2003,* vol. 1. Charleston, SC: The History Press, 2005.

Hendrix, Michael Patrick. *Down and Dirty: Archaeology of the South Carolina Lowcountry*. Charleston, SC: The History Press, 2006.

Heuman, Gad J. *The Slavery Reader*. New York: Routledge, 2003.

Hine, Darlene Clark and Jacqueline McLeod, eds. *Crossing Boundaries: Comparative History of Black People in Diaspora*. Bloomington: Indiana University Press, 1999.

Hurt, R. Douglas, ed. *American Agriculture: A Brief History*. West Lafayette: Purdue University Press, 2002.

Innes, Stephen, ed. *Work and Labor in Early America*. Chapel Hill: University of North Carolina Press, 1988.

Ivers, Larry E. *This Torrent of Indians: War on the Southern Frontier, 1715–1728*. Columbia: University of South Carolina Press, 2016.

Jameson, John Franklin, ed. *Narratives of New Netherland, 1609–1664*, vol. 8. New York: Charles Scribner's Sons, 1909.

Jones, James Rees. *Country and Court: England, 1658–1714*. Cambridge: Harvard University Press, 1979.

Joyner, Charles. *Down by the Riverside: A South Carolina Slave Community*. Urbana: University of Illinois Press, 1984.

Kelton, Paul. *Epidemics & Enslavement: Biological Catastrophe in the Native Southeast, 1492–1715*. Lincoln: University of Nebraska Press, 2007.

Knight, Lucian Lamar, Milton Ready, and Kenneth Coleman, eds. *The Colonial Records of the State of Georgia, Vol. IV, Stephens' Journal 1737–1740*. Atlanta: Franklin Printing and Publishing Company, 1906.

Kupperman, Karen Ordahl. *Providence Island, 1630–1641: The Other Puritan Colony*. Cambridge: Cambridge University Press, 1995.

Kupperman, Karen Ordahl, John C. Appleby, and Mandy Banton, eds. *Calendar of State Papers, Colonial Series, America and West Indies, 1574–1739*, vol. 28. London: Routledge, 2000.

Lee, Robert E. *Blackbeard the Pirate: A Reappraisal of His Life and Times*. Winston-Salem: John F. Blair, Publisher, 2002.

LeMaster, Michelle and Bradford J. Wood. *Creating and Contesting Carolina: Proprietary Era Histories*. Columbia: University of South Carolina Press, 2013.

Lewis, Kay Wright. *A Curse Upon the Nation: Race, Freedom, and Extermination in America and the Atlantic World*. Athens: University of Georgia Press, 2017.

Littlefield, Daniel C. *Rice and Slaves: Ethnicity and the Slave Trade in Colonial South Carolina*. Baton Rouge: Louisiana State University Press, 1981.

Lockley, James. *Maroon Communities in South Carolina: A Documentary Record*. Columbia: University of South Carolina Press, 2009.

Louis, William Roger, Alaine M. Low, and Nicholas P. Canny. *The Oxford History of the British Empire: The Origins of Empire*. New York: Oxford University Press, 1998.

Lowery, Woodbury, *The Spanish Settlements within the present limits of the United States, 1513-1561*. New York: G.P. Putnam, 1911.

Lyon, Eugene. *Santa Elena: A Brief History of the Colony, 1566–1587*. Columbia: University of South Carolina Institute of Archaeology and Anthropology, 1984.

MacLeod, William Christie. *The American Indian Frontier*. New York: Routledge, 2013.

Mann, Kristin. *Slavery and the Birth of an African City: Lagos, 1760–1900*. Bloomington: Indiana University Press, 2007.

Marcoux, Jon Bernard. *Pox, Empire, Shackles, and Hides: The Townsend Site, 1670–1715*. Tuscaloosa: University of Alabama Press, 2010.

McCandless, Peter. *Slavery, Disease, and Suffering in the Southern Lowcountry*. New York: Cambridge University Press, 2011.

McCrady, Edward. *The History of South Carolina Under the Proprietary Government, 1670–1719*. London: Macmillan Company, 1897.

McCusker, John J. and Russel R. Menard. *The Economy of British America, 1607–1789*. Chapel Hill: University of North Carolina Press, 1985.

McIntyre, Ruth A. *Debts Hopeful and Desperate: Financing the Plymouth Colony*. Plymouth: Plymouth Plantation, 1963.

Menard, Russell R. *Sweet Negotiations: Sugar, Slavery, and Plantation Agriculture in Early Barbados*. Charlottesville: University of Virginia Press, 2006.

Merrens, H. Roy, ed. *The Colonial South Carolina Scene: Contemporary Views, 1697–1774*. Columbia: University of South Carolina Press, 1977.

Merritt, Keri Leigh. *Masterless Men, Poor Whites and Slavery in the Antebellum South*. Cambridge: Cambridge University Press, 2017.

Miles, Suzannah Smith. *Writings on the Islands: Sullivan's Island and the Isle of Palms*. Charleston: The History Press, 2004.

Milling, Chapman J., ed. *Colonial South Carolina: Two Contemporary Descriptions*. Columbia: 1951.

Mitchell, Arthur. *South Carolina Irish*. Charleston, SC: The History Press, 2011.

Moore, Caroline T., and Agatha Aimar Simmons, comps. and eds. *Abstract of the Wills of the State of South Carolina: 1670–1740*. Columbia: 1960.

Morgan, Edmund. *American Slavery, American Freedom*. New York: Norton, 2003.

Morgan, Kenneth. *Slavery and the British Empire: From Africa to America*. New York: Oxford University Press, 2007.

Morgan, Kenneth, ed. *Slavery in America: A Reader and Guide*. Athens: University of Georgia Press, 2005.

Morison, Samuel Eliot. *The European Discovery of North America: The Northern Voyages A.D. 500–1600*. New York: Oxford University Press, 1971.

Nagle, Stephen J. and Sara L. Sanders, eds. *English in the Southern United States*. New York: Cambridge University Press, 2003.

Nelson, William E. *The Common Law in Colonial America: Volume II: The Middle Colonies and the Carolinas, 1660–1730*. New York: Oxford University Press, 2012.

Oatis, Stephen J. *A Colonial Complex: South Carolina's Frontiers in the Era of the Yamasee War, 1680–1730*. Lincoln: University of Nebraska Press, 2004.

O'Callaghan, Sean. *To Hell or Barbados: The Ethnic Cleansing of Ireland*. Dingle, Co. Kerry, Ireland: Brandon, 2000.

Olexer, Barbara. *The Enslavement of the American Indian in Colonial Times*. Columbia: Joyous Publishing, 2005.

Onofrio, Jan. "Johnston, Henrietta, (?-1728/1729)." *South Carolina Biographical Dictionary*, 2nd ed., vol. 1. St. Clair Shores, MI: Somerset Publishers, Inc., 2000.

Otto, John Solomon. *The Southern Frontiers, 1607–1860: The Agricultural Evolution of the Colonial and Antebellum South*. New York: ABC-CLIO, 1989.

Pestana, Carla Gardina. *The English Atlantic in an Age of Revolution, 1640–1661*. Cambridge: Harvard University Press, 2004.

Pettigrew, William Andrew. *Freedom's Debt: The Royal African Company and the Politics of the Atlantic Slave Trade, 1672–1725*. Chapel Hill: University of North Carolina Press, 2013.

Pickett, Margaret F. and Dwayne W. Pickett. *The European Struggle to Settle North America: Colonizing Attempts by England, France and Spain, 1521–1608*. Jefferson, NC: McFarland & Co., 2010.

Pollitzer, William S. *The Gullah People and Their African Heritage*. Athens: University of Georgia Press, 2005.

Prendergast, John. *The Cromwellian Settlement of Ireland*. Baltimore: Genealogical Publishing, 2009.

Purvis, Thomas L. *Colonial America to 1763*. New York: Infobase Publishing, 1999.

Ramsey, William S. *The Yamasee War: A Study of Culture, Economy, and Conflict in the Colonial South*. Lincoln: University of Nebraska Press, 2008.

Rivers, William James. *A Chapter in the Early History of South Carolina*. Charleston: Walker, Evans & Cogswell, 1874.

Rivers, William James. *A Sketch of the History of South Carolina to the Close of the Proprietary Government by the Revolution of 1719; With an Appendix Containing Many Valuable Records Hitherto Unpublished*. Charleston: McCarter & Co., 1856.

Rodriguez, Junius P. *Encyclopedia of Slave Resistance and Rebellion*, vol. 1. Westport, CT: Greenwood Publishing, 2007.

Rodriguez, Junius P. *Encyclopedia of Slave Resistance and Rebellion*, vol. 2. Westport, CT: Greenwood Publishing, 2007.

Rogozinski, Jan. *A Brief History of the Caribbean from the Arawak and the Carib to the Present*. New York: Penguin, 1994.

Roper, L. H. "Morton, Joseph, Sr." In Walter Edgar, ed., *South Carolina Encyclopedia*. Columbia: University of South Carolina Press, 2006.

Roper, L. H. *Conceiving Carolina: Proprietors, Planters, and Plots, 1662–1779*. New York: Palgrave Macmillan, 2004.

Rowland, Lawrence Sanders, Alexander Moore, and George C. Rogers, Jr. *A History of Beaufort County, South Carolina: Vol. 1, 1514–1861*. Columbia: University of South Carolina Press, 1996.

Rowland, Lawrence Sanders. *Window on the Atlantic: The Rise and Fall of Santa Elena, South Carolina's Spanish City*. Columbia: South Carolina Department of Archives and History, 1990.

Ruidiaz, E. and Caravia. "Relacion escrita por Juan de la Vandera." In *La Florida su Conquista y Colonizacion por Pedro Menendes de Aviles*. Madrid: 1893.

Salley, Alexander S., Jr., ed. *Commissions and Instructions from the Lords Proprietors of Carolina to Public Officials of South Carolina, 1685–1715*. Columbia: The State Co., 1916.

Salley, Alexander S., Jr., ed. *Journals of the Commons House of Assembly: 1682–[1738]*, 21 vols. Columbia: Historical Commission of South Carolina, 1907–1946.

Salley, Alexander S., Jr., ed. *The Journals of the Commons House of Assembly of South Carolina, Nov. 8, 1734—June 7, 1735*. Columbia: Historical Commission of South Carolina, 1946.

Salley, Alexander S., Jr., ed. *Journals of the Grand Council of South Carolina: August 25, 1671–June 24, 1680*. Columbia: South Carolina Historical Commission, 1907.

Salley, Alexander S., Jr., ed. *Journals of the Trustees for Establishing the Colony of Georgia in America, July 20, 1732–June 23, 1752*. Atlanta: Franklin Printing and Publishing Co., 1904.

Salley, Alexander S., Jr., ed. *Narratives of Early Carolina 1650–1708*. New York: Barnes & Noble, 1911.

Salley, Alexander S, Jr., ed. *Register of St. Philip's Parish, Charles Town, South Carolina, 1720–1758*. Charleston: Walker, Evans & Cogswell Co., 1904.

Salley, Alexander S., Jr. *The Introduction of Rice Culture into South Carolina*. Bulletins of the Historical Commission of South Carolina No. 6. Columbia: The State Company, 1919.

Salley, Alexander S., Jr., ed. *Warrants for Lands in South Carolina, 1672–1711*. Columbia: University of South Carolina Press, 1973.

Saunders, William L., ed. *The State Records of North Carolina, Vol. II, 1713 to 1728*. Raleigh: P.M. Hale, 1886.

Schiebinger, Londa and Claudia Swan, eds. *Colonial Botany: Science, Commerce and Politics in the Early Modern World*. Philadelphia: University of Pennsylvania Press, 2005.

Schlesinger, Roger and Arthur P. Stable, eds. *Andre Thevet's North America: A Sixteenth-Century View*. Translated by Roger Schlesinger and Arthur P. Stable. Kingston and Montreal: McGill-Queen's University Press, 1986.

Schomburgk, Sir Robert Hermann. *The History of Barbados*. London: Longman, Brown, Green and Longmans, 1848.

Sheridan, Richard B. *Sugar and Slavery: An Economic History of the British West Indies, 1623–1775*. Kingston: Canoe Press, 1974; reprint, Canoe Press, 2000.

Sirmans, M. Eugene. *Colonial South Carolina: A Political History, 1663–1763*. Chapel Hill: University of North Carolina Press, 1966.

Smallwood, Arwin D. *Bertie County: An Eastern Carolina History*. Charleston, SC: Arcadia Publishing, 2002.

Smith, Abbot Emerson. *Colonists in Bondage: White Servitude and Convict Labor in America, 1607–1776*. Gloucester: Peter Smith, 1965.

Smith, Warren B. *White Servitude in Colonial South Carolina*. Columbia: University of South Carolina Press, 1961.

Smith, William Roy. *South Carolina as a Royal Province, 1710–1776*. New York: McMillan, 1903.

Snowden, Yates and Harry Gardner Cutler. *History of South Carolina*, vol. 1. Chicago and New York: Lewis Publishing Company, 1928.

Snyder, Christina. *Slavery in Indian Country: The Changing Face of Captivity in Early America*. Cambridge: Harvard University Press, 2010.

Southey, Thomas. *Chronological History of the West Indies*, vol. 1. London: Longman, Rees, Orme, Brown, & Green, 1827.

Spruill, Marjorie Julian, Valinda W. Littlefield, and Joan Marie Johnson, eds. *South Carolina Women: Their Lives and Times, Volume 1*. Athens: University of Georgia Press, 2010.

Spurr, John Anthony, ed. *Anthony Ashley Cooper, First Earl of Shaftesbury 1621–1683*. Surrey: Ashgate Publishing, 2011.

Stange, Marion. *Vital Negotiations: Protecting Settler's Health in Colonial Louisiana and South Carolina, 1720–1763*. Goettingen: V&R unipress, 2012.

The Descendants of Hugh Armory. London, 1901. In Alexander S. Salley, Jr., *The Introduction of Rice Culture into South Carolina*. Bulletins of the Historical Commission of South Carolina No. 6. Columbia: The State Company, 1919.

Thompson, Roger. *Divided We Stand: Watertown, Massachusetts, 1630–1680*. Amherst: University of Massachusetts Press, 2001.

Rubillo, Tom. *Hurricane Destruction in South Carolina: Hell and High Water*. Charleston, SC: The History Press, 2006.

Tomlins, Christopher. *Freedom Bound: Law, Labor, and Civic Identity in Colonizing English America, 1580–1865*. Cambridge: Cambridge University Press, 2010.

Wallace, Anthony. *Tuscarora, A History*. Albany: State University of New York Press, 2012.

Wallace, David Duncan. *South Carolina: A Short History*. Columbia: University of South Carolina Press, 1961.

Wallace, David Duncan. *The History of South Carolina*, vol. 1. New York: American Historical Society, 1934.

Walter J. Fraser, *Savannah in the Old South*. Athens: University of Georgia Press, 2005.

Waterhouse, Richard. *A New World Gentry: The Making of a Merchant Planter Class in South Carolina*. Charleston, SC: The History Press, 2005.

Weber, David J. *The Spanish Frontier in North America*. New Haven: Yale University Press, 1992.

Weir, Robert M. *Colonial South Carolina—A History*. Columbia: University of South Carolina Press, 1997.

Wellburn, Ron. *Roanoke and Wampum: Topics in Native American Heritage and Literatures*. New York: Peter Lang Publishing, 2001.

Williams, Eric Eustace. *Capitalism and Slavery*. Chapel Hill: University of North Carolina Press, 1944.

Wilson, Thomas D. *The Ashley Cooper Plan: The Founding of Carolina and the Origins of Southern Political Culture*. Chapel Hill: University of North Carolina Press, 2016.

Witzig, Fred E. *Sanctifying Slavery & Politics in South Carolina: The Life of the Reverend Alexander Garden, 1685–1756*. Columbia: University of South Carolina Press, 2018.

Wood, Gordon S. *Empire of Liberty: A History of the Early Republic, 1789–1815*. New York: Oxford University Press, 2009.

Wood, Peter H. *Black Majority: Negroes in Colonial South Carolina from 1670 through the Stono Rebellion*. New York: Norton, 1974.

Woodard, Colin. *The Republic of Pirates*. Boston: Harcourt, 2007.

Wooton, David, ed. *John Locke, Political Writings*. Indianapolis: Hackett Publishing Company, 2003.

Yeager, Jonathan M. *Jonathan Edwards and Transatlantic Print Culture*. New York: Oxford University Press, 2016.

INDEX

Page numbers in *italics* refer to illustrations.

Nash, Gary, 163

Nash, R. C., 145n8

Native Americans, 1, 6, 7, 8, 47, 60, 145;
African slaves captured by, 102, 116;
Cape Fear settlement and, 52; dis-
placement of, 75; epidemics and, 168;
as slaves, 5n11, 9, 20, 23, 57–58n36,
66, 81–86, 92, 106, 110, 116–17,
125–26,

Native Americans, as slaves (*continued*)
161, 162, 164, 169; Spanish invaders
vs., 11; trade with, 62n57, 81; in Yamasee
War, 4. *See also individual tribes*

naval stores, 78, 81, 91, 98, 125, 134n27,
154, 157; bounty on, 149, 153; Native
Americans and, 86; slave labor and,
86n137, 145n8, 148; West Indian market for, 71

Navigation Acts (1660, 1663), 50

Nelson, William, 152n33

Netherlands, 18

Nevis, 29n42, 31

New Amsterdam, 45nn1–2

Newe, Thomas, 78, 84

New Hampshire, 45n1

New Jersey, 45n2, 91

Newman, Mary, 166

New Netherland, 14

Newport, R.I., 45n1

New Providence, 47n6

New York City, 112n64

Nicholson, Francis, 140–41n50

Norris, John, 78n105, 90, 107, 108

Notes on the State of Virginia (Jefferson),
16, 163n8

Oglethorpe, James, 139

Olive (ship), 18

olives, 93

O'Neill (Orrill), Philip, 65

orphans, 23

O'Sullivan, Florence, 60n45

Oyster Point, 73, 75

Pennsylvania, 45n2, 91, 112n64

Pequot War (1636–37), 23, 45n1

Percival, Andrew, 91–92n144, 146n13

Perry, Sarah, 112

Petineau, Jean, 80

Petty, William, 48n7

Philip II (king of Spain), 10–11n33

Pierce, William, 23

Pinckney, Eliza Lucas, 3n6

pirates, 60, 88, 139, 166

plantains, 20

plantation system, 15; Barbadian,
27–28n36, 71, 99, 126; Portuguese and
Dutch antecedents of, 51n17; oppressive conditions under, 155–56, 159, 164

Plymouth Colony, 18, 19, 45n1, 49

poor relief, 129–32, 144

pork, 6, 149

Portman, Christopher, 70

Portugal, 18, 154n40

Powell, Henry, 18n3, 19–20, 23

Powell, John, 18

Presbyterians, 72

Pringle, Robert, 157

prisoners of war, 23, 25

Profitable Advice for Rich and Poor (Norris),
108

Puritans, 6n15, 14, 45n1, 49, 50n12, 158

Quakers, 56n29, 72

Quebec, 14

Queen Anne's War (1702–13), 103n28,
116

Quexos, Pedro de, 9

Quintyne, Richard, 70

Raleigh, Walter, 11

Randolph, Edward, 6n16, 97–98, 102–3

Ravenel, Henry, 155–56n44

Read, John, 32

reciprocity, 33n58

*Relation of a Discovery lately made on the
Coast of Florida* (Hilton), 52